Additional Praise for
Tools for Today's High Margin Practice

"As a devout non-techie, I recognize that were it not for experts in the industry like Joel Bruckenstein and Dave Drucker, The Wealth Conservancy couldn't have evolved from being an emerging firm to being well-established and on its way to becoming an enterprise. Joel and Dave have a crème-de-la-crème reputation, and their cogent, clear writing, in layman's terms, shows they are more committed to getting the message across than impressing the reader with their technical expertise. This book is a breath of fresh air—ahhh!"

—Myra Salzer, Founder, The Wealth Conservancy, Inc.,
Author, *Living Richly: Seizing the Potential of Inherited Wealth*

"David Drucker and Joel Bruckenstein are true visionaries in the field of advisor-related technology. Many of the systems and technologies they forecast over ten years ago have come to fruition and are now mainstream needs for successful investment companies. I have used their insight and vision in my own business to great success and will continue to do so. This book provides helpful, new information."

—J. Michael Scarborough, President/CEO,
Retirement Management Systems, Inc.,
Author, *The Scarborough Plan: Maximizing the Power of Your 401(k)*

"Technology touches everything we do in our business. This book covers all-things-tech from A to Z. It is a must-read for the RIA business owner and for those responsible for tech decisions at financial advisory firms. Dave and Joel's advice will improve your bottom line."

—Tom Orecchio, CFA, CFP®, CLU®, ChFC®, AIF®,
Principal and Wealth Manager, Modera Wealth Management, LLC,
Former Chairman, National Association of Personal Financial Planners (NAPFA)

"It's a daunting task for any advisor to stay focused on the client experience and stay up on smoothly running an office. But, Drucker, Bruckenstein, and 'friends' have written THE go-to book for advisors navigating the maze of technology and advisor solutions. This is a terrific reference for every advisor's shelf, laptop, iPad, Kindle, or Nook!"

—Alex Potts, President and CEO, Loring Ward Group, Inc.,
Co-author, *The Wealth Solution: Bringing Structure to Your Financial Life*

"This book is contains a wealth of knowledge and wisdom that is mandatory for any client-centered financial advisor wanting to be relevant, efficient, and profitable."

—Rick Kahler, CFP®, President, Kahler Financial Group

"Just when you think these guys could not possibly offer even more guidance and direction in the field of technology—they write a book. Brilliant! Dave and Joel are truly the icons when we look back on how financial advisory firms tackled the tough technology decisions through each decade. They are honest and straight shooters. Why are they so valuable? So many times—money, time, and energy are saved because of the sage advice from these two experts. This is a book you want in your office."

—Diane MacPhee, CFP®, Business Coach

"David and Joel lead the industry in their insights on how to use technology effectively. What is so unique to this book is the integration of other thought leaders who bring a range of expertise and perspective. This is like a crash course in improving your business from some of the brightest minds in the industry."

—Julie Littlechild, CEO and Founder, Advisor Impact

"David and Joel have updated their definitive reference on leveraging technology for a profitable practice. Providing a consistent experience customized to your target clients' preferences practically requires that you utilize technology, at least if it is to be done efficiently. Only in this work can you find many of the top writers, commentators, and practitioners offering you tips and insights on many of the most important aspects of technology in one handy reference. I bought the first edition in 2003, and it continues to be my go-to reference today."

—Stephen Wershing, CFP, President,
The Client Driven Practice, Author, *Stop Asking for Referrals*

"David and Joel have provided all you need to know to choose the best technology for your practice. And, let's face it, in today's world, you just can't really practice without good technology to support you. Get this book, it will save you time and money, I guarantee it!"

—Deena Katz, CFP, Associate Professor,
Texas Tech University, Author, *Deena Katz's Complete Guide to
Practice Management: Tips, Tools, and Templates for the Financial Adviser*

"Building on the recommendations and predictions from their original book – which all came true, and then some!—Drucker and Bruckenstein take a deep dive into not just the latest technology tools that are available in today's marketplace to enhance the scalability and profitability of a practice, but also a look beyond into how technology trends may further shift in the coming years. Built collaboratively with an all-star lineup of contributors, *Technology Tools for Today's High-Margin Practice* is sure to become essential reading for anyone considering technology decisions in the coming years, large firm or small!"

—Michael Kitces, Partner with Pinnacle Advisory Group, Inc., and publisher of the
financial planning industry blog Nerd's Eye View at www.kitces.com/blog

"For the last decade we've been turning to and recommending Drucker and Bruckenstein for great insights on technology applicable in our businesses. Their insights and experiences have saved us hundreds of hours of redundant research, wasted time and money. In their latest offering, the gurus have assembled an all-star lineup of industry experts, each contributing in their specific area of specialty. How do you enhance a great product? Read Technology Tools for Today's High Margin Practice and you'll understand why this book is the new technology resource I recommend to all financial professionals.

—Sheryl Garrett, CFP®, AIF®
Founder, Garrett Planning Network

TECHNOLOGY TOOLS FOR TODAY'S HIGH-MARGIN PRACTICE

Since 1996, Bloomberg Press has published books for financial professionals on investing, economics, and policy affecting investors. Titles are written by leading practitioners and authorities, and have been translated into more than 20 languages.

The Bloomberg Financial Series provides both core reference knowledge and actionable information for financial professionals. The books are written by experts familiar with the work flows, challenges, and demands of investment professionals who trade the markets, manage money, and analyze investments in their capacity of growing and protecting wealth, hedging risk, and generating revenue.

For a list of available titles, please visit our web site at www.wiley.com/go/bloombergpress.

TECHNOLOGY TOOLS FOR TODAY'S HIGH-MARGIN PRACTICE

How Client-Centered Financial Advisors Can Cut
Paperwork, Overhead, and Wasted Hours

David J. Drucker
Joel P. Bruckenstein

BLOOMBERG PRESS
An Imprint of
WILEY

Cover design: C. Wallace
Cover images: Panorama Cloudscape © Tammy Bryngelson/istockphoto,
Circuit Board © aleksandar velasevic/istockphoto

Published by John Wiley & Sons, Inc., Hoboken, New Jersey.

The first edition titled: *Virtual-Office Tools for a High-Margin Practice* was published by Bloomberg Press in 2002. Published simultaneously in Canada.

For general information on our other products and services or for technical support, please contact our Customer Care Department within the United States at (800) 762-2974, outside the United States at (317) 572-3993 or fax (317) 572-4002.

Wiley publishes in a variety of print and electronic formats and by print-on-demand. Some material included with standard print versions of this book may not be included in e-books or in print-on-demand. If this book refers to media such as a CD or DVD that is not included in the version you purchased, you may download this material at http://booksupport.wiley.com. For more information about Wiley products, visit www.wiley.com.

Library of Congress Cataloging-in-Publication Data:

Drucker, David J., 1948–
    Technology tools for today's high-margin practice : how client-centered financial advisors can cut paperwork, overhead, and wasted hours / David J. Drucker and Joel P. Bruckenstein.
      p. cm. — (Bloomberg financial series)
    Includes index.
    ISBN 978-1-118-43476-5 (cloth); ISBN 978-1-118-48051-9 (ebk);
    ISBN 978-1-118-48053-3 (ebk); ISBN 978-1-118-48055-7 (ebk)
      1. Financial planners. 2. Finance, Personal-Computer network resources. 3. Investment advisors.
    4. Investments—Data processing. 5. Finance-Technological innovations. I. Bruckenstein, Joel P., 1956–
II. Title.
    HG179.5.D777 2013
    332.6–dc23

                                                              2012038305

MIX
Paper from
responsible sources
FSC FSC® C013604
www.fsc.org

Contents

Introduction

David Drucker

In 2001, I approached Joel Bruckenstein (who was known to me only as a seemingly like-minded writer for the financial trade press) and told him about a book for which I was developing a business plan. He agreed it would be an interesting project for collaboration. A year later, Bloomberg Press published *Virtual Office Tools for a High-Margin Practice* and it became an instant hit.

Of course, it's the type of book that requires frequent updating in order to remain useful to our readers and, for the past 10 years, we've opted instead to publish a monthly technology newsletter as a means of keeping the book current. Yet, after many requests from readers and from John Wiley & Sons (which partnered with Bloomberg Press), we finally agreed in 2012 to update the book for publication by the T3 Conference in February 2013.

This new book—*Technology Tools for Today's High-Margin Practice*—poses a very different challenge than did the first book, namely, that technology has changed vastly over the last 10 years since we wrote the first book. Joel and I penned the first book based upon our own technology experiences trying to assemble our own virtual offices, offices based on the use of technology and outsourcing such that we could function in a world of much larger competitors with what, essentially, remained simple home offices. Although it isn't every financial advisor's goal to have a virtual office, the principles we followed in creating ours have proven essential to creating a technologically up-to-date firm of any size and shape by gaining advantages over competitors by employing technology and outsourcing wherever profitable to do so.

In other words, what makes the smaller virtual office profitable is the same thing that makes the larger firm profitable—paying attention to the efficiencies available through technology. Technology can be used to achieve scalability either up or down . . . up by expansion of the larger firm that wants to add employees and grow indefinitely and down by the contraction of the firm that wants no employees and chooses, instead, to outsource as much as possible. Today, readers of our book still come in both flavors though expansion seems to be the dominant trend.

So, whereas, Joel and I could and did write the first book based on our own experiences, readers were taking those ideas and applying them to all manner of advisory firms—not just those seeking to remain small virtual offices but expanding

1

firms, as well. The lessons learned in the past 10 years have expanded the body of knowledge to where Joel and I decided we could produce a better product, in the way of a second book, if we engaged the help of the many experts who have emerged in the whole field of investment advisor office technology.

To illustrate how far we've come in the past 10 years, let's look at four recommendations from the first book and assess their relevancy today:

1. Recommendation: A paperless office might be beneficial to your operation. Buy a Fujitsu (or other recommended) scanner and software like PaperPort Deluxe to begin converting paper to digital records.

    Today, a paperless office isn't just beneficial, it's essential. A whole industry has grown up around the need to serve financial advisors and other small business offices looking for sophisticated hardware and software with which to escape the inefficiencies inherent in dealing with paper. Not only have better paperless office tools grown up, but they are integrated with other key systems like CRM software so that client records can be viewed in an integrated format.

2. Recommendation: Consider using flash storage devices for easy, portable backups.

    Flash storage devices, or thumb drives, as we knew them back then, are ubiquitous now. Storage capacities have climbed to as much as 32 gigabytes while prices have plummeted, making flash storage devices handy gifts rather than the moderately expensive backup devices we saw them as 10 years ago.

3. Recommendation: In the earlier book, e-mail was touted as the best communication system for advisors and their clients.

    Today, we've seen all manner of embellishments on this very basic (though still essential) communications system. In addition to e-mail, advisors and clients interact through client portals, online storage systems like Dropbox, social media networks (which barely existed 10 years ago), and other systems designed to enhance the e-mail experience, making it easier to share large documents and files.

4. Recommendation: A customer relationship management (CRM) system is important to managing clients. We discussed the benefits of Microsoft Outlook and add-ons for financial advisory firms from CRM providers like Sage ACT! and Goldmine. We also recommended several industry-specific CRM systems, one of which (Junxure) has expanded to become an industry leader, the other of which (ProTracker), while still in use, has faded substantially from its earlier prominence.

The modern financial advisory firm uses a CRM as the hub of its practice, giving it access not only to client database records but client documents and, more importantly, a system for managing workflow. Where earlier CRMs were simply repositories for basic client information (computerized rolodexes, in other words), CRMs today allow the firm owner and his or her employees to track with great specificity where the firm is in serving each client's every need.

These are just a few of the recommendations made in the original book that have been completely superseded by 10 years of technological advances. At the same time, some of the chapters in this revised book represent technologies that weren't available (or were just in their infancy) 10 years ago.

So, to make sure each subject area is covered in the proper depth and with the required expertise, we set about building our list of contributing authors and hope you agree we've got a who's who in technology for financial advisors featured in this new book. Following is a listing of authors and topics.

Robert D. Curtis, founder, president, and CEO, PIEtech Inc., "The Future of Financial Planning Software"

Linda Strachan, vice president, product management, Zywave, Inc., "The Future of Financial Planning Software and the New Client-Advisor Relationship"

Curtis and Strachan bring us up to date with the changes that have taken place in financial planning software over the last 10 years and discuss the direction of software advancement today.

Jennifer Goldman, president, My Virtual COO, "Virtual Staff Sparks Growth, Profitability, and Scalability"

Goldman discusses the state of the art in outsourcing, a trend we identified and wrote about in the first book, that has since expanded greatly. Today, advisors can find virtual staff to fulfill almost any function within the firm as the low costs and other advantages of virtual staff become apparent.

Davis Janowski, technology reporter at *Investment News*, "Selecting the Right CRM System"

Janowski discusses the many decisions that go into selecting the right CRM for one's advisory practice. Where the decision used to be easy—Microsoft Outlook—there are too many offerings today to default to Outlook, and those offerings differ greatly from one another, making the decision a critical one.

Mike Kelly, president, Back Office Support Service, "Portfolio Management Software"

Kelly discusses the many varieties of portfolio management software and the opportunity to run these in-house or seek out an outsourcing arrangement through a firm like his.

David L. Lawrence, founder and president, EfficientPractice.com, "Building an Efficient Workflow Management System"

Lawrence discusses building an efficient workflow management system. Workflow systems are usually embedded in one's CRM but are important enough to constitute a subject of their own within the new book. Designing workflow so that everyone within a firm knows his/her duties and is able to carry them out in a uniform manner is a critical process whether married to a CRM or not.

Dan Skiles, executive vice president, Shareholders Service Group, "Electronic Signatures"

Skiles discusses the state of the art of digital signatures, something not really present on the technology scene 10 years ago, but now an important part of streamlining workflow within organizations both large and small.

Marie Swift, principal, Impact Communications, "Managing Your Online Presence"
Swift discusses the advisor's online presence and what he or she must do, over and above just creating a website, to maintain an online presence in order to stay in front of clients and prospects alike.

Bart Wisniowski, co-founder and director, AdvisorWebsites.com, "How the World Wide Web Impacts the Financial Advisor"
Wisniowski discusses the more narrowly focused marketing topic of website deployment—the right way and wrong way of doing it.

Timothy Welsh, president and founder, Nexus Strategy, LLC, "ROI—The Holy Grail of the Technology Purchase Decision"
Welsh discusses Return on Technology Investment. How does the advisor know he or she is anticipating all of the costs and all of the benefits of a technology purchase decision? There's more that goes into it than initially meets the eye.

Bill Winterberg, consultant, FPPad.com, "Client Portals and Collaboration"
Winterberg discusses portals and means of collaboration with clients and other professionals over and above simple e-mail.

John Patullo, managing director, technology product management, TD Ameritrade Institutional, "Achieving Growth and Profitability with Technology Integration"
Patullo discusses TD Ameritrade's efforts to create an integrated platform of software and trading functionality online for advisor clients. As integration of disparate software programs becomes essential for efficient operation, custodians like TD are at the forefront of creating these integrations for advisors.

J. D. Bruce, president, Abacus Wealth Partners, "The Cloud"
Bruce discusses a growing trend toward operating in the cloud, that is, creating operating systems for online rather than desktop operation.

Louis Stanasolovich, founder and president; Christopher Kail, director of marketing; Sherri Slafka, communications coordinator; Daniel Kleck, marketing coordinator, Legend Financial Advisors—"Innovative Software and Technologies Implemented at One of the United States' Leading Advisory Firms"
Stanasolovich, a marketing expert in the financial advisor community, discusses the technology behind his marketing systems and the opportunity every advisor has to market more intelligently using technology designed for that purpose.

All together, our expert authors provide a blueprint for the technological redesign of a financial advisory firm. Every chapter presents a topic that must be dealt with in the formation of a firm's technology platform, and every chapter provides the answers you need (as well as the questions you need to ask) in researching and assembling your own technology platform.

We sincerely hope that as you read this book you will achieve a better understanding of the technology platform you've already created along with a clear vision of where you need to go to achieve a better integration and smoother functioning of all the pieces within that platform.

CHAPTER 1

Selecting the Right CRM System

Davis D. Janowski

Technology Reporter at InvestmentNews

When it comes to technology, few decisions are going to be as far reaching or consequential to an advisor's work life than choosing a CRM system. Whether you define it as client-, contact-, or the most commonly used customer relationship management (CRM), the software encompasses much more than the acronym might suggest.

Most advisors, and perhaps even more tellingly, two major custodians that support between them almost 10,000 advisors, are of the opinion that CRM has moved to center stage. In other words this crowd has made CRM technology the central hub around which all the rest of their technology revolves.

Historically, the hub of many types of financial services systems has been account management, and even to this day quite a few brokerages and broker-dealers continue to organize and manage their systems this way. Almost in parallel with the overall growth in the registered investment advisor industry we have seen a trend evolving in the CRM world. It began with registered investment advisors (RIA) firms bringing general CRM systems like GoldMine and Sage ACT! into their firms and trying to customize them as much as possible to the way they work. It quickly became apparent that these systems and others fell short on the features desired by advisors, features specific to their industry.

Fast forward to today.

Despite the relatively small size of the advisory industry there are more than two dozen CRM packages out there with some type of financial services slant. Sure they can all record your client notes, many can track and archive related e-mails and act as repositories for scanning and storing imaged documents. In fact, most of the available products can handle these mundane chores with aplomb. These features, however, are just the tip of the iceberg. And it is really the rest of the iceberg that will help you narrow your choices to something that best fits your needs.

With that in mind I am not going to provide you a review of each CRM package out there. One could write an entire book on the subject instead of a chapter, but, frankly the advisory industry remains small enough that this would not be worth the author's while—it would remain far short of best-seller status. Rather, I will focus on the half-dozen leaders, the brightest lights in the CRM space and examine the trends that have some of those products—despite a small market share at present— growing rapidly.

Junxure and Redtail

Let's start with the two most popular products in the space: Junxure from CRM Software Inc. and Redtail from the eponymously named Redtail Technologies Inc.

Two different advisory industry technology surveys have these two vendors leading the pack, though in reverse order. In a 2011 technology survey among advisors conducted by *Financial Planning* magazine, 32 percent of more than 3,000 respondents reported using Redtail, while Junxure was being used by 14 percent. My own publication, *InvestmentNews,* has begun to conduct its own annual survey, and in 2011, this survey found that Junxure was being used by 21.2 percent of just under 1,000 respondents, while Redtail provided CRM to 18.1 percent.

Junxure has been around for 15 years and was born from the minds of advisor and company president Greg Friedman and his developer-partner Ken Golding. About the time this book is published, a new product from CRM Software called Junxure Essentials should be available. In a nutshell, this product, a truly web-based software-as-a-service offering, is meant "to keep the Junxure DNA," according to Mr. Friedman but is more lightweight and thereby more easily delivered over the Internet than the extremely feature-rich traditional Junxure.

Many RIA firms have, over the last few years, chosen to partner with third-party providers that host Junxure for them instead of running it themselves on their own premises. The main justification for this has been offloading the expense and tedium of maintaining the software and hardware themselves. That option has proved less than optimal in terms of speed for some advisors; the application simply runs better on a local server or personal computer and was never intended to be delivered over an Internet connection.

Essentials, then, is meant to be an offering that competes head-to-head with Redtail and other CRM systems that are delivered over the Internet. That should make it of interest to quite a few breakaway types or other smaller advisory firms interested in a fairly comprehensive product that has been built from the ground up for RIAs. And that last bit goes a long way toward explaining what has made Junxure so popular among RIAs.

It was built by an advisor with other advisors in mind. Therein is also my only hesitation for calling it the best CRM product out there for RIAs: It was created by "an" advisor.

Granted the firm has gotten a great deal of input over the years from its thousands of users and has very high retention rates but even so, no two RIA firms do things the same way and some firms have hankered for more flexibility and others a less expensive solution. Its cost is acceptable for most midsize firms, but smaller ones and solo practitioners tend to find it a bit expensive.

Junxure and the upcoming Essentials application are closely integrated with Microsoft Exchange and Microsoft Outlook. Rather than totally reinventing the wheel, CRM Software long ago decided to adopt and rely on Microsoft's ubiquitous e-mail architecture as part of its own plumbing.

This is mostly a good thing given that so much of the rest of the business world continues to rely on Microsoft for this technology, too—meaning it is proven and not disappearing anytime soon. Of course, it also means that an advisory firm that wishes to get the most out of Junxure (or Essentials when it comes out) will have to run Outlook and Exchange, either its own local versions, or more likely, it will go through one of many third-party providers of this technology.

Redtail's genesis as a web-based offering and one that has easy-to-integrate document management and compliance modules has also helped boost its popularity, especially as an option among independent broker-dealers and their registered representatives. In addition though, the price also happens to be right for small RIA firms and solo practitioners for whom Junxure tends to be overkill. While it is an oversimplification to call Redtail simple, it is far less complex and in many ways less comprehensive than Junxure, the evolution of which was meant to serve what are often larger, more complex firms with an often more diverse staff and multiple roles.

Redtail is also is fairly inexpensive and, refreshingly, publishes its pricing, which is based on databases (not per-user licenses). At the time of this writing one database that supports up to 15 users costs $65 per month. Its other products, including its own e-mail and e-mail archiving as well as document management, are priced separately but are listed on its website.

One reason I have heard given by those abandoning Redtail is that it lacks the ability to support much customization by individual advisory firms. In other words, advisors starting out find it comprehensive enough for their needs initially but as their firms grow or their business model changes or becomes more complex, Redtail is sometimes viewed as lacking the flexibility to accommodate this.

That said though, another big plus in favor of Redtail is its knack for integration. It has built-in account feeds through TD Ameritrade Institutional, making it somewhat of a no-brainer for advisors that already have the majority of assets at the custodian. And this penchant for integration is one way, though not a perfect one, for advisors to add functionality to their practices by adding point-specific applications for handling particular tasks.

That said, both Junxure and Redtail have excelled at delivering a great many integrations with other advisory technology providers to their customers. I will not waste space here listing them; a quick visit to their respective websites will display these as will YourSilverBullet.net (see the resources section at the end of the chapter).

So Who Are You?

It is very likely that many different types of financial advisors will be picking up a copy of this book, among them, registered investment advisors, be they wealth managers or holistic planners who also manage assets. Registered investment advisors have the most choice when it comes to selecting their technology, usually they have a blank slate.

But advisors should think of that slate more like one big piece of a larger puzzle. Perhaps the more apt analogy is to think of CRM as a central chunk of building blocks. If you were a kid in the 1970s or 1980s, chances are good that you are familiar with Lego's plastic building blocks. At first, the blocks and kits were fairly rudimentary, but over the years they came to include far more specific scenarios and specialized pieces.

Today's kids can find kits based on themes from fairy tales to spaceships; the array of pieces and types is astounding. While most Lego pieces from one kit fit together with pieces of another, non-Lego blocks usually do not. And that analogy should help to illustrate the second most important aspect of CRM selection—integration.

In addition to the dozens of CRM system choices available to advisors, there are many dozens of other types of applications. These include other core components that will make up an advisor's platform such as financial planning, portfolio management and accounting, as well as document management. And depending on the type of practice you have or plan to build, it can include many others, such as estate planning, analytics packages, tax software, and the list goes on.

For RIAs, the selection of a CRM solution will be influenced by whether you are starting from scratch or are already established and are dumping one CRM system for something more modern or one that better fits your work. Another consideration is whether you want to transition from a locally installed system to one that is cloud-based. For RIAs, in particular, the cost of the CRM application itself—including both initial outlay for setup as well as ongoing licensing—is an important consideration.

Advisors leaving one system must also consider the costs associated with migrating their data from what they are using now into the new system, the amount of training that staff will require, and how compatible that new system will be with the other software you are already using.

Some advisors reading this book may be hourly planners or planners on annual retainer. Plenty of independent registered representatives affiliated with a broker-dealer might also be wandering through these pages seeking answers. Much as it is impossible to lump every advisor into one particular type of practice we cannot pin every firm to the same point in its lifespan either.

Some of you are going to be coming right out of a university program; others leaving a wire house; some work for an independent broker-dealer; still others might be leaving a broker-dealer and setting up shop as an RIA; and some may be mature, established RIAs in need of a modern CRM program.

Most advisors, especially those who have departed wire houses, should begin their search for the right CRM system based on who they expect their custodian or broker-dealer to be. At least, try to narrow this decision to a few choices—this will not only help you decide your business model but will assist you in making a more informed choice on the technology front, as well.

Some affiliated advisors and brokers have little choice in selecting their CRM system because either their broker-dealer or other provider requires they use the brokerage's system or dictates a certain product or provides the advisor with a set of products from an approved list. Usually products on this list have been shown to easily integrate to a broker-dealer's account management or books and records system.

For example, those who join independent broker-dealer Commonwealth Financial Network LLP do not have to worry about CRM or technology selection; the firm built its own and it was built from the ground up as a fully integrated system. That system is well-respected, and the firm spends liberally on its upkeep and development.

Quite a few broker-dealers provide Redtail as their CRM of choice or have it on their short list as a recommended product.

Salesforce, Salesforce, Salesforce

Other broker-dealers select particular systems to integrate with their back-office systems. One example is Advisor Group, the large independent-broker-dealer network that this year rolled out Salesforce.com to the more than 4,000 affiliated advisors at its three firms—FSC Securities Corp., Royal Alliance Associates Inc., and SagePoint Financial Inc.

Advisor Group worked with Salesforce to integrate the CRM system with its Vision2020 accounting platform and had plans, as of this writing, to integrate another popular bolt-on module from Salesforce's App Exchange called Chatter. That application will power an internal social network for employees at the home office and all three of its firms and is another example of why Salesforce can be a compelling choice for larger, more distributed organizations.

The App Exchange has a lot of other potential components, too. One built specifically to help advisory firms create workflows is called ProcessComposer. That app was spun off from efforts at RIA firm Orchestrate LLC, which is owned by Foster Group Inc., a wealth management company with 800 clients and $1 billion in assets under management.

Orion Connect is another Salesforce App Exchange application that should be mentioned. Orion Advisor Services LLC, which is known for its high-end portfolio management and performance reporting, had requests for such an application from some of its large RIA customers.

Thanks to the open application programming interface from Salesforce, development was fairly quick and easy—a good illustration of why Salesforce is growing in popularity. While it appears that Salesforce is taking over the world of CRM, it is a good time to remind readers that the company will likely not hold the hand of smaller advisory firms in a manner they may be accustomed to.

There are a handful of consultancies and firms that have built overlays. Think of them as sort of a customized framework set down on top of Salesforce proper that attempts to make it into a tailored solution for advisors. A case in point is Concenter Services, a consultancy in Texas that does this very thing. Its overlay is called XLR8 (sounds like accelerate) and costs $75 per month per user (at the time of this writing), with all the customizations it claims an advisor would need right out of the box, including a workflow creation engine.

Salesforce itself is all about sales, not customer service, and has sold millions of licenses across dozens of verticals. It first launched an advisory-specific version—Salesforce for Wealth Management—in 2008. By and large, though, that version was seen as too limited for most RIA firms, which, if they purchased the application then had to spend a significant amount of money and time customizing it for their needs.

When it comes to RIAs and Salesforce it is the custodians that are starting to take on the role of intermediary and/or reseller.

Both Schwab Advisor Services and TD Ameritrade Institutional have worked the last two years to bring out versions of Salesforce heavily integrated with their respective back-office portfolio management and accounting systems. TD, for its part, built out Salesforce integrations with its Veo account management system along with a batch of 50 automated workflows, as well as several other third-party applications in mid-2011.

Workflows provide a template for how a firm should handle its everyday tasks in a uniform, consistent manner, for example, the new account opening and client onboarding process, which was one of the 50 prebuilt workflows found in the initial TD Salesforce offering.

Just as important, the workflows and other integrations are meant to help ensure that account and client data from Veo or other back-office account systems can be passed seamlessly to Salesforce (or other integrated CRM systems). This was completed as one part of TD's larger Veo Open Access/Open API initiative begun in 2010. In essence, TD created an RIA-specific version of Salesforce.

Intelligent Integration Can Be Confusing

Schwab Advisor Services (SAS) announced completion of something very similar shortly thereafter—its own turnkey Salesforce-centered Integrated Office platform. For the uninitiated, things in Schwab-Advisor-Services-land can get confusing quickly. So here is a brief tutorial. Everything available in terms of technology platforms for RIAs at SAS falls under what is called Schwab Intelligent Integration.

Within that initiative are multiple offerings; I like to refer to them as flavors. One of them, the most straightforward and simplest to describe is Schwab Integrated Office (SII). It has at its core a highly customized version of Salesforce CRM that is completely integrated with the Schwab PortfolioCenter portfolio management application. A unit of SAS develops, sells, and maintains this turnkey system itself and handles any advisor support needs.

The other flavors of SII all fall under what are called the Schwab OpenView Gateway offerings. A different business unit within SAS handles this set of offerings and each flavor has a different CRM.

In an oversimplified nutshell, these include the previously mentioned Junxure (which actually has a long history with Schwab—Schwab even owned its own version of Junxure for a few years) as well as a version of Gateway for Salesforce and Microsoft Dynamics. With these gateway offerings, Schwab builds the integrations between its back office and the CRM applications, but advisors purchase those applications on their own.

By the summer of 2012, Schwab, too, had announced the availability of 33 universal workflows in its own library. Those workflows can mean a big boost in efficiency for advisors using the turnkey version of Salesforce or the Gateway version of it or Junxure.

At the time of this writing in mid-2012, Schwab reported that 250 firms were on board the Gateway platforms, evenly split between Junxure and Salesforce. And 20 firms had signed on for the turnkey platform with Salesforce at its core.

Factor in Your Favorite Apps, if You Have Them

Integrating all your other technology is another big piece of completing the CRM puzzle.

As we discussed, most advisory firms are going to make their CRM system the core around which the firm's other applications and processes revolve. That is why, if you are fairly sure about the type of firm you will build (or already have built), it is important to determine the other technology applications you will rely on most before settling on a particular CRM solution.

For many advisors, financial planning or portfolio management will represent the other core components of their work. Established firms will already have technology they use and hopefully replacing a CRM system does not also mean dumping other key technology.

If you are happy with what you're using in these two areas, then good, it will make your task of identifying a new CRM that much easier—simply start with the portfolio management, financial planning application, and/or document management system(s) you already have and find out what CRM systems they integrate with.

If you happen to be that breakaway broker starting from scratch or an established firm shedding everything, keep in mind that there are more than a dozen of each type of application (portfolio management and accounting and financial planning) that are fairly popular in the industry.

Matching this number of financial planning and portfolio management applications with a compatible CRM application results in a daunting number of possible combinations. To keep things simple, let's say you use MoneyGuidePro, the very popular goal-based financial planning software from PIEtech Inc. You will find the firm has built integrations with many other advisory software providers, including six dedicated CRM applications.

Many of the other providers of popular financial planning systems have done the same thing, including Zywave (formerly Emerging Information Systems Inc.) purveyors of the popular NaviPlan and Profiles planning applications.

Once you have narrowed down the number of providers that you are looking at, it is time to examine the actual level of integration that they provide to the CRM systems you have your eye on.

For the sake of efficiency, seek a set of applications that can seamlessly share data and that bring in data from custodians and other providers automatically, rather than having to perform multistep downloads of files.

Again, attempting to cover the gamut of integrations of just the more than a dozen fairly popular portfolio management and performance reporting vendors goes beyond the scope of this writing, but if you have favorites start with their websites to begin finding what integrates with what.

Other Considerations

There are a few options that will render much of what I have written null and void.

What am I referring to? Simple, going with an all-inclusive system. Two leap to mind, although neither is going to be a panacea for everyone, as you will see shortly.

The first is a firm that has gained a lot of traction over the last five years: Tamarac. What used to be known as Tamarac Inc. was acquired in 2012 by the cloud-based hosted-asset-management firm Envestnet Inc. (The Tamarac division within the company has now been renamed Envestnet | Tamarac). For years, Tamarac was best known for its sophisticated portfolio rebalancing technology, but in 2010 it launched its own all-in-one all-online software as a service RIA platform, called Advisor Xi in its most recent form. The modules making up Tamarac's platform include its Advisor customer relationship management system (built on Microsoft Dynamics), its reba-lancer, and its Advisor View billing application.

Advisor Xi is also integrated with other core advisory applications, including Schwab PortfolioCenter for portfolio management, a proprietary performance-reporting module, as well as MoneyGuidePro for financial planning, and ByAllAc-counts for those seeking to bring in a view of clients' held away assets through account aggregation.

Advisor CRM, as it is called, is organized around easy access to client information and, as noted, is a highly customized version of Microsoft Dynamics CRM, which was built from the ground up to work in tandem with Microsoft Outlook.

In May 2012, Schwab Advisor Services announced that it would be partnering with Tamarac to build integrations. While at the time of this writing it remains to be seen just how deep those integrations will go or when they will be completed, in theory they will provide a real-time conduit for custody data from Schwab to flow from the Schwab Advisor Services back-office systems directly into the Advisor Xi platform.

It is important to keep in mind that Tamarac is custodial agnostic; it takes in feeds of data from all the major custodians.

So what is the downside? Well, for quite a few midsize to large RIAs, there really is no downside. For smaller firms and those breakaway advisors salivating at the idea of getting, in one fell swoop, much of what they left behind at their wire house in terms of a cohesive all-in-one solution there is the cost.

Most firms will probably end up paying at minimum $50,000 a year for the full Tamarac platform. Another all-in-one technology option is Solution 360° consolidated wealth management platform from Interactive Advisory Software Inc. better known as IAS. Version 5 of that product was released in 2012 and included a much-needed interface upgrade completed in 2011.

As the name would suggest it is a highly integrated system, indeed that is its chief raison d'être: all the core applications, including home-grown CRM, an advisory firm requires powered by a single central database. The firm has been around since 2001 and has never achieved a mass following but does have a loyal one composed of around 200 RIA firms around the country, quite a few of which are managing more than $1 billion in assets.

IAS is a web-hosted software-as-a-service model (though it began life as an on-premises client-services system).

Solution 360° combines multiple applications including client relationship management, portfolio management and reconciliation, financial planning, performance reporting, and online client portals, again, all running off a single central database.

And therein is also the only major complaint I have heard among advisory firms, all smaller shops, which migrated from the system—it was too much for their needs. Too comprehensive, too difficult for a few people to master, overkill in other words and it can cost more than $2,000 a month. It will resonate with midsize to larger firms on a growth trajectory.

Innovation Continues

As I stated at the beginning, this chapter is not meant to be a soup-to-nuts review of the more than two dozen products on the market that specifically target advisory firms. Rather, I sought to present the leaders and the trends driving them.

Junxure and Redtail are two companies with offerings that many advisors use, each has strong momentum and a loyal following among advisors, but custodians are spending a lot of money on their platforms. That has given Salesforce.com a lot of credibility it did not have in the advisory space before.

Similarly, Microsoft Dynamics seems to be claiming growing market share as well and cannot be dismissed. It also makes up one of the choices in Schwab's Gateway product line though Schwab Advisor Services has not developed its own integrated version the way it did with Salesforce.

Schwab has instead chosen to partner with other independent software vendors, the first of which is Salentica, a company that already offers a highly customized version of Microsoft Dynamics used by wealth and asset management firms (called Salentica Advisor Desk). At the time of this writing, Schwab Intelligent Technologies and Salentica announced availability of Advisor Desk with Schwab OpenView Gateway after completing a pilot. Advisors using it can view real-time information on their clients' financial holdings within their CRM. Data available from Schwab Advisor Services includes account balances, profiles, positions, transactions, and alerts. Schwab Advisor Services and Salentica have also completed the first version of an integration plug-in for advisors who had purchased Microsoft Dynamics CRM 2011 directly from Microsoft. The plug-in is meant to provide both the integrations with Schwab that Salentica had built for data as well as some customizations specific to advisory firms.

There are also quite a few small, independent players in the CRM space that will resonate with advisors, as well. There are three in particular that I would be remiss in not mentioning.

The first is Grendel from Big Brain Works LLC, which its creators define as an information management system for advisors that happens to provide customer relationship management, account aggregation, and document management (the company does not like to be pigeon-holed as purely a provider of CRM). It also serves as a client portal so that clients can access their account information, and the whole thing is web-based and used by both registered reps affiliated with a few broker-dealers as well as a few RIAs.

The solution has built-in integrations; for broker-dealer iterations there is a supervisory module for overseeing reps; and several external integrations, including MoneyGuidePro, links to Albridge Data Aggregation, a Google application that synchronizes with Microsoft Outlook, and Laser App for form filling.

The second is ProTracker from ProTracker Software Inc., which has a small but loyal following among RIAs. It has both a desktop and cloud offering and a suite of compliance modules.

Finally, there is Advisors Assistant from Client Marketing Systems Inc., which has developed quite a following among advisors who specialize in insurance. It provides CRM with optional portfolio management and insurance management modules.

Resources

I have to put in a plug for the *InvestmentNews* Tech Directory, which has listings and contact information for 252 providers, 32 of which offer CRM products.

Those with a paid membership to the Financial Planning Association should get the FPA-ActiFi Adviser Technology Reports: CRM Edition, published in 2010. At the time of this writing the reports had not been updated but perhaps they have by now. Even if they have not, the reports contain a great deal of detailed information on many of the products discussed here.

Advisors should also visit the website of Your Silver Bullet LLC (yoursilverbullet .net). This alliance of 18 (at the time of this writing) technology providers have paid dues to maintain a website tracking integrations between all their software offerings. Currently that includes four dedicated CRM vendors (CRM Software Inc., makers of

Junxure; Client Marketing Systems Inc., makers of Advisors Assistant; ProTracker Software; and Redtail Technology). I said dedicated because Tamarac is also a member and while its Advisor View CRM that is built on top of a customized version of Microsoft Dynamics cannot be used without buying into the Tamarac Advisor Xi platform, it is nonetheless a comprehensive CRM package.

The YourSilverBullet site can help advisors in determining the right combination of software applications for them and is especially helpful for advisors that might already be using a piece or two of their technology (for example financial planning software). In that case, the advisor will have a starting point and can narrow their search just to applications that work with it/them.

Keep in mind that the membership is by no means exhaustive (I regularly track more than 100 firms in my day-to-day work) but does represent a cadre of future-looking providers, many with the best interests of both themselves and advisors in mind.

Advisors who are considering outsourcing their technology or some of their technology-related operations should pay a visit to VirtualSolutionsforAdvisors.com. The site provides lists of consultants and companies; those that pay a small fee have links to their websites. It can at the very least provide a novice advisor a place to start from and company names to start a web search for.

Finally, one should not discount the usefulness of social media these days. Advisors who are members of the Financial Planning Association have their own networking system called Connect where you can search among various "communities" and "networks" for advice and reach out to other members.

In addition to membership organizations like FPA, NAPFA, and others, there are plenty of advisory groups to be found on social networking sites. In particular LinkedIn.com has a burgeoning population of dedicated financial advisor oriented "groups" that are easy to search. A few that might be of interest are the Financial Advisor Network group or FAN, RIAMarketplace, and InvestmentNews for Advisers, each of which already has thousands of members.

Several of the authors of this book also frequently write about CRM products or related topics as part of their regular writing too. Searches on CRM at the websites for Financial Planning Magazine, Bill Winterberg's excellent FPPad.com blog, and InvestmentNews.com will bring up a great deal of content on the subject.

CHAPTER 2

The Future of Financial Planning Software

Robert D. Curtis

Founder, President, and CEO of PIEtech, Inc. and Designer of MoneyGuidePro

The rapid advances being made in financial planning technology will cause fundamental changes in the future delivery of financial advice. The purpose of this chapter is to look at what those changes are likely to be and how they might affect the future of your practice. But since major changes always have their genesis in what came earlier, we need to begin our discussion in the distant past (which, in our business, is only about 25 years ago).

The Distant Past

The evolution of the financial planning profession has been significantly influenced by the evolution of the software available to support it. The first phase of planning might be called the "yellow pad" era, when the only technology available was a pad, a pencil, and a calculator. The task of manually creating a 30-year retirement plan severely limited both the availability and usefulness of planning services. The early practitioners were saved by the arrival of computer spreadsheet programs, beginning with VisiCalc, quickly advancing to Lotus 1-2-3, and then Excel. Advisors developed proprietary spreadsheets that modeled their personal approach to financial planning. Like the trusty yellow pad, spreadsheets provided unlimited flexibility. Advisors could control every assumption, and determine how every number was calculated. Spreadsheets, however, allowed them to develop far more complex plans than was possible with a yellow pad. They could create almost unlimited rows and columns of detailed data, projecting, with great precision, their clients' financial condition 30, 40, and 50 years into the future. The first detailed cash flow financial planning program was born. Advisors became so comfortable with their custom spreadsheets that even today, more than 20 years later, a surprisingly high number still prefer using their familiar spreadsheets instead of changing to one of the many specialized financial planning programs available.

Spreadsheets, while clearly a major improvement over the yellow pad, were, and still are, a tough beast to master. They are difficult and time consuming to build, hard to modify (particularly by anyone other than the creator), and can easily convert a minor programming error into a major error in results. It was to address these shortcomings that specialized financial planning programs were developed. Financial planning software allowed the advisor to provide sophisticated financial planning without having to be a programmer. It handled more complex planning issues, and created impressive reports for delivery to the client, making it possible to deliver more comprehensive financial planning services. However, there were still major challenges for advisors who switched to the new programs, since they essentially automated the detailed cash flow model of spreadsheets, but with even more detail and complexity.

The new software was difficult to learn, required a great deal of time and knowledge to create a plan, and the results were hard to explain to clients. These results were printed in a massive report that advisors used to present "The Answer" to the client, with little opportunity for client interaction. If the client requested even one simple change, like retiring a year later, the entire report had to be redone. Even worse, the report was obsolete as soon as it was printed. Despite their limitations, comprehensive, detailed cash flow planning programs became state-of-the-art in the profession, but their complexity limited their usefulness and adoption. While other, simpler programs also gained popularity, they were never considered to provide real planning.

The Past Five Years

During the last five years, three major changes have impacted financial planning software. The first is the most obvious—the broad availability of high-speed Internet. The Internet, and the browsers that are used to access it, have changed everything about how software is designed, developed, and used. The best financial planning software package is no longer the one that requires the most data, crunches the most numbers, or prints the biggest report. Today, the best software program is the one that makes it easy for you to engage and motivate your client. Software must be visual, intuitive, easy-to-use, and available to you anywhere, at any time, and on any device. Today's programs must empower your client to fully interact with you, whether it's in your office on the big screen, sitting at home having a glass of wine, or on your iPad at Starbucks. All these capabilities are already being used every day by advisors whose financial planning software is in the cloud.

The second, less obvious change is that financial planning has finally broken free of its spreadsheet origins. It has moved away from an accounting orientation and finally placed its focus where it always should have been—on client goals, and how best to attain them. This change in focus has allowed new financial planning programs to accomplish what previously had been thought contradictory—to become simultaneously easier to use and more sophisticated.

The third change is a direct result of the first two. More advisors can now provide more clients with quality financial planning services. More advisors offer goal-focused planning because it's easier, faster, more effective, and less costly. More clients want goal-focused financial planning because it's more engaging, more relevant, and more understandable. Plus, it creates a more enjoyable process for both parties.

The Now

So how will financial planning software change in the future and, more importantly, how will these changes affect you? Before we can answer these questions, we need to determine where you are today. Have you gotten to the technological "now" yet?

To find out, read the following statements and select the group that best reflects the state of your current technology.

Group A
- I require every new client to complete a long, data-gathering questionnaire.
- I use Excel spreadsheets for planning.
- I present "The Answer" to my client with a 100-page report.
- I believe that providing my clients with online access to their own plan would reduce my value.
- I think financial planning must be detailed and complicated to be good.

Group B
- Clients can enter their own data online if they want.
- I have a large screen in my conference room for interactive presentations.
- I have responded to clients questions by reviewing and adjusting their plans on my iPad.
- I offer all of my clients online access to their plans, and encourage them to use it often.
- I have updated a financial plan while sitting on the beach (or some other non-traditional location).
- I only provide a printed report if my client requests it.

Which group best fits how you do business? If it's Group A, you aren't taking advantage of the valuable benefits available from today's technology. You may be a successful advisor and not see why you should change a way of doing business that has worked well for you in the past. That's certainly understandable, but there are at least two reasons why you might want to reconsider. First, better technology can improve even the most successful practice. It can save time that can be redirected to higher-value activities. It can help you create a stronger level of engagement with your clients, and maintain that engagement through difficult markets. It can improve your responsiveness to client questions and concerns. And, most importantly, today's technology can help you substantially improve the overall client experience, which leads to happier clients and more referrals.

The second reason for embracing current technology is the risk it creates for your future if you don't. When your competitors are implementing new technology to improve their businesses, it puts you at a disadvantage. You're not only falling behind your competitors, you're also failing to keep pace with the technology expectations of your customers. Consider how most of your clients use technology today, not only for e-mail, Google searches, and Facebook postings, but to manage their financial lives.

- They go online to check bank balances, pay bills, and transfer money.
- They access their 401k accounts online to check values and make changes.
- They use Mint.com to manage their budget and aggregate all their investments in one place.
- They use Yahoo.com to watch the market and Morningstar.com to evaluate their investments.
- They do all the above on their iPhones and iPads, wherever and whenever they want, and most of it's free.

Clients will expect their financial advisor to be at least as technologically savvy as they are. And, I believe, clients will expect you to make technology options available to them and will place value on the technology you offer, even if they don't use it all. Demonstrating that your firm is technologically competent and competitive is a benchmark you are judged against. It used to be that having a glossy brochure, a nice looking office, and a fashionable suit were sufficient to establish credibility. Now, you need a well-designed website and software in the cloud. Unfortunately, I'm told, you still need the suit.

For those of you who still feel comfortable staying in Group A, consider this. The pace of technological advances is quickening (think iPad). The speed with which people adopt new technology is also quickening (think Mint and Facebook). If you're already behind the technology wave, where will you be three or five years from now? You can't be prepared to respond to the challenges future technologies may bring, if you haven't yet adapted to today's technology.

If you're already in Group B, congratulations. You've embraced the use of technology in your practice, and should be realizing significant benefits. You are well prepared to gain even greater benefits from the advances that are coming soon.

The Near Future

Now that we've examined how financial planning software has evolved to its present state, we have a better chance of predicting the direction it might take in the near future. So, here are my personal predictions. There will be three major trends in the development of financial planning software, which I will call smartness, accessibility, and centering. Each of these trends has distinct characteristics and consequences of its own, but they are also interrelated.

Smartness refers to the sophistication and intelligence built into the software. Smart programs look simple, because the complexity is hidden inside. It's like being at Disney World, where all the complex activities of running a huge amusement park are underground, hidden from the guests.

Smartness is the trend that's easiest to identify. It's obvious that financial planning software has been getting smarter every year and certainly will continue to do so. Smarter software is already making your job easier, by doing more for you. As an example, here's how we make software smarter at our company. We start by learning from the advisors. How do they use the program to create great plans? What are the best practices? Then, we automate as many recurring operations as possible. Sometimes, it's a simple task that is boring and time consuming (like entering data). Or it may be a task that requires many manual iterations to find a result (replaced by SuperSolve in our software, MoneyGuidePro). Smartness includes sophisticated capabilities like maximizing Social Security, finding the least-risk portfolio, and solving multiple variables simultaneously to create a plan recommendation. But smartness also includes simple tasks, such as better defaults, conditional data entry, and automatic Social Security estimates.

You'll notice that I didn't call this trend artificial intelligence (AI), although some might label it as such. AI seems a little pretentious for what financial planning software needs to do. We're not predicting the weather or competing on *Jeopardy!*. Calling it AI makes it sound like it's doing work of such complexity that it's beyond the capability of us normal people. Smartness means something different. Generally, it's doing what any knowledgeable and experienced advisor would (and could) do, if she had unlimited time.

All the smart capabilities I just discussed are available in financial planning programs today. As computers get faster, smartness will increase. Here are a few of the capabilities I expect smartness to provide in the near future:

- Automatically recommending specific strategies to improve plan results.
- Automatically updating plans with no advisor or client intervention.
- Automatically testing plans for assumption sensitivity (e.g., what if your inflation assumption is wrong).
- Providing embedded, on-demand assistance that is personalized to each client.
- Grouping similar types of clients and making suggestions that fit their group.
- Automatically generating plans—specific client contact opportunities (e.g., I reviewed your plan and noticed that . . .).

I'm confident the capabilities I've predicted here will come soon, along with much more that I can't yet foresee. Increased smartness will have major benefits for you and your practice. Smarter programs:

- Are easier to learn.
- Make it faster and easier to create plans.
- Require less experience to handle sophisticated issues.

- Create plans that are more personalized to each client.
- Reduce frustration.
- Reduce costs.

Smartness will play an important, very positive role in my third trend, called centering, which I'll address shortly. But first, I'll discuss another benefit from smartness that might appear troubling to some of you—smartness will accelerate accessibility.

Accessibility means that everyone will have access to high-quality financial planning programs. And I mean everyone—every broker, banker, advisor, accountant, or other provider of financial services. But it will also be readily available to every individual consumer of financial products. This is where you might feel a little uneasy. Today, your clients have access to hundreds of financial calculators, available for free on the web. But you know these tools don't provide real planning. In fact, it's my opinion that retirement calculators often are a disservice to investors. In their efforts to keep it simple, they dumb down the retirement planning process. They provide over-simplified results that can easily mislead the investor. They certainly cannot compare to the programs you use today (or even your Excel spreadsheet).

Smartness, however, is rapidly changing what's possible. As software gets smarter, it gets easier to use and easier to understand. It doesn't have to be dumbed-down to be usable by consumers. In only a few years, your prospects and clients will have access to professional quality financial planning programs, either for free or as a low-cost premium service on the web. This is already happening with trading, portfolio management, and even legal software.

So, is accessibility a threat to your business? If you ignore it or fight it, the answer is yes. If you plan for it and embrace it, no. The ready availability of high-quality financial planning programs will help engage more consumers in the financial planning process and make them better informed potential clients. But they will also become even more overloaded with information than they are today. We know that individual investors are terrible at making financial decisions—better software won't change that. Financial planning programs are great at analyzing, illustrating, and comparing the potential outcomes of various financial choices, but they are incapable of providing personalized counseling and advice. That requires a knowledgeable person clients can trust. That requires you.

Embracing accessibility will let you personalize your services for each client. If your clients have access to the same software that you are using, you can encourage them to be as involved in the process as they want. Some may choose to create only their goals online, since that's the most enjoyable part of the planning process. They can sit at home, relaxed and unhurried, and design their perfect future life. Then they'll turn it over to you to design a plan to attain the life they envision. Others might want to enter all their own data and review the results themselves, before coming to you for validation and investment advice. And many, just like today, won't want to enter any of their own data—they'll still want you to do it all. But they'll want online access to their plan, so they can easily try other options whenever they want. The key is that it's always their choice. You can tailor your services, and even your pricing, to fit each client's preferred way of participating in their own planning process.

Here's another opportunity created by accessibility. It will be easier for you to work with clients who live anywhere. If your specialty is divorced women who own yoga studios, every one of them in the country can become your prospect. The entire planning process can be done online, with you and your client sharing and collaborating within the same program.

Now let's move a short time into the future, and imagine a common client story. John and Ann Walters have been your clients for several years. They're in their mid-50s, are finished with college expenses (with no boomerang kids) and are looking forward to a freer lifestyle now, with a comfortable retirement coming later. You crafted a well-designed goal plan for them when they first engaged you, and have kept it up to date since. John and Ann both have online access to their plan, and you've noticed that Ann checks it fairly often. Consider the following vignettes.

- While reading the Sunday *New York Times* on her iPad, Ann sees an article about a retired couple facing some serious financial challenges. The husband had complications from surgery, and required an extended stay in a nursing facility to recover. The unexpected expenses they incurred depleted a significant portion of the couple's retirement assets and left them concerned about their future. This makes Ann wonder if she and John could handle such a health emergency. Ann clicks into her Financial Snapshot, where she views the current status of their retirement plan. She then uses the health care slider to see what would happen if she and John incurred a similar expense. She is pleased to learn that even with the expense they're still in their confidence zone. Feeling relieved, she clicks into the Entertainment section of the paper and enjoys the rest of her morning.
- When you come into your office on Monday morning, you check for alerts from your financial planning program. One is about John. It reminds you that he plans to purchase a new car in the next six months, at a cost of $35,000. You send John an e-mail, suggesting that he discuss financing options with you before looking for his new car.
- You notice that inflation has been in the news almost every day. Some experts claim that long-term inflation will be higher than expected. All your plans assume a 3 percent inflation rate, and while you still believe this is appropriate, you also want to make sure your clients aren't worried by the news reports. You ask your financial planning program to automatically rerun all plans with a 4 percent inflation rate, instead of 3 percent and identify any plans that fall outside their confidence zone. You then send an e-mail to your clients explaining why you think 3 percent is the appropriate assumption for inflation, but that you tested their plan for 4 percent just to be safe. If their plan result was still okay, you suggest they can see for themselves by going to their Financial Snapshot and using the inflation slider. If the 4 percent inflation rate caused their plan result to fall below their confidence zone, you suggest a call to discuss it.

Let's jump ahead another year. The stock market has been terrible. The economic news has been worse. The media is into its cycle of doom and gloom. It's time to reassure your clients.

You ask your financial planning program to rerun every plan. It starts by automatically updating the value of all positions, both held and held-away. It calculates the new probability of success for each client. Clients still in their confidence zone are notified that their plans are still okay, so they can relax. For clients who are now below their confidence zone, the program automatically generates suggestions of what changes would be required to bring them back into their confidence zone. You call these clients to discuss options before they call you and yell, "Sell!"

These advisor-client interactions provide great examples of the potential value of increased smartness and accessibility. They are also examples of our third future technology trend, which is centering.

In most of the financial services industry today, the primary focus of the client relationship is their investment portfolio. Investment options and investment performance dominate advisor-client communications. Even advisors who specialize in financial planning services are likely to find that most of their time, energy, and conversations with clients revolve around their investments (unless they provide only financial planning with no assets under management). Your investment committee meets regularly to review products and managers, you watch the market constantly, you send quarterly reports that compare your performance to benchmarks, you explain the benefits of asset allocation and rebalancing and dollar-cost averaging and concentrated positions and standard deviation and . . . and . . . and . . . well, you get the point. Because investing is complicated, volatile, and emotional, it demands your attention and doesn't leave much time to focus on the benefits of financial planning. After all, no advisor gets sued because he didn't identify a client's goals properly.

The trend I've called centering means that financial planning will move to the center of the advisor-client relationship. Not just in theory, but in everyday practice. Every client needs, and deserves, a well-crafted financial goal plan before they make investment decisions. It provides the reason to save and invest wisely and creates the anchor clients require to maintain an effective long-term investment strategy.

The benefits provided by improved technology will drive the move to centering:

- The cost to deliver high-quality plans will be greatly reduced.
- The value of financial planning to the advisor will increase dramatically, as illustrated in our story of John and Ann.
- Clients are going to expect and, soon, demand a plan before they invest.
- Advisors who adopt centering will be more successful.

Here's how you'll know you've become centered around the financial plan. When a client calls because she's upset about the latest losses in the stock market, you're first response is, "Let's see if you're still in your confidence zone." When a new prospect walks in your door and asks you to manage his $500,000, you'll say, "First we have to create your goal plan. Then I'll be able to give you advice about investing your money."

Conclusion

Predicting the arrival of any totally new technology, such as the iPhone or Facebook, is impossible. The predictions I've made in this article, by contrast, are logical extensions of what's already happening today. They are not dependent on any surprise breakthroughs. I'm confident the smartness and accessibility of financial planning software will continue to advance rapidly. The harder prediction is how fast centering will take hold, because it's dependent on the willingness of advisors to adapt to a new way of thinking.

Traditionally, the advisory community is not viewed as a group that readily embraces change. I have been amazed, however, how rapidly advisors have adopted mobile technologies. Most already have smart phones and iPads and are gaining immediate benefits from their use. What's different? Maybe the problem with adoption of technology by advisors isn't so much their unwillingness to change but poor design of the technology. If it's hard to learn and complicated to use, it can't provide clear value to their practice. It's my hope that the technological advances I've predicted for smartness and accessibility will accelerate the move to centering by making it easier to deliver high-quality financial planning to every client. Centering will become the new standard for advice delivery.

CHAPTER 3

The Future of Financial Planning Software and the New Client-Advisor Relationship

Linda Strachan, PhD
Vice President, Product Management, Zywave, Inc.

Kory Wells
Product Director of Data Analytics, Zywave, Inc.

The best financial planning has never been about the software; it's always been about the story—a story that, with the help of software, the advisor helps the client define, understand, and achieve. As advisors search for new ways to deal more efficiently with more clients, powerful forces are now changing the story and the way to leverage it profitably.

Like professionals in most businesses, advisors are striving to deal more efficiently with more clients, thus increasing productivity and profitability. It's no secret that software tools are key to addressing this challenge, but the best tools are changing, just like advisors themselves, to adapt to new conditions. For the first time in our industry's brief history, both advisors and their clients and prospects increasingly represent different generations. A one-size-fits-all approach to advisor-client interactions simply doesn't work anymore, and optimal technology solutions will use this fact as a guiding principle in the years to come.

In Chapter 2 we've established that smartness, accessibility, and centering will be important trends to expect in the future of financial planning software. Let's look at how these other dynamic factors will impact advisors, particularly independent advisors and registered investment advisors (RIAs), and particular types of prospects and clients in the near future.

- **Advisor and client demographics** and other characteristics are changing expectations for the story.
- **Social media** is changing how the story is collaboratively written, constantly revised, and ultimately perceived.
- **Technological advances** such as the iPad and HTML5 are changing how both advisors and their clients and prospects experience the story.

Advisor and Client Demographics

For most of its brief history, the financial planning industry has been one of baby boomers serving baby boomers. But that's now changing rapidly, and advisor-client interactions are changing accordingly. Different clients require different stories. For example, while the analytical highlights of a retirement plan—save, grow, track, retire, withdraw—are consistent for all clients, the story used to engage a 35-year-old single woman may be quite different from the one used for a 50-ish couple who've suddenly realized they've ignored retirement planning for too long.

Generational Differences

Although client demographics are becoming more varied, the general wisdom of "know your client" is not changing. Let's look at some of the characteristics of the cultural generations and how they affect advisor-client relationships.

Baby boomers, generally considered those born in the post–World War II baby boom period of 1946 through 1964, are the generation that has been most targeted by financial planners due to its size and affluence. Boomers have also been the primary focus of popular financial planning publications for the last decade. Among this demographic are high net worth and ultra-high net worth clients who have historically used advisors of all sorts; the financial advisor is just one of their many trusted advisors. Interestingly, most advisors are also boomers, so the following characteristics may have evolved as a result of both advisor and client influence:

- Boomers often demand sophisticated planning, such as cash flow analysis and tax and estate planning, supported by robust software solutions like Profiles and NaviPlan.
- Boomers typically expect multiple, personal contacts per year—by letter, e-mail, and phone call—and prefer periodic face-to-face meetings to maintain the relationship.
- Older boomers, now at or near retirement, have lived through various economic crises and need reassurance that they will not run out of money.

Younger generations—both Generation X (born in the mid-60s through about 1981) and Generation Y (born from about 1982 through 1999)—are generally accumulating wealth and may be balancing lower paychecks with student loans, education costs for their children, and mortgages. For advisors who are compensated based on assets under management, these types of clients may be less attractive. The clients themselves may also be less interested in financial planning or unable or unwilling to justify the expense of a plan, perhaps because they're unconvinced they need a comprehensive financial plan at this stage of their lives.

Despite the apparent reluctance on both sides to engage in the manner and depth that advisors and boomers have enjoyed, advisors must now focus on Gen X and Gen Y to achieve business growth in the years ahead. Admittedly, advisors will find the contrast to servicing boomers remarkable:

- Both of these younger generations are accomplished consumers of digital technologies. Today's most common financial activity for Gen Ys is to use their smart phones for checking account balances; the vast majority of mobile users under age 44 own a smart phone, according to a 2011 Nielsen study, and are also comfortable using more interactive applications in a mobile format.
- Similarly, many members of these generations, and especially Gen Y, actually prefer digital to personal interaction. They would much rather use an app—or refer to Google or social media—than talk to someone to solve a problem or get a question answered.
- For a variety of social and cultural reasons, the next generations seek peer validation more than expert oversight. Even those who seek advisor oversight will tend to self-educate and be more involved in planning than many boomers were.
- These generations are generally inclined to mistrust financial organizations.

Given these characteristics, it's clearly imperative for advisors to find engaging yet cost-effective solutions to attract and retain these generations of clients.

Gender and Other Differences

Another major demographic difference, which has received recent industry attention, is gender. In matters of personal finance, a Barclays survey reported in AdvisorOne (Fischer, 2012) showed that women:

- Tend to be more risk averse.
- Have less confidence in their knowledge.
- Express an interest in greater discipline with regards to learning about and achieving financial goals.

Women also have unique planning needs due to their increased likelihood of working in entrepreneurial or nontraditional enterprises and to factors like taking time off to care for children or elderly parents, their own longevity, and need for more late-life care. Planners should also consider "the collaborative and community-oriented style in which women traditionally learn," counsels Eleanor Blayney in the *Journal of Financial Planning*.

In addition to employing different approaches with women, advisors may also want to interact with clients differently depending on their vocations and avocations: Creative thinkers, for example, likely respond best to a softer, less analytical story than engineers. As we'll see later in this chapter, technological advances are going to make a more flexible approach to client interaction easier than ever before.

Social Media

"I couldn't tell you how much my dad earned," says a Gen X woman, referring to the privacy with which her parents have held their finances for their entire lives. In tremendous contrast, she's aware of friends who are posting information about their salaries, spending, assets, savings goals, and debt pay-down progress in specialized online communities such as Bundle.com and Wesabe.com.

Led by Facebook, Twitter, blogging, and a plethora of niche community sites, social media has permeated our culture so deeply that some of us now willingly share personal information—including financial data—in a public format, eager to see how we compare to others of a similar demographic. Those of us who aren't ready to take such a step may at least peruse an investment site to check out crowd-sourced wisdom about a particular stock. Even some of us who are advisors aren't immune; we share information in online communities, follow our most respected colleagues to glean their advice, and at least think about the elusive "content" we ourselves should be generating in order to engage prospects and clients. When we read something that's valuable, we expect to have buttons to "Like" or "Share" it with others. Undoubtedly, social media represents a low-cost, powerful tool for advisors to expand their reach and connect with clients on a deeper level.

Yet many advisors have been slow to experiment with, let alone embrace, social media, often due to potential compliance issues with state and federal regulators or the mistaken notion that their clients are not interested. On the regulatory front, guidelines are becoming better established so that advisors will be able to operate in the social media space with greater confidence. Their customers are certainly there: 50 percent of all adults use social media sites, and social media is turning increasingly "gray" with older users (Pew, 2011). Depending on the focus, social media may help advisors relate to the population of a geographic area (in the advisor's city) or to a certain demographic the advisor focuses on (the unique planning needs of divorced women regardless of where they live, for example). A few tips to advisors include:

- Don't feel like you have to do it all—Facebook, Twitter, LinkedIn, Google+, blogging, and community sites. Pick a couple of formats where you're most comfortable and invest time and consistency there.
- Monitor financial planning media and your particular areas of interest using technology tools like Google Alerts, Pocket (recently known as Read It Later), Flipboard, Pulse, and Taptu.
- Try to deliver real value in your social media posts. It's fine to mention your services occasionally, but you'll have more success if you talk generally about

financial planning and other news of interest to your target community. You can also promote free content or prospecting tools associated with your financial planning software, such as Profiles Professional's Retirement Consumer Facing Application. For a boost to your social media success, consider contributing to conversations and community forums among other advisors, as well.

Just as advisors need to take the long view with developing younger generation clients, they also need to take the long view with investing time and effort in social media and developing a presence that will engage the younger generations—both prospects and clients—in their own backyard, so to speak. Advisors also should not overlook the power of social media as a format for interacting with their peers across the nation.

Technological Advances

While advisors differ widely in terms of expertise and approach, they generally have two desires: to serve clients better and to achieve increasingly higher profits, even in the face of declining or flat markets. Independent advisors have an advantage over enterprise financial service organizations because of their ability to more quickly respond to a changing landscape. To maximize this ability, however, advisors need to be at the forefront of technology, especially in terms of delivering a better client experience. Those who leverage their client relationship skills with cutting-edge technology will realize a more efficient and effective business practice.

New technologies are continuously evolving, of course, and one challenge for both financial planning software vendors and the advisors they serve is to be adaptable to the latest technology trends. At the forefront of those trends today are tablet and mobile computing, robust data integration, and leveraging "best of breed" applications—an advantage that independent advisors have over enterprise organizations.

Tablet and Mobile Computing

User interfaces today are more graphical and engaging than ever, thanks to technology such as tablet computing and HTML5. Due to these advances, both advisors and their clients expect tools that provide value without being cumbersome. Many advisors are already using iPads both for general business purposes and for specific financial planning tasks such as client presentations. For example, an advisor who formerly used a large flat screen in his boardroom for client presentations now drives presentations from an iPad while the client or clients across the table follow along on their own devices. This is an interesting modification to traditional face-to-face meetings that stands to make each client feel more personally involved.

The HTML5 language is one of the latest core technologies for structuring and processing content for the Internet. It's especially notable because of its ability to deliver video and other media to smart phones and tablets without requiring another common—and now aging—tool, Adobe Flash. (Flash is not even supported on Apple iOS products [iPads], and Adobe has announced plans to focus on HTML5.)

Understanding the significance of HTML5 is one example of how, when selecting or upgrading financial planning software, advisors and their organizations may need to consider:

- The software's support of multiple browsers (for both desktop and mobile devices).
- The ability of the software to provide value on tablets such as iPads and Android devices (as well as whatever the future brings).
- Interface issues such as touchscreen typing requirements.
- Security concerns.

Successful implementation of software that exploits these new opportunities and the ability of various types of advisor organizations to implement and deploy them is likely to vary for many years to come.

Robust Data Integration

Data integration issues can be among the most frustrating and time-consuming tasks in any aspect of an advisor's operations. It is not uncommon to hear of advisors who get caught between two vendors, each pointing their finger at the other when problems arise; in fact, lawsuits occur over such issues.

There is currently no common data schema to support standardized integration across applications in the financial planning space, so while it is the hope of the future, the road ahead looks rough and long. In the meantime, when selecting financial planning software, questions like these will help advisors both gather important information and communicate to vendors the importance of integration issues, thus shaping the future direction of improvements:

- Are there videos that show what the ideal integration looks like for all parties?
- Is there really a relationship between two vendors, or is it in name only? (Some vendors have a long list of "partners" but don't have true relationships with them.)
- Can the vendors demonstrate specifically how they cooperate? Can they assure the advisor of how they take joint responsibility to resolve a problem, rather than leaving a burden of proof and resolution on the user? This is just an extension of an organization's ability to support users for all issues.
- Do error messages provide helpful text, not just meaningless codes, and indicate which vendor to contact for further assistance?

Integration isn't a panacea, but achieving better integration of data across multiple software systems will reduce work and result in fewer errors.

Best of Breed Applications and Other Independent Advantages

Admittedly, it can seem overwhelming to keep up with technical advances and jargon, data integration issues, and the constant onslaught of new technology. Even the technical information provided in this chapter will be stale by publication time. Advisors need to remember, however, that they can leverage emerging technology to achieve an advantage over their enterprise competitors.

One way advisors can do this is to be alert to best of breed tools—especially when they learn about those tools from their clients—and take advantage of those tools in their client interactions. Examples, some of which are described elsewhere in this book, include:

- Using WebEx, FaceTime, or Skype for advisor-client meetings to save your clients time. This is especially effective when geography or calendars prevent a face-to-face meeting.
- Using industry leaders such as Redtail for client relationship management (CRM), Albridge for portfolio management, Laserfiche for document management, and Tamarac for rebalancing. The industry press regularly reviews and surveys users for the best technology in each of these sectors.
- Investigating choices presented by the various custodians. Custodians are much more active in selecting and integrating the best tools into their platforms, and this may provide some additional value.

When it comes to implementing any new technology, independent advisors have several other advantages over enterprise organizations:

- Enterprises must support literally hundreds of applications on an infrastructure designed for the lowest common denominator of applications. For example, while independent advisors have no trouble upgrading the to the next release of Internet Explorer, or Chrome, or Safari, enterprise organizations are often hamstrung into staying on older versions until *all* of their applications can support the new version. This may include proprietary applications that need updates and compete for the same IT budget.
- Enterprises have been slow to adopt emerging social media trends, since their size often limits their ability to control messaging. An independent advisor or smaller firm can more readily control policy and messaging and more easily manage the volume of monitoring needed to interact effectively in the social media sphere.

Of course, being nimble enough to take advantage of newer technologies is only one part of the equation—advisors must also identify and learn about those new technologies. And while it's certainly possible to learn from colleagues, clients, vendors, and online resources, advisors who attend industry conferences such as Technology Tools for Today (T3)—the premier technology conference in the industry—and the Financial Planning Association's (FPA) annual conference will be best positioned with industry-specific knowledge to build and refine more sophisticated platforms.

An Advisor's Planning Tool versus Consumer Planning Tools—Working Together or Apart?

It seems increasingly inevitable that most financial planning clients may use or be familiar with needs analysis tools on their banking and investment sites. Many may also be using financial account consolidation and monitoring tools such as Mint.com, and some may even be aware of online financial plan providers or robo advisors, such as Personal Capital, Wealthfront, and FutureAdvisor. The perceived level of conflict between these systems and the services offered by traditional advisors are as varied as the systems themselves. While these self-service models may seem to threaten the advisor, comprehensive financial planning software combined with the expertise of an advisor is a far superior model. "Some professions have a fundamentally human component that will never be replaced by computers, machines, or algorithms," Mike Alford writes in *Forbes*. Advisors who seek to make their business more scalable, personal, and accessible to clients and prospects and who avoid an "either-or" perspective concerning these tools will effectively neutralize their threats.

But how will advisors' planning tools differ from these consumer tools? Financial planning software that has the following characteristics will increasingly become the norm:

- Increasingly flexible presentations.
  - Ability to focus on different demographics or objectives—for example, retired clients need a different story than clients who are still accumulating for retirement (offered by both NaviPlan and Profiles solutions from Zywave).
  - Support for regional language and graphic requirements to better represent the client.
  - Option to address a single need at a time as a simpler, step-by-step method of gradually leading the client in the fact-finding process. This allows the advisor to demonstrate value in small increments and clients to limit how much information they have to divulge at once, thus providing an alternative path to advisor-client engagement and trust.
  - Client self-service for some simple purposes, such as retirement needs assessments as a prospecting tool.
  - Ability to expand simple needs assessments into a comprehensive analysis that uses the full power of a sophisticated planning tool.
  - Interactive "what-if" presentations as opposed to a hardcopy report or book.
- Electronically deliverable client reports.
  - Reports will be built on templates and defaults, but advisors will have customization control over certain content areas.
  - Options to control configuration of reports, such as choice and ordering of columns.
  - Options for advisors to personalize recommendations, action plans, and product recommendations.

- Opt-in options to new software features so advisors don't have to learn a new feature until they're ready.
- A continuance of popular wizard-type interactions but with options that require even fewer clicks of the mouse.
- Options to run planning software online and/or store data in the cloud.
- Options to personalize the user interface and even modify the software itself to suit specific needs.
  - Ability for user to define preferred paths through the software, thus simplifying available controls and features for everyday use.
  - Ability for users to brand the application and reporting to differentiate themselves.
- Reactive abilities, as discussed in the previous chapter, so that clients will receive alerts regarding factors that impact their plan. Such alerts will sustain the advisor's value to the client throughout the year and help avoid big changes or surprises at the time of the annual review.
- Data integration, as discussed earlier in this chapter, and also an important element in implementing reactive features.
- Ability to integrate goals and changing plan factors with web-based marketing and content tools to automate education-oriented, automatically scheduled outreach to clients.
- Integrated user feedback, including the ability to vote up and down for suggested software enhancements.

Conclusion

In summary, advisors who are active in social media, proactive about learning new technology, and anticipatory of their clients' changing demographics and characteristics will use financial planning software to its fullest potential. The best advisor planning tools of the future will be built on decades of research and development in planning techniques and a demonstrated commitment to timely tax and legislative updates. More flexible and customizable than ever before, these tools may seem as simple, slick, and accessible as popular consumer planning tools, but they'll also provide deep, comprehensive analysis and consistent results across all levels of functionality, allowing advisors to fully leverage changes in the market to drive profitability. In other words, they'll be both sexy and smart. As a result, presentations and reports won't overwhelm prospects or new clients, and their easy adjustability of the story as a client's life circumstances change will strengthen how clients perceive their advisors' expertise, accessibility, and personal skills.

References

Alfred, Mike. 2012. "Why Betterment, Wealthfront, and Other Online Investment Firms Are Wrong about Financial Advisors." www.forbes.com/sites/brightscope/2012/05/02/why-betterment-wealthfront-and-other-online-investment-firms-are-wrong-about-financial-advisors/ (accessed June 26, 2012).

Blayney, Eleanor. 2012. "Empowering, Educating, and Engaging Women Clients," *Journal of Financial Planning* (July). www.fpanet.org/journal/CurrentIssue/TableofContents/EmpoweringEducatingand EngagingWomenClients/ (accessed June 29, 2012).

Fischer, Michael S. 2012. "Challenge of the Sexes: Big Differences on Financial Planning." www .advisorone.com/2012/02/07/challenge-of-the-sexes-big-differences-on-financia (accessed June 28, 2012).

Madden, Mary, and Kathryn Zickuhr. 2011. "65% of Online Adults Use Social Networking Sites." http://pewinternet.org/Reports/2011/Social-Networking-Sites.aspx (accessed June 29, 2012).

Nielson.com. 2011. "Generation App: 62% of Mobile Users 25-34 Own Smartphones." http://blog .nielsen.com/nielsenwire/online_mobile/generation-app-62-of-mobile-users-25-34-own-smartphones/ (accessed June 29, 2012).

CHAPTER 4

Portfolio Management Software

Mike Kelly
President, Back Office Support Service

Before we can discuss portfolio management software we must define it. This is particularly important as the different flavors of financial software expand and the edges become blurry. For purposes of this chapter, portfolio management software is software that allows a user to obtain, manage, and report on client data. At a minimum, that includes the acquisition of client financial data from various sources, calculation of internal and/or time weighted rates of return, calculation of management fees, and generation of reports for clients. This is, admittedly, a very broad definition but still delineates features beyond what advisors will have available using just their custodian's standard capabilities.

This brings us to the next distinction we are going to use. The focus of this chapter is on software used by independent investment advisors, financial planners, and small broker dealers that we will collectively refer to as advisors. We will not be covering programs such as Albridge, which are oriented toward institutional usage. Nor will we be covering software provided by custodians that ties you to that custodian.

Throughout the chapter, we will provide current examples of portfolio management software that exhibit certain characteristics. The examples are not meant to be a complete listing but a representative listing. Also keep in mind that new vendors may appear on the scene at any time.

The information in this chapter will cover portfolio management software from three vantage points. In "My Place or Yours?" we will examine programs based on the responsibility for maintaining the operational environment. Your office? Hosted? Hybrid? Does it matter?

Next, in "All for One or One for All?" we will examine portfolio management software based on business approach. Does the software attempt to be all things to all people? Does the software act as a focal point for integration with other financial software? Is there a combination of both? Does it matter?

"Keeping Up with the Joneses" examines system maturity. What about software that has a long track record? What about software that is revolutionary but doesn't have much of a track record? Does it matter?

I am sure you noticed that each area included the question, "Does it matter?" To which you should respond, "To whom?" Your circumstances will determine what is important to you, so we will try to highlight considerations for different categories of advisors such as breakaway brokers, new advisors, and those who are considering a change from one system to another. On to the big top.

My Place or Yours?

An early consideration in the evaluation of portfolio management software is the responsibility for maintaining the software environment. Historically, the most widely seen implementation of portfolio management software has been the purchase (technically lease) of the program from a vendor who then expects you to provide the environment in which it will operate. That could be on a single desktop computer, a local-area network, or even the placement of the software in a separately staffed data center. The key point here is that you, not the software vendor, are responsible for the hardware that operates the program. The company that produces the software will provide technical support for installation, but it is your responsibility to maintain that system and to install any updates provided by the vendor. Once the software is installed, you can expect the software vendor to provide some form of continuing support. There is usually an annual fee that covers the cost of ongoing support and upgrades to the program. Examples of software provided this way include PortfolioCenter, Axys, FinFolio, Captools, PowerAdvisor, and Principia CAMS.

Increasingly, advisors are seeking ways to move the responsibility for the hardware out of their office. With this approach, the software is hosted by the vendor. There is no installation although there will still need to be some customization of asset classes, billing specifications, report selection, and so on to reflect the way you do business. Vendors such as Morningstar, Tamarac, Interactive Advisory Software, and Advent-Black Diamond provide the platform and access so you can process your data and run reports. Other firms such as Orion and AssetBook bundle their software with a service bureau offering. You cannot get one without the other.

What difference does it make? There are three key considerations: data, information technology (IT) maintenance, and cost. If you purchase and run the software in your environment, there is little doubt about control of the data, access to the data, ownership of the data, and the responsibility for protecting and backing up the data. When you use a solution hosted by the vendor, the responsibility for backing up and protecting the data becomes theirs, but you may not have full access to all your data. You need to know what your options will be if you decide to move from the hosted solution in the future. What data will the vendor provide you? Will it include all historical prices, transactions, performance calculations, and so on? (The most common issue that comes up is the lack of prices in the provided data.) Can it be used as is anywhere else or does it need to be converted? If it needs to be converted, are there companies that can/will do that? While these are valid questions whether you host the data or not, you have less access to the data when it operates in the vendor's hosted environment.

Using a hosted solution will eliminate many of the IT-related headaches. This includes such things as server problems, network problems, and updates to the software. If you already have IT staff, then this is not as significant. If you do not, then it helps to simplify your operations.

Cost is not as easy as it sounds. The cost of just the software will be less when you are responsible for the operating environment. When comparing the cost to a hosted solution, however, do not stop there. Do you need to pay for a stronger server? Do you need to purchase more expensive related software (such as SQL) to operate the program? How will it affect your time or your IT costs? Will part of the cost of hosted services be offset by other savings in staff or time? (The host may perform daily posting, for example.) Your portfolio management software touches a major portion of your operations. When you consider costs, examine the impact on time and related costs as broadly as possible.

All for One or One for All?

Another way to look at portfolio management software is to segment by scope. Is the primary focus of the vendor a fully integrated product or a best of breed approach? Integrated programs provide functionality beyond our definition of portfolio management software as part of a single program. Most portfolio management software includes some form of rebalancing as part of the software. The features are usually provided in the form of a report. Integrated packages, on the other hand, go beyond rebalancing and may include more sophisticated features such as order entry, block trading, and tax lot optimization as part of a trading module. Examples of this are Tamarac, Orion, Interactive Advisory Software, and Morningstar. Every portfolio management software program offers some form of contact management. The information is necessary to keep track of clients and accounts within the system. Portfolio management software with more sophisticated CRM capabilities will provide more customizable fields and direct integration of contact information with e-mails and calendars. Examples of integrated CRM include Orion, Tamarac, Interactive Advisory Software, and Morningstar.

While CRM and trading are the most common additional components of an integrated system, they do not represent the full list of additional features in the marketplace. Morningstar Office and PowerAdvisor add investment analytics and Interactive Advisory Software adds financial planning features.

On the other hand, solutions such as Axys, PortfolioCenter, and AssetBook use a best of breed approach, which places more emphasis on the integration of functionality from third-party vendors allowing the user to determine the best choice in each category. Best of breed is a different approach to solving the needs of advisors. If we continue with the trading example, an advisor might select TRX, TradeWarrior, RedBlack, or some other trading package that works in tandem with the portfolio management software and meets the specific needs of the advisor. An advisor could then select a CRM package from Redtail, Junxure, Salesforce, or ProTracker to best meet their specific needs.

What difference does it make? As was the case with "My Place or Yours?," there are three primary considerations. In this case, they are cost, convenience, and functionality. Let's take those in reverse order as understanding functionality is critical to a fair assessment of convenience and cost.

Understanding what you do and how you do it are determining factors in assessing whether a piece of software will enhance your business. A best of breed approach will give you more options in matching your needs and more flexibility if your needs should change. While a greater number of choices can increase the odds of finding the best match, it is still appropriate to ask if a specific integrated solution meets your needs. If it does, then having another set of choices is not of value unless your style of business changes. The challenge for integrated software is that it provides a particular solution for each category, and you must find a good match in each category within the same software package. First and foremost—does it meet your needs?

In most cases, a best of breed approach will rely upon some form of data transfer between the programs as a means of integrating the functionality. While data transfers are becoming more automated and some can run in the background, the current state of the art is such that an extra step may be required. In most cases an integrated program will share data in real time. That means that an update to the number of shares held or price of a security is instantly available to the trading module in determining what kind of trade makes sense. A best of breed approach may require a new export of data. Let's circle back to your needs. If you are a high-frequency trader, this may be very important. If you trade less frequently, then the importance will diminish. That is not to say that it becomes as convenient, only that the inconvenience becomes very small. If you are outsourcing and your outsource provider does that part of your work, the issue may be moot. When it comes to convenience and the transfer of data between unrelated software, it should be noted that several major custodians are actively engaged in the development of platforms that will streamline and automate the transfer of data. The end result may focus on something other than the portfolio management software as the hub of the data transfer but the end result is likely to be that performance, trading, CRM, or what have you will talk to one another with much greater ease than is the case today.

Finally, time to pay the piper. The cost of integrated portfolio management software is going to be higher than a system that uses a best of breed approach. This should not be a surprise as the scope of features is broader. You can't just look at the cost of the portfolio management software in this case. You must look at the broader scope of software requirements for your firm. As you analyze your needs and determine what software can meet them, add the cost to your shopping list. Your best of breed portfolio management software is the first building block in a comparison. What do you need to add to that? Does your business style require a more sophisticated trading approach? If so, the cost of the software must be added to the portfolio management software cost for a fair comparison. Do you also need to add a separate CRM package? If so, add the cost to the running total. If not, leave the cost out.

Let's suppose that you need CRM capabilities beyond what a nonintegrated system will provide but don't need the extra trading features of the integrated platform. Aren't you paying for extra features you don't need? Irrelevant. If the cost of the integrated system is less than the total cost of the nonintegrated components, then the lower cost still prevails. What about the reverse? Suppose the integrated cost is higher but there are extra features that you don't currently need. Isn't there some value for the additional features? No. Not unless you can reasonably expect that you will use them in the future. If your needs change, you might use the additional features or you may need to go to separate software to meet those future needs. If it is likely you will use the features then there is value. If not, then you are paying for extras you don't need.

Keeping Up with the Joneses

We all understand that an advisor's business relies on relationships and that fact is a constant. The only constant in technology, however, is that it is constantly changing. This is just as true for portfolio management software. There are programs that are headed to pasture, new arrivals, and all the programs in between have added new features since this chapter was written.

When you consider the purchase of portfolio management software, be sure to inquire about the development schedule. What new features are going to be added and what is the timetable for those releases? It is not likely that the features will actually be available on the target date, but the question should give you some insight into the mind-set of the vendor. Another question is how many firms (not users) they have using their system and how much has that changed over the last year. If there is even the slightest doubt about the future of the program, be absolutely certain that you have an exit strategy that allows you to retain your data and move it to another system. At the time of this writing, Principia CAMS falls into the category of "headed to pasture."

Exciting new technology does not require that a new company be involved. Orion and Black Diamond continue to push the envelope with regard to the use of tablets and cloud computing and many vendors are not far behind. The initiatives by custodians will continue to make the integration of all data easier and easier but will take several years to mature. Innovations do exist, however. Blueleaf uses a completely different approach to the processing of custodial data with the potential to significantly reduce the cost of daily processing. New companies, whether they use a new approach or an old approach, require the same caution as fading companies—plus an extra wrinkle. Just like the fading company, you must have a viable exit strategy. Additionally, know that you will likely have more software issues than with a company whose software has been tested in the marketplace for many years.

Another consideration when being impressed with a new company and new software is the scope of features. New software will likely have a more attractive interface, but that does not automatically transfer to ease of use. Software that has been around for a while will have developed a rich feature set. New software will go through the same evolution. It bears repeating. Does the software have the features you need/want based on the way you do or will do business?

Putting It All Together

Moving from one portfolio management software package to another involves considerable time and cost and should not be undertaken unless you perceive a significant benefit to your firm. Benefits might include improved reporting, lower cost, ease of use, or features not available in your current software. When considering additional features, I cannot overemphasize that extra features mean nothing unless the features contribute to the way you do or will do business. Software that automatically reminds you of the next scheduled launch of a space shuttle has a special feature but will not contribute in any way to your bottom line or enjoyment of your business. Also consider features that you may lose. Just because a software package is using a newer technology does not mean that all of the features you take for granted are present.

Consider that most vendors charge more for the first-year license than they do for a renewal of an existing license. If outsourcing works for you, you can overcome the initial cost hurdle by moving to an outsource provider that supports the software you have chosen. Your current portfolio management software may be used in conjunction with other software. This may be as subtle as a spreadsheet that has been designed to import data in a specific format. What will you need to buy or change to complete the same process with new portfolio management software? The answer can be in time, money, or both. Another cost consideration is lost productivity as you and your staff become accustomed to new features and processes.

New software will entail a learning curve for you and your staff. You should strive to make this work for you rather than against you. Insure that key members of your staff are involved in the evaluation process. Let them identify the areas of weakness in your current system and how those will improve with a new system. Will improved ease of use save them time? Can activities run on the side using spreadsheets be more effectively integrated into the workflow with new systems and processes? What current processes will take more time or effort? Use the evaluation process as a means to challenge your current work habits and those of your staff. If they actively participate in the process, you will be surprised at some of the new ideas you will hear, and your staff will be more inclined to constructively work through the unexpected issues that will come up.

The process of evaluating portfolio management software is not the same for everyone. We will suggest considerations for three common circumstances where advisors might be evaluating portfolio management software; new advisors, breakaway brokers, and portfolio management changes for established advisors moving from an existing system to a new one.

New Advisors

For our purposes, a new advisor is any advisor who has not been using portfolio management software. The advisor may have been in business for many years using spreadsheets or be a recently licensed advisor. The key is that new advisors are just starting out with portfolio management software. There may be a temptation to look at the various offerings, choose the newest, coolest one and let that define the way you will do business. The end result may be that you have the coolest, nonfunctional business in town. That beautiful new convertible may simply not be the best vehicle to move the dirt from your weekend gardening projects.

First, get a high level view of what portfolio management software can do. You can get that from vendor websites, discussion groups, professional organizations, industry conferences, and discussions with your peers. Next, focus on business objectives. Based on your business model, what do you want from the portfolio management software? Are you going to have lots of face-to-face client meetings or update your clients electronically? What kind of information do you want to present to your clients? Where are your client accounts?

A few key considerations are important. Do not focus on duplicating the process you have now. Focus on the best way to get the end results you want. A good example of this is billing. Prior to using portfolio management software, most fee-based advisors use spreadsheets to calculate management fees. There is a high degree of control and comfort in this process but it is not efficient. Most portfolio management software includes very flexible billing components that will give you the end result including an accurate invoice, in a fraction of the time it takes to process spreadsheets. That brings me to my next point—scalability.

If you have a small practice and intend to keep your practice small, then this is not critical. Otherwise, not implementing portfolio management software is simply very poor planning. When you have 10 clients, it may not seem like spending 10 minutes each to get their reports ready each quarter is a problem. That is less than two hours per quarter. Think about what your practice will be like with 100 or 300 clients. What is now two hours becomes 60 hours and that is on top of additional client contact, marketing, analysis, trading, administration, and so on. Do not wait until the bottlenecks force you to reevaluate your processes. The amount of time it will take to fix hundreds of accounts later will give true meaning to Murphy's Law. It will be much more disruptive to your practice the longer you wait. Consider how the features and ease of use of portfolio management software will streamline and complement the workflow you want with a larger client base. As you examine your workflow, consciously try to remove exceptions in favor of processes you can automate within the portfolio management software. This does not mean you have to move to a one-size-fits-all approach. Portfolio management software today offers considerable flexibility within the areas of billing, allocation, reporting, and custom field usage. A key consideration in selecting the best solution for you is the determination of which package best complements the workflow you are seeking.

Finally, as you do the workflow analysis, keep in mind that your workflow may be complemented by third-party software. If that is the case, whether for trading, contact management, or portfolio reporting consider how well the platforms will work together. Will you be sacrificing beneficial features for ease of use or vice versa?

Breakaway Brokers

The needs of brokers leaving a wire house environment are, in many ways, similar to the needs of new advisors in the sense that you are looking to set up portfolio management software from scratch. With regard to portfolio management software, your focus should be on the services formerly provided by your broker-dealer that you will now have to take care of yourself. The two of greatest concern to most breakaway brokers are billing and reporting. The billing section of most portfolio management software will provide all the flexibility you need. Some of the commonly available features include the ability to bill in advance or arrears, tiered or flat rate, by individual account or in aggregate, with or without discounts, and the ability to assign different clients to different billing structures. If you have already completed your Form ADV, the billing disclosure from that document will provide enough information for your billing setup. If you have not completed the Form ADV yet, keep in mind that simpler is better. It will be easier to set up, easier to maintain, and easier for your clients to understand. The one billing structure that is not available in most portfolio management software is performance-based billing where your compensation is based on the extent to which your performance exceeds that of a benchmark.

When you leave a wire house, you gain control over the contents of the reports that your clients see. When rates of return are provided in wire house reports or those of a mutual fund company, the returns are generic returns for a specific security over a month, quarter, year, and so on. They are not the returns for a specific investor that will be influenced by when the client first invested and whether or not the client has added or removed any funds during the period. Portfolio management software, on the other hand, provides performance detail based on the specific circumstances of the client. The information can be presented as an internal rate of return or a time-weighted rate of return, over different time frames and against different benchmarks. This is the first and most fundamental difference between the reports your clients have seen in the past and what your clients will see in your new practice.

Consider the contents of your reports carefully. Content is king. Do not get hung up on a specific layout of information. The question you need to answer is whether or not the information *you* want to present is displayed in a manner that can be easily understood by the client. What performance parameters are important? Will you want to focus on the most recent performance or long-term performance? To what extent do you want to provide information already provided by the custodian such as holdings and gains and losses. You may wish to duplicate the data so the client only needs to look at one set of reports. Only after you have considered what information you want your clients to have should you examine the reporting capabilities of a portfolio management software package. Most systems today have more reports than you should ever consider putting in front of a client. If a portfolio management solution has only four reports but they are the reports you need, then it doesn't matter that there are fewer reports. Your needs will still be met. Once the content threshold is passed, then consider aesthetics. If you fail to consider content first, you will spend a lot of time explaining your reports rather than focusing on building your practice and managing your client's assets.

Another decision you will be facing will be the manner in which reports are delivered. Remember that your objective is not to kill trees but to impart information. Do you want to provide the information electronically instead of, or in addition to, paper reports? If so, how does the portfolio management software you are considering facilitate that?

When reports are considered, advisors often focus so much on what their client reports should look like, they forget that there are business needs that must be met as well. Whether it is as simple as a cross-reference report, performance across all clients with a given investment objective, or deposits and withdrawals made by your clients on any given day, you should carefully consider your business practice reporting needs, as well. When you do this, do not focus solely on the paper reports that a system can generate. Some portfolio management software has fewer reports but provides the information you may need on-screen. As is the case with client reports, focus on what you will need to run your practice and then find out if/how that information is available in any given portfolio management software package.

Changing Your Portfolio Management Software

If you have portfolio management software in place and are considering a move, your evaluation is a little bit different from that of a new advisor or breakaway broker. As we mentioned earlier in this chapter, such a move should be considered very carefully. The two reasons we hear most frequently for an advisor moving from one portfolio management software package to another are changes in business needs or acquisition of more useful features.

A change in business needs may, or may not, be something over which you have control. A decision to use a specific money manager may force the use of a specific custodian or a specific portfolio management solution. On the other hand, if you are merging your practice with another practice or have acquired another advisor's business, there are choices you do control. The common approach is to convert the smaller amount of data to the other format. While this will usually result in a lower conversion cost, it should not be an automatic default choice. Instead, you might take the opportunity to compare the two software packages to determine which has the features best able to facilitate the new business. It does not matter why either package was purchased originally, only which is the best choice at this time. A decision to outsource the operation of your portfolio management work may result in changes in your workflow but will probably not force a change in portfolio management software as most of the systems on the market are supported. It may, however, present an opportunity to reduce the learning curve while gaining additional features you like in a different program.

Adding a new tool to a workbench provides a benefit with few downsides other than cost and the empty space it removes. The same cannot be said of gaining extra tools by changing your portfolio management software. That is true whether the extras are in the form of enhanced reporting, a cleaner interface, or any new features your current system does not have. The pros are more obvious than cons. Consider the move from both a feature and a workflow point of view. A change in workflow may be required and may actually be beneficial. On the feature side, however, a common error is to assume that all features in your older current system exist in the newer, faster, better system. Do not make this assumption. The newer the portfolio management software the greater the chance the developer hasn't gotten around to adding some of the features of your current system or that the developer may believe that a different search approach is warranted. A new developer, for example, may prefer the ease of a menu-driven search process over the power of writing SQL scripts to extract data. Understand what you are giving up before you make the leap.

Any of these choices will result in the need to convert your data from one performance management system to another. Plan ahead. Do you need all of the data from the legacy system? Reducing the amount of data you convert will decrease the cost of conversion. Is any portion of the data you want to convert incomplete? It may not be possible to answer that question without an understanding of the differences in operation between two programs. One system may be set to look back a week, a month, or a year to find a price it needs for a calculation. Another program may look back only a few days for such a price. Information would be complete in one system and missing in the other. One system may be built around accounts while another may be based on assets. Do custom fields in one system have a counterpart in another system? If not what will happen to this data?

Summary

The portfolio management software marketplace is constantly changing. To get updated information on available options, consider talking with your online resources at www.yoursilverbullet.net and www.advisortechtools.com. Portfolio management software does and will continue to cover a wide range of features and price ranges. All of them, however, will allow you to track and manage your client's assets, communicate with your clients, bill your clients, and manage your practice with greater ease than ever before. Come on in to the marketplace to select the best choice for your style of business. This week there is a sale on efficiency.

CHAPTER 5

Achieving Growth and Profitability with Technology Integration

Jon Patullo

Managing Director, Technology Product Management, TD Ameritrade Institutional

---

Creativity is just connecting things.
—Steve Jobs (*Wired*, February 1996)

The growth of the registered investment advisor (RIA) business has been remarkable over the last several years, resulting in around 20,000 firms in business today managing nearly $2 trillion in assets. This opportunity has not been lost on technology vendors and has resulted in a variety of innovative choices for advisors. Traditionally, advisors were forced to spend on technology in order to meet a need. Now advisors have both the ability to turn that expense into an investment and the ability to increase their technology investment returns by ensuring integration of the systems and software they buy.

This wave of technology innovation has so far failed to produce the ideal, one-size-fits-all solution. Vendors and custodians have attempted to make this dream a reality, but advisors continue to demonstrate their independent spirit when building their technology landscape. Today's advisor wants to choose the best solution for each component of their technology investment, and they expect those solutions to work together as one. While this reality is attainable, it takes a little work to reach the summit.

Technology choices are so much simpler for the advisors who are forced to use the systems that are provided to them. However, that situation doesn't necessarily provide for an ideal outcome—and it certainly doesn't allow for any choice or flexibility or help better service clients. Just as RIAs choose the best investment solutions for their clients, they also want to choose the best software available for meeting their unique business needs, client needs, and clients' goals. So how do you find the best solutions for your firm and, at the same time, ensure that they all work together?

Wading through a Wealth of Choices

Vendors have targeted every aspect of the RIA's front and back office. Some software applications—such as those related to customer relationship management (CRM), client portals, social media capture, document management, and other tasks—can be adopted from other industries. But many of an advisor's tasks call for specialized applications in areas like proposal generation, financial planning, portfolio management, and risk analytics.

Today, hundreds of specific applications exist to streamline and automate all parts of the financial planning and wealth management process. RIAs can choose from them to build a portfolio of technology tools to help grow their businesses in the way that best meets their firms' needs. Yet business solutions sometimes lead to new problems, and the challenge of choosing the best-in-class product from a variety of vendors leads to the challenge of *integrating* those products—getting them to work together effectively. This integrated state would be as if the apps in Apple's App Store weren't simply separate applications on a common platform but were connected and working together. Imagine the possibilities of that: Your preferred weather app could, upon noticing that there was a 100 percent chance of rain this coming Friday, automatically check your calendar, find the tee time you have booked with your client that day, immediately cancel that tee time by contacting your club's app, and notify your client.

Integrated technology is about this kind of efficient data sharing, and the impact of that on the advisor's bottom line. The first, most basic way that impact is felt is in getting the most mileage out of the existing technology investment. RIAs don't typically go into a software purchase with a blank slate; they already own applications in which they've invested time and money for licensing, installation, and training. This means that the ability to integrate any new software with existing applications can, and should, actually drive purchasing decisions. This was reflected in the 2011 *InvestmentNews* RIA Technology Study, which found that 41 percent of firms were already purchasing systems based on integration. In fact, that same study showed that the top-performing firms spend about the same amount as other firms on technology but are more likely to maximize the potential of their existing systems as they do so.

SPENDING YOUR TECH DOLLARS STRATEGICALLY

- **Technology is best viewed as an investment, not an expense.** It's important to focus on the long term and on getting the maximum value from what you purchase.
- **Have a strategy behind your investment.** It's helpful to have a clear idea of how the time you can save with your technology solution can be reinvested in the firm to enhance performance.
- **Technology should enable profitable growth.** Think of deploying your solution in order to achieve scale and generate revenue growth by using existing resources more efficiently.
- **It takes people to make technology work.** Involve your staff to make sure you have buy-in on the decision. Align your human resources and technology strategies so they support the same goals.
- **Recognize the importance of training.** Don't just allocate dollars to software; invest in training your people, as well. Follow the lead of top-performing firms, which are nearly three times as likely as other firms to be investing in this area.

Based on findings from major studies, including the 2011 *InvestmentNews* RIA Technology Study, the 2010 *InvestmentNews*/Moss Adams Financial Performance Study of Advisory Firms, and a 2012 Advisor Index survey conducted by Maritz, Inc. on behalf of TD Ameritrade Institutional, a division of TD Ameritrade, Inc.

Preserving Quality, Increasing Profits

Coming out of the recession of 2007–2009, many advisors recognized that they needed to become even more efficient than they already were. All of an advisor's clients don't usually call at once, on the same day. But when panic strikes, as it did back then, the phones just might start ringing off the hook. Such dramatic increases in client contacts quickly reveal the very real need for highly effective practice management techniques and highly efficient technology solutions.

This is especially true in an environment of volatility and fear, when clients may more likely feel uneasy with their investment performance . . . and might decide to move their business elsewhere. Because carefully chosen technology increases productivity, it can increase the time advisors have available to spend with clients and prospective clients. An integrated solution only adds to the overall gains in productivity.

Technology integration can help achieve the level of efficiency that makes two critical things possible: providing better client service and achieving the scalability that leads to growth. By 2011, in fact, 50 percent of advisors said that investing in new technologies was their top profitability initiative, according to the *InvestmentNews*/ Moss Adams Financial Performance Study of Advisory Firms.

Increased efficiency means saving time and effort, which means maintaining quality service while having the capacity to add clients. As Mark Pearson of Nepsis Capital Management noted, "When it's that much more efficient to bring in AUM [assets under management], everyone gets back to work much faster driving new business." And after all, adding clients to an infrastructure that's already paid for comes close to dropping additional account management fees right to the bottom line.

One advisor who actively sought this kind of increase in efficiency and profitability is Richard Brown of JNBA Financial Advisors in Minneapolis, who started out in the business by taking over a firm (his mother's) that had no computers. He quickly changed that, and by 2007 had four teams of people, "and everybody was doing the same task a little differently," Brown says. "But we wanted to be a firm with a consistent reputation and values, so we built an end-to-end process for how each task would be done. Integrated technology was key to doing this. It puts you in the position to be a scalable, effective, disciplined firm."

For JNBA, the integration-based consistency didn't just apply to back-office functions. They also used integrated portfolio rebalancing software to evaluate and ensure that the firm's investment strategies were being followed consistently by all advisors.

Integrated technology can also drive profitability by promoting the workflows that support informed decision-making and create consistent processes for everyone in the office. Over the last decade, financial advisors have seen advances in information technology that far exceed anything available to prior generations. Prior to the Internet age, a state-of-the-art online display meant viewing a stock quote and a news headline. But the emphasis now is not on the availability of data (advisors would be overwhelmed if someone in the office printed out all available information on each asset class). Instead, tech integration that drives profits will emphasize delivering information that clarifies the available choices *at the point of decision*—both at the right time, and within the application that the advisor is currently using.

For example: While rebalancing a portfolio, the advisor sees that a client deposit cleared, then sees that the available balance has risen to the minimum investment level for a new fund allocation.

In terms of investment decisions, an advisor can obviously never guarantee that clients will achieve their goals. An advisor can, however, explain to clients that they rely on this kind of an integrated decision-making process. This can help reassure clients that each investment decision is made by seamlessly melding the best available market data with the client's documented risk profile and financial goals.

Building such integrity into a technology-dominated process becomes a way to build trust. And clearly, trust in the process can lead to client referrals and promote client retention—especially during the inevitable market downturns. This is the ultimate integration of advisor relationships with the systems supporting them.

Much More than Data Access

Establishing and understanding the building blocks of integration is essential, because there is more to integration than the seamless, automated exchange of data. Of course, eliminating the need to reenter client data is among the simplest ways to reduce errors. In terms of integration, though, that's the all-important foundation, but it's also just the beginning.

The deeper advantages of integrating software applications lie in workflows—as in the rebalancing example described above. "It's more than just sending data back and forth, it's how you work every day," noted Tony Leal, CTO of MoneyGuidePro, makers of financial and retirement planning software. "The systems need to lend themselves to navigate that way; the software has got to match your workflow."

The critical areas in which integrated applications can improve workflow include:

- **Onboarding:** Bringing new clients on board can prove a real test of back-office operations at both an RIA and the analyst's custodian. Using electronic signatures to facilitate the signing of new account and transfer paperwork and automatically populating client data files can cut steps and time from the process.
- **Billing:** When processing quarterly management fees, advisors can automatically send fee instructions directly from their portfolio management system to the custodial platform. Then, management fees can be automatically deducted from the designated accounts.
- **Client service:** Having a snapshot of all client information—such as his financial plan, performance reports, CRM information, as well as his available balances, positions, and history—on one consolidated dashboard when the client calls enables an advisor to proactively address any opportunities and possible gaps in the big picture of the client's financial situation.
- **Trading:** RIAs save time and gain accuracy by validating and submitting orders to their custodian without ever leaving their rebalancing tool, eliminating the need to download and upload trade files. Additionally, they can review order status and corresponding warning or error messages without going to their custodian platform.

There's also the simple question of speed. In less volatile times, overnight batch processing of files between applications, resulting in the RIA receiving a start-of-day view, worked fine. Today, everyone (including the client) expects real-time information. Applying market and account data across applications on a real-time basis means achieving efficiency in whatever actions are taken intraday.

So the benefits of integration are clear. The ways to achieve it, however, are not all equal.

As in many industries, technology speaks its own lingo. Some terms—like "data mining," "portal," "social network," and "the cloud"—become so ubiquitous that they achieve something like celebrity status. The result is that definitions of these terms tend to broaden and blur over time.

Consider, for example, "open architecture," "open access," and "open API (application program interfaces)"—all terms that are frequently used to tout the degree to which a technology product or platform can interact with other software applications.

Today, open APIs help drive revenue at such technology giants as Google, Facebook, and Twitter. That's because an open API brings the programming power of multiple vendors' software teams to the table. It sets the stage for the discovery and building of solutions that are beyond the capabilities of any single entity's IT department. True openness facilitates innovation and creativity in the industry.

In other words, open wins. Open architecture makes all of the benefits of technology integration even better, because it broadens the extent to which integration is possible. The approach enables vendors to innovate and to harness their nimbleness in order to get integrations completed quickly, in sharp contrast to the slow approach of bundled offerings. By making data easily available and creating the ability to transmit transactions, open architecture makes deeper and broader integration possible. TD Ameritrade Institutional was even able to use its API to more quickly deliver applications for devices such as the iPad and smart phones; mobile applications were the product of putting that menu of data to work. This strategy of being open has been embraced by advisors and vendors, and has even prompted the rest of the industry to be more open. Open architecture also allows for the most choice and flexibility, allowing RIAs to take maximum advantage of (in other words, continue using) more of the software they've already purchased, grown familiar with, and rely on every day. Eric Clarke, president of Orion Advisor Services LLC, which provides portfolio accounting software, describes it as the approach that "allows the advisors to pick the best tech platform as opposed to the one-size-fits-all attitude."

The Key Early Efforts

Early attempts at technology integration were often driven by the software vendors themselves. In the groundbreaking case of Your Silver Bullet, it was driven by Greg Friedman—a vendor *and* an advisor. Friedman was running Junxure, which provides a comprehensive CRM solution. But first and foremost he was—and remains today— an advisor who envisioned what kind of tools he needed to make his workday more efficient. He saw one-off integrations of the software tools he used happening, but he also saw advisors like himself clamoring for more.

Friedman knew the CEOs and CIOs of several tech firms, and he knew that together they needed to create a consortium of those who were committed to developing integrations and getting information to advisors. This consortium, Your Silver Bullet, came to life in 2007. It was intended to be for the good of the industry, not for the profit of Junxure or any other firm. To firmly demonstrate this, his first call to invite someone to get on board with the effort was to a direct competitor, Warren Mackensen at ProTracker Software Inc. From there, a circle of trust was established among a select group of small, entrepreneurial firms dedicated to integration as the path to meeting advisors' challenges.

Said Friedman, "These were firms run by people who were deeply committed to our industry and excited about the prospect of making it better. Their response when I described what we [Friedman and Ken Golding, co-founders of Junxure] wanted to do was, 'You had me at hello.'"

Your Silver Bullet was designed to promote and push forward these tech integrations and to improve them. Friedman purposely made the effort a high-visibility one, a public relations event, and his efforts did help raise awareness of the fact that this was an extremely valuable undertaking.

Next, the industry needed an even broader unifying solution, one that would bring all the players together. Ideas and aspirations began to form around achieving an even more open approach, one that was open to even more players, players of all sizes (because sometimes the best ideas start in garages). With the exposure it brought to the topic, Your Silver Bullet helped speed up the efforts to begin realizing this vision.

The Custodians Get on Board

Custodians, given their central role in supporting RIAs' back offices, were the next natural candidates to drive innovation. It was logical for them to step in and help advance integration still further: As the keepers of client account books and records, they clearly had to become part of the effort. Many did so, in fact, providing bundled solutions that offered advisors a small subset of vendors to work with.

Against this backdrop, TD Ameritrade Institutional conducted a strategy and feasibility review, and grew determined to provide choice. In other words, the company wanted to allow any vendor that could meet its technology and data security standards to seamlessly integrate and securely exchange data with Veo, the firm's core trading and account management platform.

In late 2010, the firm began discussing this plan with industry leaders, including Joel Bruckenstein, coproducer of the annual T3 Technology Conference for financial advisors. When Bruckenstein initially met with TD Ameritrade Institutional to discuss its integration approach, he was not just unimpressed, but doubtful. "And I wasn't the only one," he said.

"Clearly there would be substantial costs involved with vetting the firms. Were they willing to commit to that?" Bruckenstein remembers asking. Skepticism also circled around the meaning of open access, he said. He wondered what would actually be allowed.

"The direction TD Ameritrade Institutional was taking was different from anything else being done," Bruckenstein said. "The others out there doing this at the time were taking a best of breed approach: getting one good provider for each software category, then maybe expanding later with two or three per category. They were never saying they would welcome all comers."

Many of the initial integration partners immediately understood what the value of the open system could be. "There was never any doubt in my mind," said Bruckenstein, "that they would get on board with the initiative."

An Open Invitation

In March 2010, after meeting to discuss feedback from TD Ameritrade Institutional's Advisory and Operations panels, the firm called an integration summit. Representatives from industry-leading technology vendors, leading industry consultants, and TD Ameritrade Institutional management got together to talk about how to solve integration for their mutual clients. The goals? Listen carefully, share viewpoints, and think big. The event reflected the company's commitment to gathering firsthand feedback on best practices, features, and capabilities. As Chris Valleley, director of technology solutions at TD Ameritrade Institutional, explained, "We look to the entrepreneurship and ingenuity of providers to deliver new and inventive ideas together with us. We really partner with them in idea creation and to deliver choice, flexibility, and efficiency to our mutual clients."

"It was the first time we were invited to anything quite like that, and I was skeptical about even going," said Leal, of MoneyGuidePro. "In large companies, it's hard to act and get commitment. Sometimes technology is used as a differentiator for marketing purposes, but, in fact, there's no product behind it. But here, the right people were invited. And it was unique that the TD Ameritrade Institutional's tech, business, and marketing perspectives were all at the table."

But what really persuaded industry leaders like Leal to attend the event was the agenda structure. "Each invitee got time to explain what we think integration is about, and what we think is important in order for advisors to have a better experience," he said. "Instead of sitting there listening to people talk about things that may or may not be delivered, I appreciated having the floor to explain what I thought the process should be."

The summit attendees agreed with the pursuit of an open API approach, and with the implementation strategy that was designed to deliver as much flexibility, choice, and efficiency as possible.

Taking advantage of a truly open API required a certain amount of tech savvy on the part of vendors, and while it became clear that not everyone was up to the challenge, some, like Orion, were way ahead.

Eric Clarke explained that Orion had launched an API before the TD Ameritrade Institutional summit, and he was asked to bring his tech staff to the event. "We knew what APIs were capable of," he said, "so we were pretty excited about it."

This type of collaboration proved so productive that summits have been held annually since the first one in 2010. Attendance has grown to over 30 participants, all eager to help create improved integration for RIAs. Shortly after the initial event, TD Ameritrade Institutional became the first custodian to launch an open API, and in quick succession launched single sign-on with context—which saves time by allowing for intuitive, seamless access between applications—as a critical first step. Later and larger rollouts involved multiple APIs to pull and push different types of data between a variety of applications. In other words, the flexibility of data moving between applications now enables different types of transactions to be initiated from one application to another.

"Working hand-in-hand with advisors and vendors, we were able to help lay the foundation for integration to really take off," said Tom Bradley, former president of TD Ameritrade Institutional. "We're proud of what we achieved in a short time, and that we helped to change the strategy, attitude, and approach of our industry."

Advisor demand and vendor responses have driven the rapid progress the firm has seen with integration since that first Technology Summit, and the event has grown each year since then.

The Next Generation

It's probably harder to predict the closing price of the Standard & Poor's 500 Index next week than it is to predict next year's breakthrough in technology. Still, RIAs must continue to do their technology due diligence—and their custodians must continue to deliver the tools and opportunities that drive growth and profitability.

As president of TD Ameritrade Institutional, Tom Nally, for one, is on board with that. "With technology, you're never done. In our industry, if you stand still when it comes to technology, you're going to get left behind. There's always the next innovation to incorporate," he noted. "We are committed to helping advisors get better integration and more efficiency."

Those next innovations will definitely be exciting ones. This industry, like so many others, has changed so much already, but stands to make still more tremendous leaps in productivity and efficiency in the near future. Especially with custodial platforms opening up further, the promise of fully integrated technology remains to be seen.

Integrations will be pushed even deeper. For example, they will need to continue focusing on integrating social media with CRM and other systems. This will help pave the path for appealing to children of existing clients, the next generation of investors who are essential to an RIA's future growth.

More fully developed dashboards will also remain a focal point. Already in play to varying degrees of complexity, dashboards hold the potential to customize tasks to the way an advisor wants to work and to be customized for each role in the firm. Their promise is delivering all critical data in a single display and in an *actionable* format. Many even see this concept as something to be extended to clients, who are asking for and getting access to more and more powerful online tools from many of the vendors. Advisors will need to stand out, especially with the tech-savviest clients, by being the trusted partners that provide their clients tools for data sharing and analysis that they can't find elsewhere.

Fortunately, with an open access custodial platform, the core data and account/ market processes running in the back office stand ready and waiting to be integrated into any new front-office function. As more and more vendors offering tech solutions reach the downhill side of the integration learning curve, integration will become part of the software design process—not something to be dealt with post-launch. So each new application will not only integrate more seamlessly and more efficiently, but it will do so in version 1.0.

Helping the next generation of RIAs prepare for all of this is something that Richard Brown of JNBA has taken on. In addition to his workload as an advisor, he teaches at the University of Minnesota–Duluth business school, because he feels a responsibility to help the next generation of RIAs to understand how the business works today.

"What we're teaching is what an operations person, a compliance person, an investment person, the client service role, a planner, and a rainmaker look like today for an independent RIA," said Brown. He wants it to be clear that if a new RIA wants to achieve longevity for his firm, all of these roles need to be on board with integrating technology. He wants it to be clear, in fact, that utilizing integration is *the* great opportunity to grow an advisor's business.

At some point, each new level of technology becomes table stakes for a business to survive. Some examples are more obvious than others (try running a service business today without e-mail). The current level for RIAs is real-time integration of best-in-class software applications for portfolio management, financial planning, and CRM.

The RIAs with the best knowledge of the markets and their client base will determine the best-in-class software. By seamlessly integrating those technology solutions, they achieve the highest form of efficiency and make the best-informed decisions for their clients. Those RIAs become the most profitable. Those who leave integrated technology decisions solely up to their custodian or some other technology vendor, have given up some of their independence—a key to their success.

And as Tony Leal stated: "It's not just about adapting to technology. It's embracing it."

The future of our industry rests with those who are actively diving into the exciting opportunities for working in new, more efficient, and more profitable ways.

CASE IN POINT: A MONEY MANAGER USES INTEGRATED TECHNOLOGY TO GROW BY ACQUISITION

Mark Pearson and Mark Clark of Nepsis Capital Management in Minneapolis, Minnesota, believe in technology, and in their firm's brand, which stands for clarity. "If we're going to preach clarity, we need to live in clarity," Pearson said, "and technology allows you to have clarity in how you run your business."

When Pearson came to the financial services industry as an advisor in 1994, he brought with him a solid background and interest in technology, having worked in that industry just as firms like Oracle, Intel, and Microsoft were starting to take off. Right away, he saw technology as a productivity booster and sold his colleagues on that view.

And Nepsis clearly stood to benefit from streamlined, integrated tech setup. As a third-party money manager, their workflows include wholesalers, solicitors, the financial advisors who work directly for Nepsis . . . and must incorporate all of the different needs, data, and agreements that must be in place for all of these parties.

Six years ago, Nepsis went completely paperless. Today, the firm relies on an integrated technology platform—one built on Salesforce and relying on DocuSign, Morningstar, TD Ameritrade Institutional's Veo, and more—to achieve:

- **Lean operations:** Nepsis manages a substantial book of business with very few support people.
- **Up-front, consistent communications that support their brand:** They can easily track who is and isn't reading their regular updates and analysis on markets and portfolios, and thereby spot someone who might be at risk of sliding toward dissatisfaction.
- **Smooth transitions of client accounts:** Nepsis is capable of moving business in quickly, to the benefit of the advisors it works with, and those advisors' clients. Not

uncommon was this occurrence in 2012: With no hassles or hiccups, Nepsis brought in $25 million from over 200 accounts (nearly 100 households) within a month. All paperwork—including integration of fee schedules—and all other transition tasks were handled by only two people with some part-time help.

- **Real and significant business growth:** Aiming for very aggressive growth in new assets annually, Nepsis looks to open offices around the country, and to work with more advisory firms to manage assets for them. The company's tech platform is the critical foundation for achieving that—it makes the necessary level of productivity possible, and makes the process of joining forces that much smoother.

In short, Nepsis's tech setup is a tool for scalability and sales, as well as a competitive advantage.

Today Nepsis continues to work toward achieving deeper integration across the multiple custodians, annuity companies, mutual fund companies, and other entities it works with. It wants to deliver a complete picture of client data and Nepsis processes, from onboarding on.

"At the end of the day," Pearson said, "it's all about clarity. Give the advisor more clarity on the process—the how and the why—and the more successful they're going to be. We're all going to become more productive and therefore more profitable."

FIGURE 5.1   Shaping the Future Together, Orlando, Florida, February 2012

Over 30 technology vendors came together as a community at TD Ameritrade Institutional's 2012 National Conference in Orlando, Florida (see Figure 5.1). Advisors

(Continued)

were able to experience, firsthand, integration between multiple applications as a result of the shared knowledge and vision of all participants in Veo's open access initiative.

FIGURE 5.2 Integration Analyzer

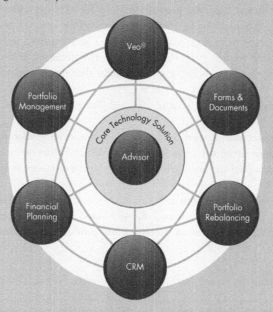

TD Ameritrade Institutional's Integration Analyzer (see Figure 5.2) shows the ability of software applications to work with one another in four basic categories:

1. *Data exchange/single sign-on.* An RIA logs in once and can move data between software applications by manually transferring files. Example: Transfer trading history from the custodian's database to the CRM running in the RIA's office.
2. *Automated web services.* With no keystrokes or other actions, real-time data flows seamlessly between software applications. Example: The office CRM receives changes to client account positions or balances as they occur in the custodian's trading system.
3. *Intuitive navigation between applications.* In one click, an RIA can complete a task that combines similar features within two separate applications. Example: To send a client a check, the RIA clicks a button in the CRM that launches and populates the check-writing page on the custodian's platform.
4. *Embedded functionalities and workflows.* An RIA can stay on the same screen within one application while triggering a series of requests in a second application. Example: A portfolio rebalancing application generates a series of orders and delivers them to the custodian's trading system for execution without leaving the rebalancing tool.

TD Ameritrade Institutional and all third parties listed above are separate unaffiliated companies and are not responsible for each other's services or policies.

CHAPTER 6

How the World Wide Web Impacts the Financial Advisor

Bart Wisniowski

Co-Founder and Director, AdvisorWebsites.com

Jason Lindstrom

Managing Partner, AdvisorWebsites.com

Few people today would argue that the Internet has not had a tremendous impact on the way that they conduct their lives. Have you been online today? It would be difficult to imagine that as a financial advisor you haven't at some point today searched, researched, compared, shopped, communicated, or validated something by using the web.

For most consumers, the Internet has become their go-to resource for problem solving and decision making. For advisors, the Internet has drastically changed how your clients and prospects interact with you compared to just a few years ago.

In a 2012 study published in an e-book titled, *Winning the Zero Moment of Truth* by Jim Lecinski, Google set out to find precisely when and why a prospective buyer becomes a customer. From this study, the term "zero moment of truth" (ZMOT) was coined to describe the very moment when a shopper decides to pull the trigger. To no one's surprise, the trigger point, or ZMOT, represents a new marketing phenomenon only made possible with the advent of the Internet. Essentially, today's shoppers use the Internet with the help of powerful search engines to extract as much information as possible from customer review sites and forums, blogs, and social networks in addition to the information available from old media such as TV and publications. According to the study, for 84 percent of Internet shoppers, the ability to extract buying information from the Internet became the ZMOT—the point at which they decided to buy—a stark difference from a few years ago when most shoppers waited until the "first moment of truth," which occurs while standing at the product shelf.

The book bottom-lines the challenge for businesses, producers, and marketers who must find ways to ensure that prospective customers find them at the ZMOT lest they eventually become invisible to their market. And, in the vast digital space of the web where information is sought from an ever-expanding universe of mediums, including e-mail, social networks, social media, blogs, forums, and websites, it is imperative that you be able to place yourself in the right place, at the right time, with the right message.

Your Website as a Hub

As the web continues to evolve and grow, we are noticing that advisors' websites are increasingly becoming the central hub of their interaction with clients, tying the key elements of their marketing activities together. By placing their website at the hub of their marketing strategy, linking their entire social media apparatus, they can create a more visible online presence.

Websites in 2012 are more than just repositories of information. Today's website is a place where Internet users—clients, prospective clients, and Curious Georges—can walk inside, take a look around, and then have that ZMOT moment. Because of this fundamental shift in approach, today's websites must make the dramatic leap from the static content of yesterday's websites to interactivity. No longer are websites built and then left to languish for years on end without updating. Today's websites are built to achieve specific objectives—build brand awareness, increase traffic, spur interaction, create new customers, and add value to existing relationships. They must be simple to navigate and polished to your brand specifications. And, of course, they must be compliant. Above all else, they need to include a variety of metrics that enable users to track and measure their online performance and quantify results.

The design of your website should reflect your specific goals. Each goal will have a direct impact on a website's design and overall usability. Some websites will serve a more marketing-based purpose, whereas others can be viewed as a portal for existing clients to interact with your firm. The key to establishing goals for your web strategy and design is to make sure they are realistic and measurable. While the ultimate goal of any marketing strategy is to increase revenues, the actual measures of your marketing initiatives should be based on your specific goals, such as increasing qualified leads, establishing your authority, generating more referrals, or expanding your market reach. Revenue is a direct measure of your client interactions, which should increase if your marketing objectives are achieved.

Websites today also create more opportunities for interaction with your prospects and clients through clearly defined calls to action. These could include contact buttons, seminar or meeting registrations, and requests for more information. Current clients may be able to access additional information not available to the general public via private password-protected pages. This saves advisors time and resources and enhances the client-advisor relationship.

Building a Web Presence

Building a website is now easier than ever. From easy-to-use templates, to custom designs with videos, rotating banners, and the full spectrum of colors to choose from, websites can be built to meet most specifications and suit any brand. Technology advancements have made features that were cutting edge just three years ago easily attainable at minimal or no cost. Working with experienced and industry-specific web-design providers, there is virtually no limit in the flexibility, customization, and access to technology one needs in order to create a world-class website. Likewise, from a technical standpoint, putting together social media profiles on the social media sites is typically a quick process with only minimal computer skills required.

Mobile Considerations

In just 10 years, the smart phone—and mobile browsing—has ratcheted from oblivion to a technological necessity. Performing more than simple calling and texting functions, today's phones can thank mobile networks for their ability to browse the Internet, utilize GPS technology, and act as a mobile entertainment center. Additionally, tablets, such as Apple's iPad and Samsung's Galaxy, have also latched onto the mobile browsing trend, providing most of the features of a smart phone (in addition to others) in a more vision-friendly format.

In the latest Cisco Visual Networking Index (VNI) Global Mobile Data Traffic Forecast Update, it was estimated that mobile browser usage is set to increase 26-fold between 2010 and 2015, and mobile-connected tablets will generate as much traffic as the entire mobile network in 2010.[1] And mobile browsing is not just for the young. A 2011 Nielsen study shows that the number of people over the age of 50 accessing social networks through their mobile devices has doubled in the last few years.[2]

Although mobile banking and financial transactions have been slower to catch on, a study by comScore reports that the number of Americans accessing their financial accounts online crossed the 30 million threshold in 2010, a 54 percent increase in just one year.[3]

From the perspective of financial advisors, the opportunities to interact with clients and prospects are still limited to applications provided by their firms and custodians that enable mobile access to account information. Although mobile marketing is fast becoming a major initiative of an increasing number of financial services companies, financial advisors are constrained by some of the same compliance issues that had limited their use of social media.

For now, financial advisors should be aware that mobile devices are quickly becoming the preferred browser for all segments of the population, so their websites should be designed with small screens in mind.

Easily Convert Your Existing Website

Tools such as Mobify, Wiremode, Onbile, and Moppin Mobilier utilize copy and paste code blocks to easily install onto your website. When users are browsing your website, these tools detect whether a mobile browser is in use, and will then redirect the user to the mobile version, optimizing their browsing experience.

These tools need not be expensive—Mobify even offers a free mobile domain name, although you will have to pay extra to remove the Mobify logo from your site. These tools will likely appeal to small firms that do not have the resources required to build a dedicated mobile website. The downside is reduced customization. Some website vendors in the financial services development space also offer this feature right out of the box.

SEO for Mobile: An Imperative Consideration

According to a June 2011 Mashable blog post, Google's Eric Schmidt noted that mobile search is growing much faster than desktop search.[4] As mobile increasingly becomes a primary gateway to the Internet, it is crucial for companies to incorporate forward-thinking SEO practices into their mobile strategies to ensure their mobile sites are easily detected by search engines and found by consumers.

Having a mobile-optimized website will help increase page rank. Usable, fast sites with accurate screen rendering and functioning features will rank even higher. In this case, mobile sites will offer an advantage over their nonmobile-friendly peers. Traditional search engine optimization strategies (keywords, outbound links, relevant content, etc.) still persist, but may need to be modified to work in a mobile context where less is more.

Mobile Development Considerations

Clearly, mobile browsing is a big deal—but what goes into mobile-friendly website development? Design best practices include web browser and device considerations. With the advent of smart phones and other mobile browsing devices, today's technology permits users to do much of what they could previously do on a desktop computer anywhere. With its exponential potential, mobile browsing technology is sure to be a societal fixture, and your organization must make sure that it isn't losing ground. By following best practices including a comprehensive needs analysis and effective design, your organization's content will be accessible and informative to clients, partners, or other individuals interested in your website.

If we had to sum up mobile, it would be to make sure you realize you are working with much less screen real estate than a traditional computer and as long as your visitors can use their thumbs only to navigate your entire site, then you are in good shape.

Social Media and Websites

Social media is here to stay, and today's websites capitalize upon this. Websites now include integrated links to your Facebook, Twitter, LinkedIn, and YouTube accounts, with advanced websites featuring an ability to update social media platforms directly from your website, saving you valuable time. Your social media sites and your website have a symbiotic relationship—think of social media as your website's chatty, outgoing wingmen or wingwomen.

With the advent of Facebook, Twitter, and LinkedIn, social media has become a ubiquitous tool within the marketer's arsenal of strategies to connect with potential clients. While it provides an informal yet informative avenue to share knowledge, cultivate relationships, and connect with clients, social media integration within the financial services sector lags behind that in other service industries. This provides financial advisors with websites an excellent opportunity to take advantage of the power of social media's reach.

Why Is Social Media Such a Big Deal?

Nothing has garnered more attention on the World Wide Web than the phenomenon of social media and its influence on the way people congregate and communicate. With hundreds of millions of people digitally connected through the Internet cloud, the world has suddenly become a cyber community no bigger than the size of a computer screen. In addition to radically changing the social mores of relationships and networking, it has transformed the way in which businesses market to their constituencies and build their brands.

While financial advisors have been slow to adopt social media, largely due to compliance and regulatory ambiguities, they are quickly discovering the powerful attraction that it holds for their target markets and its potential as a business development tool. A recent study showed that 60 percent of financial advisors are actively using social media channels and that half of those users reported receiving quality referrals as a result of their use.[5] Another survey showed that financial advisors believe that social media is second only to face-to-face opportunities for establishing and cultivating new relationships.

Financial advisors are learning what other businesses have known for a while, and that is that social media has become one of the most effective and efficient ways to build their brands and get their messages out to their target markets. Here's what business users say are the top benefits of their social media use:

TABLE 6.1 Top Ways Small Businesses Benefit from Social Media[6]

Generated exposure for my business	85%
Increased traffic/subscribers on my site	63%
Resulted in new business partnerships	56%
Helped us rise in the search engines	54%
Generated quality leads	52%
Helped to sell products/close business	48%
Reduced overall marketing expenses	42%

Clearly, social media's reach is expansive and effective.

A Symbiotic Relationship with Your Website

Social media provides an excellent jumping off point into an organization's website. Conversely, it also provides visitors a personal view into your organization. For example, relevant content, promotions, or blog posts can build rapport and establish your organization as a thought leader. Existing clients who are happy with your services will also share or "like" your organization, providing a valuable feedback mechanism that signals to others that they should check out your organization and create your zero moment of truth.

As your organization posts more content or is mentioned more frequently on social media sites, your website's search engine ranking increases as more traffic is linked to your site. Integrating social media with your website can be fairly easy, requiring just a simple copy and paste of the social media site's URL into the input fields located in the code.

What Does Social Media Integration Look Like?

Social media integration is seamlessly incorporated as a result of simple icons, such as "retweet" buttons, or by embedded media that may invite viewers to follow your organization, join a discussion, share content, or provide feedback. Additionally, the number of likes and retweets can be displayed, providing your organization feedback on the social success of your posts or your organization's reach.

Video Social Media Integration: Another Simplified Process

Online videos (like the ones you see on YouTube) are an excellent way to share content, market your organization, or provide how-to or instructional advice. Financial advisors are generating followers by creating and posting informational videos on core financial planning topics. Go to YouTube.com and type in the words "financial planning" to see the number of postings and the number of hits they are getting. Popular formats include interviews with industry experts, simple how-to subject matter, questions and answers on timely topics, or simply posting a webinar. Video postings are an effective way to increase traffic to your website and increase your overall web presence. Your videos can go a long way to building your brand image, so it is important that they meet a minimum quality standard and have good audio and lighting.

In the past, embedding was often problematic due to coding issues or incompatibilities. These days, you simply copy and paste the embed code given by YouTube, Vimeo, or Viddler to embed your video and add an interactive touch to your website.

Social Media Integration: Part of the Big Picture

Having so many different options for social media can be quite overwhelming and keeping up with updates and what's happening in your networks can be a full-time job if you let it. You may find it extremely valuable to use a tool like HootSuite to help you bring all of them under one umbrella and use a centralized dashboard to make your efforts significantly more effective while saving a ton of time.

The benefits website owners stand to gain by integrating popular social media tools with their marketing strategy are tangible. With a little time investment, and some copying and pasting, today's websites can provide a plug-and-play environment that harmonizes different web platforms into one cohesive marketing apparatus. This allows each component to add value, ultimately helping your organization to achieve its bottom-line objectives.

Blogging

Blogging can have a very positive impact on your online marketing efforts. A blog is much like a digital journal, a self-publishing device on a website that enables you to share your thoughts, ideas, and insights on a nearly unlimited scale. It's very much like a newsletter you may distribute; only with a blog there is the potential to reach far beyond your direct mailing list.

From a marketing perspective you'll notice several benefits including:

- Increased traffic to your website.
- Greater number of search terms your site will be indexed for with the search engines.
- More pages indexed.
- Leverage of your visitors social networks through the use of "share this content" buttons.
- Increased visibility as an authority and thought leader.
- Higher recognition as an expert in your field.
- Larger community of readers and brand ambassadors.

An increasing number of financial advisors now include a blog as part of their marketing efforts. Maintaining an active and relevant blog can be time-consuming, which is why many advisors choose to outsource their writing to ghost-bloggers. Of course, compliance oversight needs to be a consideration when producing frequent blog updates.

Content and Website Maintenance

On the wonderful World Wide Web, content is king. It's the primary reason people go online—to be informed, to find answers, to solve problems. The content needs to be good and relevant as the ease with which Internet surfers can click out of one site and onto the next renders a content-poor site into a fleeting flash of colors, buried for good in the history archive. Although not nearly exhaustive, here is a list of popular content found on many advisors' websites. This can be a great starting point if you are looking to start a website or freshen up an existing one:

- Personal and company biographies
- Community involvement
- Products and services
- Useful resources
- Social media integrations
- A blog
- Timely articles of interest
- News updates
- Event announcements
- Data, market, and RSS feeds

In 2012, you don't need to be a computer programmer to update your website. Today's content management systems (CMS) are easy to use with simple text input fields—there is no need to understand complicated coding language—the CMS will do it for you. Users who are familiar with updating Facebook profiles will have no trouble with these systems. There should be no need to hire a website specialist for the great majority of updates. With that said, leading website developers will understand that not all users are comfortable with technology and will provide customer support and knowledge bases to help users get on their way (and will usually not charge extra for the guidance). CMS providers in the financial services industry like Advisor Websites will go a step further and offer a compliance moderation portal for the websites where updates are time-stamped and archived and can be set up to send to compliance for review and approval.

Marketing

An effective website presence requires a good web strategy that can range from basic tasks you can do in a few minutes to advanced techniques that could take months or even years to implement correctly. From a practical standpoint, we've seen the best results when advisors focus on a couple of key elements at a time and build up their strategies piece by piece over time. While not exhaustive, here are some of the more common tasks we've seen advisors use.

Web Marketing Basics
- E-mail Signature. Include a link to your website and social media profiles as a part of your signature. Consider using a slightly larger font to make it stand out and you can include a call to action (i.e. "Check out my website at . . ." or "Connect with me on LinkedIn," etc.)

- Business Card and other Physical Marketing Collateral. These pieces should all contain links to your website and social media profiles. You may want to highlight to draw extra attention to them or use a QR code with a link back to your website.
- Social Media Sites. Add your website address to each of your social media profiles. Remember these count toward your search engine rankings.
- Voice Scripts. Include references to your online resources in your sales and marketing voice scripts, voice mail, and client communication pieces.

Building Traffic

Getting a good amount of visits to your site consists of a variety of factors. Here are great starting points.

- Quality of content: unique, timely, and targeted to your audience. Content is becoming the most important factor in search engine ranking success.
- Quality inbound links to your site: inbound links (i.e., links to your website not from your website) are one of the most influential factors. Quality of websites linking to yours is of the essence.
- Social media links: participating in conversations that contain back links, forums, and blogs is a great and easy way to get quality links back to your site.
- Blog: we briefly mentioned blogging earlier but the takeaway is that sites that blog (all else equal) will receive significantly higher traffic than those that don't.
- Articles shared with others: you could write articles for others (i.e., a personal finance blog) and include link information back to your web presence.
- Social bookmarking: sites such as Digg, Del.icio.us, and StumbleUpon allow audiences to bookmark your site, share it among their friends, or submit excerpts to aggregator sites, giving you tremendous potential reach.

Pay per Click Advertising

An easy way to drive traffic to your website is to pay for it. Using an auction system like Google AdWords allows you to bid for keywords that are typically used by your target market when using the search engines or social media sites. This will increase the chances that your ad will appear each time a keyword is searched. If someone clicks on your ad, you are charged a fee depending on the market value of that word. More competitive words (like "financial advisors") will tend to be quite expensive and it may be challenging to get a good ROI, but you could do quite well targeting and narrowing down your searches by focusing your term a bit further (i.e., "financial advisors specializing in doctors San Diego"). Most search engines and social media sites offer a pay per click service. You may have to experiment a little to find one that works best for you.

Calls to Action

It's important to have calls to action on a website as these turn your visitors from tire kickers into solid leads. A call to action can be as simple as a registration box so they can opt in to e-mail updates. Here are the most common calls to action to consider on your web properties:

- e-newsletter opt in
- Text update opt in
- Request for more information
- Client review request
- Invitation to join social networks
- Seminar or webinar registration
- Tell a friend form
- Join social media groups
- Download article
- Book a meeting button

Monitoring and Measuring for Results

Finally, analytics should be used to track the performance of your website. Many website platforms offer the ability to integrate with Google Analytics, which will allow you to find out who your users are, what content they are most engaged in, what browsers they are using, and where they are located. The data generated will then enable you to find out how to optimize your search engine ranking (search engine optimization). From this information you can more easily pinpoint how to build longer interactions with users by developing more relevant content and improving certain elements of your website. Analytics provide an important feedback mechanism, and facilitate decision-making so website owners can get the most out of their websites. Some social media sites also provide great insight into your reach and how users in your networks interact with you and your connections.

Compliance

Unquestionably, financial advisors today face increased oversight and scrutiny. While technology is here to make life easier through a variety of solutions, common sense still needs to be applied and exercised when using any web medium. In order to mitigate deception and to protect clients, the Financial Industry Regulatory Authority, or FINRA, and the U.S. Securities and Exchange Commission have established a number of policies for web interaction with clients, giving compliance departments the guidance they need to issue guidelines for social media and web marketing practices. Fortunately, one of the biggest compliance concerns—adequate reviews and archiving—is built into many web platforms customized for financial advisors. Leading website developers and social media services providers include integration for compliance departments, making adherence to required record keeping a painless endeavor.

By no means do we consider ourselves the experts on compliance issues, so our purpose is not to offer any specific advice along these lines. However, based on our experience, working closely with the professionals in your specific compliance department and environment will provide a frictionless experience.

Conclusion

Compliance issues aside, the number one reason given by financial advisors for not implementing a web strategy is that they don't know where to get started. This lack of knowledge, when combined with the fear of being the newbie in the room, has kept many of them out of the game. But, for advisors to be able to compete in the digital world, they must develop the web and social media acumen that enables them to communicate with their clients and their markets. Having said this, there are now more resources than ever available to advisors who want to take advantage of the World Wide Web. It all begins with a first step and a little bit of perseverance.

Additional information, education, and product resources can be found on www .advisorwebsites.com/blog, www.webvisorbook.com, and www.advisorwebsites.com.

Notes

1. Cisco® Visual Networking Index (VNI). Global Mobile Data Traffic Forecast Update (2010–2015).
2. Nielsen, NM Incite. "State of the Media: The Social Media Report (Q3 2011)." http:// blog.nielsen.com/nielsenwire/social.
3. comScore. "Mobile Financial Advisor Report." March 2011. www.comscore.com/ Press_Events/Press_Releases/2011/03.
4. Jason Taylor. Mashable Social Media blog. http://mashable.com/2011/06/03/mobile-seo.
5. Olivia Glauberzon. "Social Media a Hit with Advisors." *Investment Executive*. September 2008.
6. Michael A. Stelzner. "2011 Social Media Marketing Industry Report." www.socialmedia examiner.com/social-media-marketing-industry-report-2011/.

CHAPTER 7

Managing Your Online Presence

Marie Swift

Principal, Impact Communications

Pete Alepra, a senior vice president with RBC Wealth Management in Cedar Rapids, Iowa, was sitting at his desk when the phone rang that day.

"Hi, Pete. I'm a part of the news team at KCRG-TV9 in Cedar Rapids. I found your name in a quick Google search for financial advisors in Cedar Rapids. I need your help. As you probably know, 20 shipping department coworkers at the Quaker Oats plant in Cedar Rapids will, on Wednesday, be claiming their shares of a $241 million Powerball jackpot—the largest lottery prize won in Iowa since the state lottery's inception in 1985. We're doing a story on how this will change their lives and are hoping to get some advice from you as a financial advisor. Is now a good time to talk?"

Remembering the media training sessions he'd recently completed with Impact Communications, Alepra took a deep breath, composed himself and said sure thing; he'd be happy to help.

"The absolute first thing you have to do is slow down," he said with a deep authoritative voice. "Take a step back and enjoy the moment because I am guessing the next 24 hours will probably be one of the most incredible days of your lives. They're probably in a state of shock and the long-term decisions they need to make, they can put off a month, two months, or six months. Any decision they make now will be from an emotional perspective rather than a long-term perspective."

Alepra passed the journalist's initial test and was invited into the local television studio for an interview. An article with his advice also appeared on the television news site.

"The amazing thing is," said Alepra in a subsequent telephone interview with me as I prepared to write this chapter of the book, "that until very recently, I really didn't even have much of an online presence. I had a website, but not a very good one.

People couldn't even find me unless I gave them the URL. Basically, I was nonexistent on the web.

"I'm very thankful now that I took your advice to improve not just my website but my overall online presence. The fact that this journalist just called me out of the blue—and that a number of my clients and people in the community have been saying, 'hey, I saw you on TV,'—is amazing to me. It's really created a snowball effect for my business," Alepra said.

"The television appearance has been a nice supplement to the articles I've been writing for *The Gazette* newspaper," he explained. "It really improved my clout and visibility, creating a kind of allure and buzz in the community."

What made the difference for Pete Alepra? Pete worked with one of the marketing consultants on my team who helped him write and place carefully worded news releases on news aggregation sites. In addition, Alepra also engaged an Internet marketing consultant to analyze his website titles, keywords, and metadata.

"We added a number of essential keywords to my website and have been cross-linking to other relevant sites. So that's been driving up my search engine rankings," Alepra said. "And I learned that I should always ask for—or put into the content I write and place on news sites—a link back to my site. Now when you search for 'investment advisor cedar rapids' I come up on the first page on Google.

"What I've learned over the past few months is that when it comes to building your online presence, two plus two equals six. Everything you do multiplies. It's not just putting up another piece of content, it's creating a viral effect online."[1]

Being Seen (and Heard) Online

Alepra's story is not surprising. This type of happy "stumble upon" event happens all the time.

Sometimes it's not a journalist who calls.

"I suppose the largest client deal I can attribute to my online presence is worth $1.5 million," said Rick Kahler, CFP, in an e-mail exchange with me in June 2012. "I can't really give you a firm count as to how many new clients have come from my online presence, but I can say last year my client roster grew by over 25 percent. I cannot attribute any other activity to this increase other than doing what I've always done—having a strong online presence," Kahler said.

In addition to having a rich and engaging website that includes audio, video, and lots of visually appealing graphics, Kahler is active on top social media sites such as YouTube, Facebook, Twitter, and LinkedIn—not so much to market and promote his services as to reach current clients.

"I learn much more about what is happening in their lives—like my client who is touring Italy this week or another who is leaving for Germany in a few days. I learn about their kids and often learn of events that we address in reviews that impact their financial plan, like the client who recently announced on Facebook that they have listed their home for sale. Where was that in their financial plan? It wasn't."

Kahler, who is a NAPFA Registered Financial Advisor and president of Kahler Financial Group Inc. in Rapid City, South Dakota, believes that financial planners who don't use social media or establish a strong online presence are ceding potential clients to those who are.

"I can't imagine they will maximize their opportunities for growth over the next five years. I embrace and use technology extensively. We are totally paperless, even with our client communications. A consultant recently told me only 8 percent of financial planners are actually paperless. Amazing," Kahler said.[2]

Lou Stanasolovich, CFP, has been building his online presence for some time now. He told me in a July 2012 telephone interview for this book that over the past 9 to 10 years his firm has been receiving approximately 50 percent of all new client inquiries due to web searches. In fact, the firm received two $4 million account inquiries in the same week, and when the firm was profiled in the *Wall Street Journal* in July 2007, it brought in over $50 million in new assets.

"People will use the Internet to search before they call you. Typically they see you somewhere, do an online search, or were referred in to you," Stanasolovich said. "Google AdWords never really worked for us, but working with the media and improving our online presence more organically really has."

A well-known advisor in the industry, Stanasolovich is founder, CCO, CEO, and president of Legend Financial Advisors, Inc. and EmergingWealth Investment Management, Inc. Stanasolovich is also the editor of Risk-Controlled Investing, a subscription service that guides financial advisors on how to build investment portfolios with lower risk, and Global Economic and Investment Analytics, a subscription service that provides economic and investment oriented research, analysis, and educational content for financial advisors. He is using more video in all of his firms' communications and believes so strongly that video should be a key element in his communications campaigns that he is building a professional video recording studio right in his office building.[3]

Stories of other advisors who can directly attribute new client activity and business growth to their online efforts continue to trickle in.

In November 2011, an article by Lavonne Kuykendall published in *Investment-News* proclaimed, "Adviser's YouTube Video Attracts $1M Client: Video on Suitability, Fiduciary Standard Gets Extra Clicks."[4]

An InvestmentPal.com blog post on January 19, 2012, provides "8 Notable Stories on How New Clients Were Won" including these stunners: "Wealth Manager Wins a $3M Account from a Prospect Who Followed His Firm's Facebook Page for 8 Months" and "Wealth Advisor Wins a $2.6M 401(k) Rollover Account from an Acquaintance Whom He Noticed Had Checked Out His LinkedIn Profile."[5]

So it's amazing to me when, in the face of all these success stories, I meet an advisor who doesn't even have a website, let alone a good LinkedIn profile, a YouTube channel, Facebook page, or Twitter stream.

Creating a Great First Impression Online

The reality is that traditional marketing methods like print advertisement and direct mail still work, but they are no longer the most effective way to impress clients.

"Prospects today will look for you online first," said Cynthia Stephens, chief marketing officer of ByAllAccounts, a leading data solutions provider in the financial services industry, in a meeting with me in May 2012. "Even if they are referred to you, you can bet that the first thing they will do is Google your firm and see what they can find out about you online."

In order to get in front of your prospects and create a favorable first impression, Stephens says you need to learn and master the new marketing methods that include inbound/content marketing, e-mail marketing, and social media strategies.

But a recent survey of advisors conducted by ByAllAccounts shows that only 62.4 percent of the advisors who responded use a website (Figure 7.1). While I was not surprised to see that just 21.4 percent of the advisors who responded use social media—after all social media is still a fairly new phenomenon, something that many advisors are still trying to understand and integrate into their overall communications plan—it is stunning to think that 37.6 percent of those surveyed do not think having a website is all that important.

FIGURE 7.1 Top 10 Marketing Activities Utilized

Top 10 marketing activities utilized

Which of the following marketing activities do you currently utilize? (please check all that apply) (Responses n = 173, multiple responses allowed)

byallaccounts
data for smart decisions

Activity	%
Websites	62.4%
Events/Seminars	56.1%
E-mails	51.4%
Newsletters	47.4%
Direct mail	30.1%
Social media	21.4%
Content creation (white papers, etc.)	19.1%
Print media advertising	18.5%
Press release	18.5%
Search engine optimization	15.0%

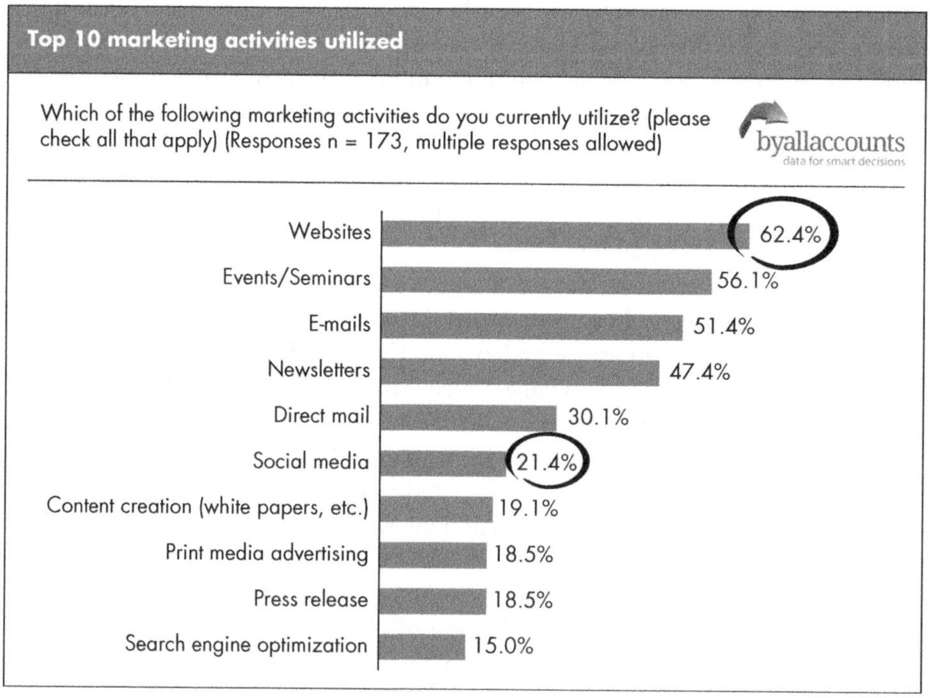

Source: www.byallaccounts.com.

I think the business case for having a good website as a financial advisor today is very well established. In today's world, you don't exist as a viable business unless you have a good website. And, as we saw in the lead story in this chapter, just having a website is no longer enough. Advisors who fail to embrace the World Wide Web are missing the opportunity to build share of mind, streamline communications with current and prospective clients, and position themselves as modern, relevant firms.

In my opinion, your website should serve as your online hub. While you may have digital outposts such as a blog, a LinkedIn profile, a Twitter or Facebook account, profiles on advisor directories, and so on, not having a website would be like not having a central meeting place to conduct business in the physical realm. Think of your website as your virtual office. It's important that you have one central presence that captures the best qualities of you and your firm and presents that public face to the world.

Really, there is no excuse for not having a good website anymore. A host of service providers have sprung up to serve the growing demand for individual advisor websites. I've worked with all of the companies listed below and think they are worth a look, whether you are just now setting up your first website or are ready for a total overhaul. In addition, there are scores of other companies that build websites for small and large businesses. The vendors listed here specialize in building basic sites for financial advisors.

FMGSuite.com
AdvisorFlex.com
AdvisorWebsites.com
AdvisorDesigns.com
AdvisorProducts.com
AdvisorSquare.com
EmeraldConnect.com
Lightport.com
Morningstar Advisor Websites
MarketingLibrary.net
FinancialVisions.com

Using these services can reduce website development time and provide a fresh flow of educational and market content. More advanced advisors, however, may choose to engage a web architect firm, marketing consulting firm, or freelancer to build a custom website that better reflects their personalities and businesses.

"It may sound like a no-brainer, but surprisingly many financial advisors have never had a website and others are mistakenly abandoning their website and solely using social media outlets as their online contact. A website may not be a direct tool for gaining clients, but it is an important staple of any business," said Kirk Hulett, executive vice president, Strategy and Practice Management, for Securities America Inc., during a conversation we had at a recent industry conference. Hulett leads Securities America's Practice Management Group, which provides consultation to investment professionals on how to improve the efficiency and profitability of their practices. Hulett is also one of the creator/producers of AdvisorPod.com, an online practice management portal that contains podcasts, videos, worksheets, and marketing advice.

"Smart advisors turn their websites into a learning resource," Hulett said. "By building an educational library with brochures, letters, articles, and other information on products you offer and general financial advice, you can transform your website from a simple contact page to a resource that clients and prospects can use to find and share important information." Creating relevant content also helps your search engine rankings.

"Keep in mind that today's tech-savvy consumer will likely visit your website before ever making contact with you in person or by phone," Hulett said. "The same is true of centers of influence such as attorneys and accountants, who may be unwilling to make referrals to a business with an inferior website—or no website at all. And making your website mobile-enabled—meaning you can read it on the smaller screen of a handheld device—gives you even greater exposure and flexibility."[6]

"Social media does not replace a website," said Josh Gilliam, president and managing director of Gilliam, Mease & Associates in Louisville, Kentucky. "If anything, it makes websites more critical, as your goal with all social media is to drive them to your website and eventually you."[7]

While the growing trend in the industry is to promote yourself via LinkedIn, Twitter, and Facebook, business websites are still valuable to existing and future clients. Make sure you are making the most of your professional website while embracing social media.

Other Digital Outposts

As I said, and it bears repeating, just having a good website is no longer enough. You should create other profiles and online posts, including publishing news releases and bylined content on credible third-party sites (always trying to build in a link back to your site). The goal is to build a spider web of digital assets and positive media mentions that appear whenever someone looks you up online or is perhaps searching for a particular topic or what you have to offer.

Other digital assets or Internet outposts to consider:

- FinancialAdviceNetwork.com
- FeeOnlyNetwork.com
- BoulevardR.com
- InvestorsWatchDog.com
- BrightScope.com
- FigSig.com
- Vestorly.com
- BetterBusinessBureau.com

- Google+
- About.me
- LinkedIn.com
- A personal or company blog
- A Facebook business page
- A Vimeo or YouTube channel
- A Twitter account
- A robust newsroom on your website that links out to stories about or by you
- A search-engine-optimized news release service such as PRWeb.com or 24-7PressRelease.com
- Listings on membership sites such as FPA, CFP Board of Standards, NAPFA, Garrett Planning Network, Kinder Institute, Sudden Money, Money Quotient, fi360, and so on.

Certified Financial Planner professional Dan Goeken of Insight Financial in Norfolk, Nebraska, knew the importance of having a website available for his clients especially during the short time while he was moving his office and rebranding.

"With everything else going on, including the physical demands of the move, we didn't have time to focus on creating a brand-new website from scratch," Goeken said. "Working closely with Securities America's marketing department while rebranding, they suggested using the Financial Advice Network. One 30-minute phone conversation later, and hardly any effort on our part, we had a great resource to point our clients to while we transitioned."

Financial Advice Network builds a powerful online profile using information provided by the advisor and an online search. It then strategically connects the profile, cross-linking it to media quotes, articles, news releases, community organization websites, professional association sites, and the advisor's own website. Once Insight Financial was officially branded, Goeken used website vendor Emerald Connect to create his current website.

"I don't look at a website as a generic need or a want," Goeken said. "I look at it as a service that clients need for account access or linking to educational resources. It's a client account service enhancement rather than a marketing tool."

Still, Goeken plans on continuing his use of Financial Advice Network for its search engine optimization and the credibility it builds by promoting his firm's website. That's a smart move, in my opinion. I just googled Dan Goeken and see that his Financial Advice Network profile comes up as the number one and number two listings on page one of the Google search, even higher than his website listings in the third, fourth, and fifth place on the search I did just now.

Matt Peterson, president of Make It A Great Day, Inc., a boutique marketing and technology services provider dedicated to helping financial services firms, recommends that advisors implement Google Analytics on their websites. "A new set of social reports help you measure the impact of your social marketing initiatives and evaluate the effect social media has on your goals and e-commerce activities," Peterson said in a recent blog post on www.miagd.com. "The four new reports aggregate key data points to help you see the complete picture of how social marketing and media affect your business. You'll find the Social Value Overview, Social Sources, Social Plugins, and Conversion Reports in the Traffic Sources section of your Google Analytics account."[8]

How Do You Stack Up?

Wondering how you compare to your peers when it comes to building your online presence? Go to ImpactCommunications.org and click through the Advisor portal, look for the Advisor Resources tab, and locate the Gap Analysis/Diagnostic Tool that I created to help advisors understand (1) what their peers are doing (2) best practices for financial advisors (3) where they might be missing opportunities to build a better presence online.

Use Social Media as an Extension

While you shouldn't focus all your attention on social media, you don't want to ignore it, either. Placing social media buttons on your website will let your website audience know you are up-to-speed with the latest trends and that you are open to working with them through a medium they may be more familiar with. Using social media can also showcase your networking connections within your community, adding to your credibility.

With a successful website already in place, Josh Gilliam made an intentional effort to start building a three-pronged, social-media framework nearly a year ago, hoping to efficiently use Facebook, Twitter, and LinkedIn with his business.

"We learned quickly that it's not just about having an account and being out there," Gilliam said. "You need to promote social media on your website and promote your website through social media and you can do both with the right content. Social media boils down to content, and the content you choose to put out there is important to establishing yourself as a thought leader in the industry."

Gilliam emphasizes that social media sites are not all the same. Each outlet has a different demographic and so different content should be shared.

"Social media shouldn't just be busy work, but instead should have a conscious benefit that drives it for sharing, educating, networking, and interacting with prospects, clients, and other professionals," said Securities America's Kirk Hulett.

"My best advice is to just start doing it," Gilliam said. "It's not for friends, followers, or likes. It's for building your online presence as a thought leader."

Gilliam said the goal of his social media framework is to shine a big, bright light on his website, and since its implementation, he has seen website activity increase dramatically.

"We can measure its effectiveness by how much website traffic we generate," Gilliam said. "Our goal is to drive people to our website where the majority of our content is available. A lot of our clients aren't on these sites. Facebook is not meant for business, but it is good to use socially, for client events, as an example."

As advisors flock after the wealth of the retiring baby boomer generation, social media may seem like the least likely route to go, but as Josh Gilliam believes, social media does lead to Generation Xers who will one day inherit that wealth.

"Not many advisors have a lot of Generation X clients," Gilliam said. "We pick up a lot of retirees because people who are looking for someone they trust often look to their children for guidance, and those children are the Generation Xers who are more computer literate and tech savvy. They expect you to have that strong online presence."

By generating, aggregating, and sharing unique and significant content for clients and prospects, and distributing that content through all available outlets, advisors package themselves as credible, knowledgeable, and engaged.

"Embrace social media as a way to communicate, but don't forget about your website," Gilliam said.

Communication Essentials

The first thing to keep in mind about building your online presence is the golden rule of technological progress: No matter the innovation, don't forget the fundamentals.

"It is easy for advisors to get so caught up in tweeting or blogging that they let the technology become an end in itself, instead of a facilitator of essential human communication," said William Chettle, chief marketing officer of Loring Ward, in July 2012. Loring Ward is an investment management and practice management solutions provider to thousands of registered investment advisors and registered representatives in the United States.

"No one will become a client because of your Twitter feed. What they should find valuable are the ideas you express and the inextricable you-ness of you—your personality. Remember that the number one reason most clients are with their current advisors is simple chemistry: They like you. Make technology an enabler and extender of your likability."

With all that said, Chettle believes the best way to build an online presence—an area most advisors are just starting to explore—is video. Video allows prospective clients to see and hear you, and it is a powerful way to showcase your personality.

"Every advisor should have a video intro on the homepage of his or her website," Chettle said. "This does not have to be a major investment. Costs are going down. The technology is getting easier to use and it's higher quality. If you are halfway tech savvy (or have kids who are) you can even do this yourself."

According to Chettle, a good introductory video should be no more than two to three minutes long (some Internet marketing experts would even say that that is too long) and highlight your background, your philosophy, and your client commitment. "Create several videos and place them on the relevant pages of your site," Chettle urged. "Even better, start a YouTube page (it's free) and host at least four or five short videos there. Remember, YouTube is the world's second most popular search engine after Google," he said.

Chettle "walks his talk" by helping the company mastermind and produce educational videos for Loring Ward's website and YouTube channel. One of the most compelling videos produced by Loring Ward is titled "My Biggest Investment Mistake." The three-minute video shows real people sharing their financial mistakes and investment blunders. The company put an ad on Craigslist to find and interview consumers who were unaffiliated with Loring Ward. The end result is a compelling video essay with these investors sharing the pain of trying to time the market and make financial decisions on their own. "I should have hired a financial advisor to help me," says one of the consumers. Loring Ward encourages advisors to link to and share this video content as a way to spark a reaction that leads to client engagement.[9]

Finding Your Social Media Groove

What once was a meeting place for business colleagues and college alumni has now become a powerful marketing tool used by big brands, small business owners and, more and more, by financial professionals like you.

While social networking sites are still a popular resource for people to communicate and interact with friends and family, today they are also one of the best places to build and maintain strong relationships with clients and prospects online.

According to Cynthia Stephens at ByAllAccounts, there are five reasons advisors should be embracing social media:

1. Networking opportunities with centers of influence such as certified public accountants and attorneys.
2. Attracting clients in their niche by creating content that addresses their issues and positions themselves as experts in the space.
3. Increasing traffic to their websites by showing up higher in search engine results organically.
4. Learning more about clients and prospects so the advisor can ask for better referrals to people in their networks.
5. Participating and engaging in conversations with their prospects—especially if they are focused on acquiring Gen X and Y children of their baby boomer clients.

"Online interactions and conversations are happening with or without you," Stephens said. "Part of managing your online reputation is knowing what's being said about you and participating in the dialog. You don't want to be the last to know."

Where to Spend Your Time

Here are some interesting findings from a HubSpot survey of 611 advisors in various business models, which was conducted in 2011:

- Sixty-one percent of the advisors using LinkedIn acquired a client through it.
- Forty-seven percent of the advisors using a blog acquired a client through it.

- Forty percent of the advisors using Twitter acquired a client through it.
- Thirty-five percent of the advisors using Facebook acquired a client through it.

It would not be a big stretch to assert that the percentages of success above have been and will be going up as more and more advisors get the hang of and embrace social media as a part of their overall marketing plans.

The established social networking sites listed above are, of course, just the beginning for advisors who want to ramp up social media strategies, Google+ is gaining traction among advisors because users can sort their contacts into groups and tailor content to those groups. Instagram allows users to easily share photos. Pinterest allows users to share videos, photos, and other content centered on areas of interest.

While it can sometimes be difficult to determine what exactly in the mix of online activities is producing the results (I believe your overall online perception is just as important as the social media component), the HubSpot survey of advisors points toward the importance of LinkedIn and blogging as high-value activities.

Furthermore, another HubSpot blog post (dated January 30, 2012) says that LinkedIn is 277 percent more effective for lead generation than Facebook and Twitter.

"In a recent study of over 5,000 businesses," said author Rebecca Corliss, "HubSpot found that traffic from LinkedIn generated the highest visitor-to-lead conversion rate at 2.74 percent, almost three times higher (277 percent) than both Twitter (0.69 percent) and Facebook (0.77 percent)."

"People join LinkedIn to showcase their career, work expertise, and find content and information to make their professional lives better. So businesses that target other businesses will naturally find a higher concentration of their target market on LinkedIn. Also, when someone visits LinkedIn, the person is most likely in a business-focused mind-set, helping businesses' content perform inherently better," Corliss explained.[10]

LinkedIn

Every advisor should have a LinkedIn profile. It has become a business essential. Having a great website as your online hub that is cross-linked to a great LinkedIn profile (both a personal page and a business page) are the two "must have" foundational elements. Then pick one or two other social media platforms and master them before you move on to another and another.

While a good LinkedIn profile almost always ranks high in search engine page ratings and is a good place to showcase your expertise, your LinkedIn presence can be much more than just another static profile page. Add connections strategically and take the time to look at whom your connections know; ask for and make introductions. Participate in discussions on Groups. Use some of the widgets to embed a Twitter feed or a SlideShare presentation or a reading list on your page. Post events that are open to the public using the Events feature.

Use industry keywords throughout your LinkedIn profiles and include working URLs with your company name embedded into the hotlink (not "company website" but rather "Smith Financial Planning"), so your profile will appear higher on Internet searches.

To see how other advisory firms are using LinkedIn company pages, log in to your LinkedIn account and enter these company names in your "company search" box:

Trovena, LLC
Know Your Options Inc.
SCS Financial
Loring Ward
KeatsConnelly

Blogging

"To build online influence in the age of social media, you must build a powerful online presence and consistently publish your thought leadership insights through a professional blog site," said Stephanie Sammons, founder of Wired Advisor, a company that helps advisors set up search engine optimized blogs. "Blogging allows you to attract your target audience, cultivate relationships, accelerate referrals, and showcase how and why you're different!"

While Sammons asserts that an advisor's blog should be his or her online hub, and I take a slightly different bent by insisting that the advisory firm's website should serve as its online hub, we do agree on this: Blogging helps you build a strong online presence in a couple of ways.

First, frequent blog postings on your site or a credible third-party site (especially if crossed-linked to your website or a secondary blog) can significantly improve your search engine page rankings. Second, blogging can position you as an expert in your field and a contributor to a body of work or a community of interest. Blogs don't always have to be just words, so if writing is not your strong suit, consider video blogging or posting audio content instead.

Andy Millard, CFP, a NAPFA Registered Advisor and president of fee-only advisory firm Millard & Company based in Tryon, North Carolina, has mastered the art of producing good-looking video clips—without the help of a professional video team. This allows him to script and capture his thoughts more frequently. He posts his videos on the company website and a stand-alone blog, cross-linking the two and using social media sites to "buzz up" the new content. He also uses an e-newsletter to push out the blog posts and videos to his "house e-mail list."

"My clients and strategic partners love the videos and blog posts," Millard said at the FPA national conference last year. "It's really added a richness—a sense of 'knowingness'—to our business relationships."

Millard continues to use the free Blogspot page he created while at one of the Social Media Boot Camps I led for FPA in 2010; he uses a mix of audio, video, photos, and text.[11]

Twitter

Since Twitter is closely correlated to blogging—after all, it is really just microblogging—and is fairly easy to do (especially if you automate some of the tweets you post), I would also encourage you to consider adding that to your top-tier social media tactics.

I encourage advisors to post short, catchy headlines and shortened links on Twitter. Learn to "bottom line it" and create a bit of intrigue. Think of yourself as a reading service, pointing the way to good information. Then try to engage people who follow you. Retweet their posts. Comment on their posts. Mix it up with about 75 percent business reading service and about 25 percent personal insights and character-revealing posts.

See how I do it on my custom-branded Twitter page at www.twitter.com/marieswift.

If you are new to Twitter, just start an account and follow a few people or entities you know and trust such as @finplan, @marieswift, @napfa, @sherylgarrett, @byallaccounts, @bobveres, @daviddrucker, @fintechie, @michaelkitces.

Once you listen and watch for a while, it will all begin to make sense.

Facebook

Facebook is gaining popularity with financial advisors as they determine how to post the right mix of business formal and business social information.

"Facebook is an excellent platform for social interaction, which is of course why it is called a social networking website," says Loic Jeanjean, sales and marketing director at Advisor Websites. "Most visitors come to Facebook because they love to interact with their friends, post their photos, and do other social activity. However, it can still have room and prospect for a financial advisor to promote their brand or financial product. However, since the line between personal and professional is very narrow, it may be challenging for anyone to make use of social media overtly for business purposes. Additionally, unlike other businesses, financial institutions have some compliance restrictions laid down by Financial Industry Regulatory Authority (FINRA). But despite these spikes, financial investors and entrepreneurs have been able to get solid business traction by creating a successful media presence on Facebook," he concludes.

The currency of Facebook is visuals so I always encourage advisors to think of their business Facebook pages as an electronic scrapbook. Posting lots of photos, videos, images, multimedia presentations, and so forth, with just a little text and a few select links is a good strategy for financial advisory firms' Facebook pages.

You might think of your Facebook page as a "celebration page" where you post photos of the firm's employees doing community service projects together, conducting a seminar or town hall meeting, or hosting a client event. If you occasionally add a photo and simple caption of you on vacation or with your family, or doing something you love—for instance, sailboat racing (which shows character and agility)—then people will get a three-dimensional sense of you as a human being, not just a business professional.

To see how other advisory firms are using Facebook to build their online presence, log in to your Facebook account or search for:

- Michael Kitces
- Dan Moisand
- KeatsConnelly
- Family Investment Center
- Trovena, LLC

Begin with a Strategy

By using social networking sites, advisors can get their messages out quickly, measure the effectiveness of their communication efforts, and receive feedback directly from clients.

A word of advice: Don't begin with the tools. Begin with a strategy—a social media game plan.

Think of this as a multistep process:

- Listen
- Learn
- Engage
- Act
- Measure

Listening and learning are only the first steps—you need to take action on what you discover.

Ideally, you will be engaging your audience of "friends" or "followers" right on the social media platform. Of course there will also be times that you will be acting on what you learn (most of the time you'll then be taking the conversation offline via phone, private messaging, or e-mail).

Sidenote: No one wants to follow a long, personal exchange between two people on a social media site but an occasional short, personal exchange between two people can be interesting and/or helpful for the entire online group.

Monitoring, archiving, and measurement are the additional pieces you should have in place.

Compliance

Of course compliance is always a concern so work with your compliance department or consultant to create a social media policy. Good online resources for information and possible archiving solutions are:

- www.arkovi.com
- www.backupify.com

- www.mailbanc.com
- www.socialware.com
- www.erado.com
- www.actiance.com
- www.smarsh.com
- www.hilladvisors.com
- www.corecls.com
- www.advisors4advisors.com
- www.riacentral.com
- www.horsesmouth.com
- www.protracker.com (compliance manual available for purchase, with social media module)

Training

You might also decide to engage a social media expert to conduct a workshop or series of consulting sessions on how to use social media in the right ways. Beyond the basics of how to use the tools, there is some nuance and social media etiquette that must be learned.

Resources include:

- www.echelonbusinesssolutions.com
- www.wiredadvisor.com
- www.wealthmanagementmarketing.net
- www.relaystationmedia.com
- www.financialsocialmedia.com
- www.tritonnews.com
- www.onlineadvisorcentral.com

My firm, Impact Communications (www.impactcommunications.org) offers social media strategy, training, community development, and content creation for our PR and marketing retainer clients, and I frequently lead Social Media Boot Camps and training workshops for NAPFA, FPA, broker-dealers, custodians, and advisor study groups.

In addition, *Financial Planning* magazine will be providing social media training modules on its website, www.financial-planning.com.

Guarding Your Webutation

As service providers, we must all be aware that we live in a new and ever-more-transparent world. It seems that everyone has some sort of a smart phone or digital device capable of capturing photos or video at the ready, so we must all be on our best behavior. Thanks to ratings sites such as www.Yelp.com, www.ScamBook.com and www.RipoffReport.com, and social media sites and blogs—where anybody can say just about anything, where everyone can be a critic or a fan online—we must all take precautions to guard our business brand and personal reputation on the Internet. So add that to your list of important things to do.

If you don't have time to monitor and manage your online presence, including mitigating negative comments and trying to create a sense of real-time engagement with clients and prospects on social media sites, you should consider hiring a community manager or outsourcing that function to a marketing/PR firm that really gets your brand and can serve as an extension of your everyday team.

According to a fun but informative video on CommonCraft.com, search engines are constantly scanning the web. "Their goal is to take a snapshot of every word, picture, and video on the web and save it for search results. This means that once a page has been scanned, it may be there forever. Even if the image is deleted from a site, it may still be found in the future—which is when problems can occur."

You want to be the first to know if and when something negative or problematic is said about you online; you don't want that comment to go ignored—or to go viral.

It goes without saying that you want to provide the best services possible and to nip in the bud any negative perceptions about you and your firm. Still, we can't control everything online. If you do learn of something you'd rather not have online, act quickly and ask the person who posted their opinion (or the site host) to remove the offending text; hopefully you can appeal to their sense of fair play before the search engine spiders take a snapshot of the page and catalog it by keywords.

In the social media boot camps I lead for FPA and NAPFA, I continually remind people not to post information or tweet when they are tired, emotional, or in a rush; you don't want to be on the receiving end of an upset phone call or e-mail from someone who takes issue with something you've said. I know from firsthand experience, and it didn't feel good. I'll never make that same mistake again.

On a similar note, take care not to post too much personal information about yourself. While the goal of social media and other digital communication tools is to show a more human side of your professional self, always consider how you might feel (and how others might feel about you) if you cross the line and share too much information. A Harvard University study suggests that posting personal information makes us feel good about ourselves; it provides an intrinsic value much like food and sex. A University of Pennsylvania study suggests that sharing information and feelings during times of stress can be a coping mechanism.

At a minimum, have Google Alerts set up for your name and your company's name so that you will see on a regular basis what others are saying about you and your firm online. You might also sign up for Social Mention, which works like Google Alerts and is free but is designed to troll a variety of social networking sites and send you an e-mail message when the keywords you select are posted somewhere.

Social Media Dashboards

Other higher end listening and engagement tools such as Meltwater Buzz, Vocus, and Radian6 are available, but I believe they are more than most advisors need or will pay for. I've been using HootSuite (the free version), SocialMention (free), and Google Alerts (free) for a while now and find that they do most everything I need. I did recently sign up for the paid versions of HootSuite, Viralheat, and SproutSocial (so far, I like HootSuitePro and SproutSocial better than Viralheat).

The list of social media engagement and monitoring tools grows on a daily basis, but here are a few that you might consider:

SocialMention.com
HootSuite.com
Seesmic.com
SproutSocial.com
Viralheat.com
Trackur.com
TweetDeck.com
Addict-o-matic.com
Topsy.com
IceRocket.com
Buzztrac.com

Using a social media dashboard can not only help you see what people are saying about you and your company, but they can streamline the communication process in that you'll be able to send tweets and post information across multiple platforms, schedule communications to go out in the future, shorten long links right there in the dashboard, and view several social media accounts all at once.

Locking Out the Imposters

Registering your name as a domain name, and signing up for every social network out there will ensure you have a presence and locks out others with similar names so you won't be mistaken for someone else.

Crowd out negative information online by generating positive search results that will rank as highly as possible in a search. The goal is to push the unsavory items farther down in the list. Start a blog, establish a LinkedIn profile, a Facebook page, an About.Me page, a Twitter account, a Google Profile, and so on and work to cross-link everything together. Tag your photos and graphics so that when someone conducts a search, they find positive and accurate information and attractive images for you. LinkedIn typically ranks high in search results, as do blogs that are constantly being refreshed with new and relevant information. Google yourself once a week and see what comes up. Be sure to look at the "images" section—hopefully nothing more unsavory than old photos of you with a prior hairstyle 10 years younger comes up.

As mentioned above, I strongly encourage financial advisors to sign up for a profile page with www.FinancialAdviceNetwork.com or its sister service www.FeeOnlyNetwork.com. These supercharged profile pages rank high on keyword searches and serve as a rich supplement to your primary website.

"Anyone can post rumors and fake reviews online, any time—including competitors. And the longer negative material is on the Internet, the more damage it does," say the people at Reputation.com, a service that allows you to monitor your online presence from its dashboard. You can take a free scan to see how you look online at www.reputation.com/for-business.

What makes a good online presence? According to Reputation.com:

- The first page of Google results are all positive.
- No negative results on first few Google pages.
- Top Google results are from credible sources.
- No links for other people with same name.
- Being quoted in reputable publications and working to cross-link to the online articles can not only improve your positive search rankings but can also create a favorable impression when current and prospective clients and business partners use Google to see what they can find about you.

Marketing Automation Software

One online idea that almost no advisors are currently using is marketing automation. This is a system that allows you to "read" the digital body language of your clients and prospects. Are they opening your e-mails? Where are they looking on your website? Are they watching your videos?

The marketing automation systems used by Fortune 500 firms can easily cost $30,000 or $40,000. But there are cheaper, scaled down tools available, which can be a big help in identifying your most engaged clients and prospective clients (note: these systems only make sense for advisors who are actively marketing and prospecting).

Viable solutions for smaller firms include:

CaptureTrackConvert
Act-On
Spark by Marketo
AWeber

These tools connect to your blogs, tweets, and so on and help you put together largely automated marketing campaigns. For example, if someone downloads a white paper on retirement income from your website, you can then put together a campaign to share retirement income-related information with this person (as well as anyone else who downloads the white paper). Apart from setting up the parameters and following up as necessary, these campaigns can run largely in the background, alerting you whenever a prospect shows increasing engagement.

"Whatever you do online, let the technology serve you—don't serve the technology," said Loring Ward's William Chettle. "Provide useful content, show your personality, keep everything short and to the point, and don't be afraid to stand out. The average web surfer spends less than five seconds on a page. Make sure your message is credible and intriguing."[12]

Notes

1. www.kcrg.com/news/local/The-Next-Step-What-To-Do-With-The-Millions–159143275. html; www.Alepra.com; http://thegazette.com/tag/pete-alepra.
2. www.kahlerfinancial.com; http://financialawakenings.com.
3. www.legend-financial.com; www.globaleconomicandinvestmentanalytics.com.
4. www.investmentnews.com/article/20111102/FREE/111109986.
5. http://blog.investmentpal.com/social-media-success-stories-new-clients-won.
6. www.SecuritiesAmerica.com; www.AdvisorPod.com.
7. www.gilliammease.com.
8. www.insightfp.net; www.SecuritiesAmerica.com; www.FinancialAdviceNetwork.com; www.miagd.com.
9. www.loringward.com.
10. http://blog.hubspot.com/blog/tabid/6307/bid/30030/LinkedIn-277-More-Effective-for-Lead-Generation-Than-Facebook-Twitter-New-Data.aspx#ixzz1zK24bUek; www.byall accounts.com.
11. www.low-stress-investing.com; www.andymillard.blogspot.com; /www.wiredadvisor.com.
12. www.capturetrackconvert.com; www.actionsoftware.com; spark.marketo.com; www .aweber.com.

CHAPTER 8

Client Portals
and Collaboration

Bill Winterberg, CFP
Consultant, FPPad.com

When the first edition of this book was published 10 years ago, "collaboration" as a word likely inspired images of two or more people meeting together in a conference room, capturing discussions and ideas on notepads or whiteboards. Today, you can collaborate with clients, employees, and other professionals in a remarkably different fashion, facilitated in large part by technology.

Your ability to collaborate in new ways is driven by near-ubiquitous access to high-speed Internet connections. New personal and professional collaboration tools are continually introduced that take advantage of the always-on connectivity we enjoy today. These tools, when used purposefully, have the potential to drive significant growth in productivity and profitability, two essential tenets of operating a high-margin practice.

This chapter explores several categories of collaboration tools and their relevance to internal operations, client communication, and business intelligence within the financial services industry.

Delivering Documents and Reports

One process that doesn't easily scale as advisory firms grow is the delivery of documents and reports to clients. During the typical quarterly portfolio reporting period, advisors expend considerable resources printing, collating, stuffing envelopes, labeling, and mailing reports to clients. As the number of clients and accounts under management grows, so does the amount of labor required to complete the quarterly report delivery process.

Some advisors may send electronic file attachments via e-mail instead of mailing paper reports to clients. E-mail is by far the most common way we all communicate and correspond with one another, but it should be avoided when sending information and documents containing personal or sensitive information, such as Social Security numbers and investment account numbers.

Client Portals

To solve both the scalability and information privacy issues surrounding quarterly report delivery, advisors have adopted web-based client portals and document vaults. These solutions allow them to upload an array of electronic documents to a secure repository to which clients have access where they can view statements, reports, and other documents present in their portal.

Client portals were the first technology to enable collaboration between the client and advisor without requiring a face-to-face meeting or use of overnight mail. Some client portal solutions also offer integrations with portfolio management software, streamlining the upload process for reports created in bulk.

You can choose between dedicated client portal solutions and portals that are integrated as a component of a larger software platform. We'll explore several providers in each category in the following sections.

Dedicated Portals

Dedicated client portals serve as a central online repository where clients and advisors upload, store, and share important documents. Both advisors and clients typically enter the portal by entering credentials on the portal's login screen, which is often branded with the advisory firm's logo, color scheme, and other custom characteristics.

Once logged in to the client portal, users are typically presented with a list of folders and files stored in the system displayed much like the Windows or Mac file explorers. Users can add new folders and upload or download documents, but functionality generally doesn't extend beyond that. Advisors can access a properties or settings menu to control the access and functionality clients have when uploading and downloading documents in the portal.

Selection among dedicated portal providers is limited as an increasing number of vendors now integrate client portals directly into their software solution. Current stand-alone portals are available from ElevateCDS (formerly FamilyOfficeNetwork), Advisor Products Inc. and LIGHT[PORT].

To better integrate dedicated portals with the software used to create portfolio performance reports, Trumpet Inc. created a utility called Assemblage that will customize the contents of such reports. Assemblage gives you the ability to assemble multiple documents and reports into one PDF file, apply correct page numbering schemes, and automatically upload packaged reports to the correct destination folder in the client portal.

But if you want additional functionality, you may want to consider a solution with an integrated portal to simplify the upload and management of documents to be shared with clients.

Integrated Portals

Integrated portals behave much like their dedicated counterparts with respect to the client experience. Clients generally follow the same procedures to log in, view, download, and upload documents within the portal. But you gain an advantage with integrated portals, as much of the publishing and uploading of new documents can be streamlined through automated processes.

Your choices among integrated portals feature many of the leading software platforms for advisors. They include (listed in alphabetical order):

- AssetBook
- Black Diamond
- BridgePortfolio
- eMoney Advisor
- Envestnet | Tamarac Advisor View
- Finance Logix
- Grendel Client Portal
- Interactive Advisory Software
- Junxure ClientView Live
- Morningstar Principia CAMS View My Accounts
- Morningstar Office
- NetDocuments ShareSpaces
- Orion Advisor Services

However, these integrated portals are part of larger and generally more complex software platforms that are covered in more detail elsewhere in this book. You will want to evaluate many more attributes and functions beyond a platform's integrated client portal before adopting the software in your business. Often, your desire for specific functionality around relationship management, portfolio management, trading, and other functions will supersede your affinity for the integrated portal you may like the best.

Portal Drawbacks

As client portal solutions mature, advisors have encountered one significant drawback to the products: clients, by and large, don't use them. In conversations with advisors, I've discovered that about 1 out of 10 clients actually log in to their client portal on a recurring basis to view documents. Three reasons emerge when exploring the lack of client adoption of these systems.

First, client portals require a login and password. If you're like me, you already manage dozens of login credentials for a variety of secure websites. Adding yet another password to that extensive list is rarely an appealing prospect for most clients. Second, many client vault solutions have cumbersome user interfaces. The link to the document vault may be nested among links to other portal content, and once in the vault, clients may not understand how to navigate through files and folders.

Finally, many portal solutions employ a tedious process to upload and download multiple documents. To download files, clients typically select one file from the portal and then choose the destination directory on their local computer. To upload files, clients must first browse to the destination folder in their portal, click the upload button, and then select one file from their local computer to upload. Each process must be repeated if clients want to upload or download multiple documents, an inefficient experience at best.

To eliminate the drawbacks of client portals and increase client adoption rates, you will want to consider alternative solutions to simplify document sharing. Many of these solutions are part of a category of tools called cloud file-sharing services.

Cloud File Sharing

Cloud file storage and sharing services leverage the proliferation of broadband Internet access to store, synchronize, and back up files on servers in large, remote data centers, generally referred to as "the cloud." Many of these services function as if they were a hard drive installed on your local computer, except your files reside on a remote server that you access over the Internet. Other services operate in a hybrid fashion, where your files are physically stored on your local hard drive, but they're also stored and synchronized on a remote server.

The breakthrough that cloud file storage and sharing services offer is the ability to share files and folders with other users of the service. Should you want to allow others to view and edit documents in a specific folder, simply send them an invitation to join your folder, and everything contained inside is accessible by them just as it is on your computer.

What to Look For

When evaluating any Internet-based file storage service to use with sensitive documents, you must pay close attention to each service's data privacy and protection policies. Identify the encryption scheme in place and whether it applies to documents both in transit and at rest. Also, learn where the encryption keys are stored. If encryption keys are stored "server side," then select employees of the provider can potentially decrypt your files and view their contents (for example, in response to a government request). Providers that employ "client side" encryption keys have no ability to decrypt your files, as those encryption keys are stored solely on your computer and are inaccessible by the provider.

You should also ask about any independent audits or certifications a provider has obtained. Common auditing standards include SSAE 16 Type II (formerly SAS 70 Type II) and ISO 27001. With any service requiring an online login, you should see if the provider offers multifactor authentication. In addition to supplying your username and password, multifactor authentication requires a separate security token or passphrase when logging in (the second factor), often delivered to your mobile phone via SMS text or voice message.

Also, explore what access permissions exist for documents stored in the service. Determine if you can enforce read-only permissions, prevent files from being deleted, and set expiration dates for files you share with clients.

Many services also offer desktop synchronization of the files stored on remote servers (the hybrid function mentioned earlier). This feature is the key to increasing client adoption of file sharing services, as clients can access their personal document repository just as if it were any other folder on their local computer.

File synchronization also has benefits as a disaster recovery and business continuity solution for your firm, as computers can be relegated to nothing more than an everyday appliance rather than a critical piece of hardware. When the hard drive fails on your computer, you can simply buy a new computer, connect it to the Internet, and wait an hour or two for all of your files to synchronize from your cloud service.

Compliance

Any time you elect to store files with client information using third-party services, you must take reasonable precautions to verify that the files are safe from unauthorized access.

Regulatory guidelines from both the Financial Industry Regulatory Authority (FINRA) and the U.S. Securities and Exchange Commission (SEC) will never specifically approve a cloud file service as being compliant. Instead, each regulator emphasizes that you, as a regulated provider, must implement and follow policies and procedures reasonably designed to protect client information. Therefore, you must conduct due diligence when evaluating a provider and determine whether you are comfortable with its security practices.

Dropbox

Dropbox, a small start-up founded in 2007, has rapidly grown to support over 50 million users. The company's primary aim was to eliminate the need to transfer files between computers on USB flash drives. Instead, Dropbox users install the program on multiple computers, and all files and folders saved in the Dropbox folder are synchronized through the service over the Internet.

One additional feature that allows Dropbox users to collaborate on documents with other Dropbox users is the ability to share folders. Many advisory firms configure a shared drive on their file server that all employees use to work on common files. Shared folders on Dropbox allow users to set up a similar sharing scheme, but with other Dropbox users who do not need to work in the same network environment.

For example, when one user updates a PDF document in a shared folder, Dropbox instantly synchronizes those file changes with all of the other Dropbox user accounts that are sharing the folder. It's no longer necessary to email the updated PDF as an attachment or insert version information into the filename. Dropbox takes care of synchronizing the file updates behind the scenes.

Dropbox offers a free plan with up to 2 gigabytes of storage. Folders can be shared with an unlimited number of other Dropbox users. Additional storage up to 100 gigabytes is available for $19.95 per month, with several pricing tiers in between. Dropbox offers free mobile apps for all of the popular mobile platforms, allowing users to access all files in Dropbox from mobile phones and tablet devices.

Egnyte

Egnyte is a service similar to Dropbox, but adds several features that are beneficial to the enterprise and corporate environment, including investment advisors. One benefit is Egnyte's ability to synchronize files between network-attached storage (NAS) devices, in other words, your server, and the Egnyte Cloud File Server.

Like Dropbox, Egnyte supports shared folders with other users, but the service adds capabilities such as file versioning, locking, file annotations, and notifications to enhance security and collaboration options.

Egnyte offers several pricing plans, starting with the Group plan for $24.99/month. The Group plan supports up to 5 employees and 150 gigabytes of file storage. For up to 10 employees, Egnyte's Office plan provides 1 terabyte of storage and is priced at $44.99/month. Larger offices will need the Enterprise plan, priced at $12.99/employee/month, providing 3 terabytes of storage.

All plans are compatible with Egnyte mobile apps supporting iOS, Android, Windows Mobile, and even e-readers such as Amazon's Kindle Fire and NOOK by Barnes & Noble.

ShareFile

ShareFile, acquired by Citrix Systems in 2011, takes many of the sharing and synchronization features found in consumer services and enhances them for the enterprise environment. For example, ShareFile allows you to add your company brand and logo to the website login page. Instead of seeing a generic login prompt, clients will see your company's information when accessing their own ShareFile account.

ShareFile also supports the creation of common folders, which are ideal for sharing documents like your client newsletter. Instead of copying and pasting your newsletter document to hundreds of client folders, in ShareFile you simply add the document to one common folder to which all clients have read-only access.

A plug-in for Microsoft Outlook is also offered with ShareFile, so you can continue to send documents securely to clients all from within the Outlook program. Instead of attaching documents to your outgoing e-mail, ShareFile will upload the document to its service and include a link to the file in the body of your e-mail.

Clients can also access their ShareFile folders without needing to log in to the ShareFile website. Both a Desktop Widget and Desktop Sync utility enable access to documents and files right from a computer desktop. I prefer the Desktop Sync utility as it allows both you and your clients to map folders created in ShareFile with folders created on a local computer or server. With Desktop Sync enabled, all you need to do to share files with a client is drag and drop them to the mapped folder on your computer, and they will be uploaded automatically to your client's ShareFile account. For your clients, the next time the Desktop Sync utility synchronizes with the ShareFile service, their files will be automatically downloaded to their local computers.

ShareFile supports all popular mobile devices in use today, including apps for iPhone, iPad, Android, Windows Mobile, and BlackBerry. With mobile apps installed, your clients can access and view their documents while they're on the road and away from their primary computer.

Pricing for ShareFile is more expensive than its consumer-oriented counterparts, but the service offers a number of additional features not found in other applications. The Professional plan, which supports up to 10 employee accounts, starts at $69.95 per month and allows you to configure an unlimited number of accounts for your clients. If you want to take advantage of the Desktop Sync feature, you'll need to upgrade to the Corporate plan priced at $119.95 per month. Reduced pricing is available when purchasing ShareFile in quarterly or annual installments, and the service can be cancelled at any time.

There simply isn't enough space in this book to cover all the file sharing and synchronization services available, and new ones are continually introduced to the consumer and enterprise markets. Services finding interest among financial advisors include the following (listed in alphabetical order):

- Amazon Cloud Drive
- Box
- Cubby from LogMeIn
- DocLanding
- Google Drive
- M-Files
- Microsoft SkyDrive
- NetDocuments ShareSpaces
- Nomadesk
- Octopus from VMware
- SpiderOak
- SugarSync
- TitanFile
- Wuala from LaCie
- YouSendIt

Wikipedia has an extensive matrix highlighting many of these services and their primary features that can be found on this page: http://en.wikipedia.org/wiki/Comparison_of_file_hosting_services.

Refer to this matrix periodically as it is continually updated to reflect new providers and new features adding to existing services.

Edit Documents Simultaneously

Cloud file sharing works well as long as two users don't attempt to edit the same file simultaneously. If that happens, services often create two versions of the same file, marking one as a conflicted copy. It's up to you to determine what changes were made in the conflicted copy and manually merge them into to the original document.

Fortunately, there are several solutions available that support real-time editing and collaboration of the same files. Both Google Drive (an extension of Google Docs) and Microsoft Office 365 allow you to store word processing and spreadsheet documents on their online platform and invite other users to edit those documents simultaneously with you. Any changes made to documents are saved in real time, so there's no need to return to files at a later time and manually merge updates added by other users.

Collaboration Platforms

Being able to work on documents simultaneously is very appealing, but collaboration often extends beyond the need to edit just spreadsheets or word processing files. As the modern workplace continues to evolve through the addition of mobile devices and the ability to connect and work from anywhere, collaboration platforms have emerged to allow work to be done on more than just files.

Collaboration platforms allow you to manage calendars, tasks, projects, workflow, and knowledge base articles relative to your business, all within one online platform. Basecamp, a product from 37signals, is an example of a collaboration platform that is gaining interest among financial advisors. Centered on project management, Basecamp allows users to engage in project-related discussions, add tasks and to-dos, upload and edit related documents, and schedule important milestones on a community calendar.

Pricing for Basecamp starts at $20 per month, which supports up to 10 simultaneous projects and 3 gigabytes of file storage. Several different pricing tiers are available for additional projects, up to an unlimited number of projects for $150 per month.

Again, the list of collaborating software options is extensive, so you can find more information on programs like Basecamp and many others in the following Wikipedia entry: http://en.wikipedia.org/wiki/List_of_collaborative_software.

Screen Sharing

As we've illustrated before, cloud-based document sharing applications work well for delivering files that don't require regular updates, such as portfolio performance reports or archived tax returns. However, you often need to perform financial plan illustrations and update reports in real time with clients. Collaboration platforms discussed earlier are ideal for real-time status updates among employees, but they're not appropriate for use by individuals outside your practice, including clients and other professionals.

Typically, you might schedule face-to-face meetings with clients to review financial plans and other work in progress, but clients may not always be available to meet in person. Other times, you simply need clients to quickly review and confirm information listed in a form, but want to avoid inconveniencing your client with all the formalities of scheduling an in-person meeting.

The tool best suited to collaborating in real time with individuals outside your practice is a desktop screen sharing application. Desktop screen sharing allows you to broadcast anything you see on your computer screen to one or more people via the Internet. Whatever you can show on your screen, including documents, reports, e-mails, and even videos, you can show to those who have joined your screen sharing session.

WebEx and GoToMyPC were two tools highlighted in the first edition of this book to conduct screen sharing and web-based conferencing with clients and prospects. Today, the list of providers is substantially larger, and we'll cover the most popular tools in the following pages.

A note of warning is in order before we proceed with the most popular screen sharing tools. It's your responsibility to always protect client data and maintain client confidentiality. This means that before sharing your screen with others, you must disable any pop-up windows or notifications that might contain client information. Specifically, you should disable e-mail notifications that display the subject line, sender information, and a portion of the message body, which can be viewed by others who join your screen sharing session.

Several tools offer premium subscription plans with a feature that automatically blocks windows and pop-up messages you haven't approved to share in your session, a useful feature not typically found in the free services.

WebEx

Cisco Systems purchased WebEx in 2007 and today provides a suite of applications for real-time meetings, training, and support services branded under the WebEx name. Advisors should be most familiar with WebEx Meeting Center, available for a $49 monthly subscription fee with up to 25 meeting attendees. Discounts are available through online promotions or by purchasing an annual subscription.

WebEx offers an extensive list of features, so we'll highlight those most relevant to your meetings with clients and prospects. In addition to screen sharing, WebEx allows you to share documents with meeting attendees as well as give control of your keyboard and mouse to others. Several advisors depend on this feature to let clients type their username and password credentials for held-away retirement accounts into account aggregation software. The advisor is never exposed to that information, thereby avoiding triggering any custody issues with respect to access to those held-away accounts.

WebEx also makes a whiteboard available for brainstorming during meetings, and highlighting and annotations can be marked up anywhere on the screen. The program can also record your meetings, which you can use to create training videos (for example, your process to add new securities to your portfolio management software) or archive webcasts of a presentation. High-definition video conferencing is also included, so there's no need to use separate video conferencing services such as Skype or FaceTime to conduct virtual face-to-face meetings.

Finally, WebEx Meeting Center supports meetings on a variety of mobile devices, making it possible for you to schedule, host, and attend meetings on an Apple iPad, Android smart phone, BlackBerry, and more.

GoToMeeting (and GoToWebinar)

Developed by Citrix Online in 2004, GoToMeeting is another popular web conferencing application advisors should recognize. It supports many of the features found in WebEx, including screen annotations, video conferencing, sharing keyboard and mouse control, meeting recording, and mobile device support. Like WebEx, GoToMeeting is available for a monthly $49 subscription fee with a discount available for an annual subscription.

GoToMeeting supports up to 15 meeting attendees, so if you plan on using the tool for presentations to larger groups of people, consider upgrading to the GoToWebinar product. At $99 per month, GoToWebinar allows you to host meetings and presentations with up to 100 attendees. Maximum attendee levels of 500 and 1,000 are available for a monthly subscription of $399 and $499, respectively.

Mikogo

German company BeamYourScreen GmbH released a free version of its online collaboration software called Mikogo in 2009, which attracted attention from financial advisors for its included features. Not all advisors conduct web-based meetings on a routine basis, so Mikogo was a free alternative to the paid applications for the occasional virtual meeting.

Recently, the company transitioned to a premium subscription model and offers the free version for noncommercial use only. Pricing is fixed to the number of meeting attendees per session. Mikogo Basic supports 3 attendees for a $149 annual subscription, Mikogo Pro allows 15 attendees for $249 per year, and Mikogo Pro+ allows 25 attendees for $399 per year. Lifetime subscriptions are available for each plan level.

join.me

join.me is a recent addition to the family of screen sharing applications created by LogMeIn, Inc., provider of a suite of remote access software. A free application released in 2010, join.me is one of the easiest applications clients and prospects can use to join meetings you organize. Attendees need only visit the join.me website or use mobile apps for iOS and Android and enter a nine-digit meeting code you provide.

Your meeting attendees don't need to download or install any software on their computer, and they see everything you show on your screen directly inside their Internet browser. As the meeting host, you must download and install the join.me meeting application one time in order to begin your meeting session and invite meeting attendees.

A join.me Pro account, available for $149 with an annual subscription, is required for features such as personal meeting links, transferring control of the keyboard and mouse, and more.

Skype

Skype, the popular voice-over-IP phone service purchased by Microsoft in 2011, is another free application that supports simple screen sharing between two callers. With well over half a billion users worldwide, it's likely that many of your clients are already comfortable using the service on their computers and mobile devices.

Skype supports very basic screen sharing functionality on a one-to-one basis, but should be sufficient for most meetings you hold with clients. You can share either a specific window of your desktop or display the entire screen. Group screen sharing is available under the Skype Premium plan, priced at $9.99 per month with discounts available when purchased annually.

Google+ Hangouts

Google+ is the Internet search giant's response to the exponential growth in social networking platforms like Facebook and Twitter. One feature included in Google+ is called Hangouts, which allows you to conduct video chat sessions with up to nine other Google+ users. With a Hangout session in process, you can share your screen using the link labeled Screenshare at the top of the Hangout session.

Like Skype, Google+ Hangouts screen sharing lets you choose whether to share a specific window or your entire desktop with Hangouts participants.

Again, your options for screen sharing solutions aren't limited to those covered here. You may find one of the following applications best meets your needs:

- MeetingBurner
- Adobe Connect
- AnyMeeting
- Fuze
- Yugma
- MegaMeeting

As with the other solutions covered in this chapter, you'll find a comprehensive matrix listing many of the popular web conferencing and screen sharing applications on the following Wikipedia page: http://en.wikipedia.org/wiki/Web_conferencing.

Social Enterprise

Over the last 10 years, you no doubt have witnessed pivotal changes in the way we interact and engage with one another. The dominant trend has been the rapid rise of social networking services, with Facebook the most influential of them all.

Facebook will soon surpass 1 billion active users, with most regularly engaging with the site's News Feed where one can post status updates, photos, and check-ins from a variety of physical locations. The Facebook News Feed is an effective platform where you can stay informed about friends, family, colleagues, and acquaintances who might be located anywhere in the world.

With such success in the consumer market, businesses have recognized the potential benefits of similar social services when applied to the enterprise environment. Instead of reviewing status updates on personal activities, users of social enterprise services can see updates regarding customer issues, prospecting opportunities, and business metrics.

Financial advisors can apply the same principles of social enterprise services using some of the tools mentioned in the following section.

Salesforce Chatter

Chatter is an enterprise social network from Salesforce.com, the leading provider of web-based CRM. Chatter configures a private social network that you and your colleagues can use to follow people, groups, and records relevant to your business. For example, you can follow your support staff and see when they post status updates like completing a client check request, downloading the most recent custodial data into portfolio management software, or scanning tax documents delivered by clients earlier in the day.

You can search across all Chatter updates to find up-to-date information on activity for a specific client, reducing the time you might spend tracking down a colleague in person to request an update. While you're away from the office, you can use free mobile apps for iOS, Android, and BlackBerry devices to monitor interoffice activity.

A recent update to Chatter now allows you to extend access to guests outside of your office, so you can choose to include clients on posts and updates specific to them. The product also added instant messaging and screen sharing functionality directly within Chatter using Chatter Messenger and Chatter Screensharing, so users do not need to leave their Chatter session to use third-party programs highlighted earlier in this chapter.

Chatter is available for free and can be used by everyone with the same domain name in your e-mail address. A Chatter Plus plan is available for $15 per user per month that extends the free features to include custom reports, Salesforce AppExchange integrations, and workflow capabilities.

Social enterprise is a new segment in collaboration solutions, so the list of providers and their respective functionality is constantly changing. Offerings similar to Chatter include Jive Engage, Yammer, and Regroup. Even vendors to financial advisors have enhanced their products with social enterprise features, such as Orion's Wall from Orion Advisor Services LLC. Integrated into Orion's platform, Orion's Wall permits both automatic and manual updates to a community news feed, where you can quickly see the status of new client deposits, withdrawals, and even business metrics such as total assets under management updated on a daily basis.

Wrap-Up

It's difficult to imagine that only 10 years ago, virtually none of the collaboration tools and solutions mentioned in this chapter existed. Today, there are hundreds of new technologies and platforms available that enhance the way we collaborate with others, all made possible through widespread access to broadband Internet connections.

Gone are the days when the only way to get an answer to a question was to track down a colleague in person or call a client on the phone. Now you can connect via screen sharing applications, launch a video conference call, or even monitor status updates on a social enterprise network.

All of the collaboration tools highlighted in this chapter make it easier to capture and share information in your business, permanently altering the way you interact with employees, allied professionals, prospects, and clients.

Which solutions will you start using today?

CHAPTER 9

The Cloud

Using a Cloud-based IT Infrastructure to Enhance Profitability

J. D. Bruce, MS, CPA, PFS

President, Abacus Wealth Partners

Understanding Cloud Computing

To help you understand cloud computing, I intend to explain to you how I transitioned a national registered investment advisor (RIA) firm with multiple offices from a situation that could be described as an IT disaster to a happy and content 100 percent server-free existence. My firm, Abacus Wealth Partners, will serve as a case study illustrating the pitfalls and silver linings of living the cloud lifestyle.

I do practice what I preach. This entire chapter was written in the cloud, end-to-end. The original invitation came via Gmail. I wrote the outline using MindMeister, which is connected to Box.com for storage. The draft was written using Google Docs, also connected to Box.com. Also, I only listened to music on Spotify. Interestingly, I did most of my writing on planes, so feel free to suggest your own cloud puns.

I'm a firm believer that there is no one right answer to running an RIA, and I'd love to continue the conversation about the best way to do so. Feel free to contact me via twitter (jdbrucecpa) or LinkedIn (jdbruce) to ask questions, poke fun, or challenge my conclusions.

What Is the Cloud?

If you ask 16 tech guys to define "the cloud" you'll get 16 wildly different answers. It's similar to asking certified financial planners about a safe withdrawal rate. I'm going to dispense with the tech jargon and avoid categories like IaaS, PaaS, and SaaS and words like "multitenancy" and "virtualization." If you're a tech geek like me, search Wikipedia for cloud computing and enjoy a great introduction. For the rest of you, I'm going to define it my own way and use descriptions that my eight-year-old son understood when I explained it.

According to my son, "Cloud computing is what you get when you throw your computers away, not all of them, just the ones you don't want." That's about the best explanation I've ever heard. In my words, the goal of moving to the cloud is to reduce costs and/or increase convenience by eliminating your internal servers. The cloud is simply what happens when you rent applications, computing power, and data storage instead of buying it.

History and Evolution of the Cloud

I'll keep this section short and leave out a lot of important historical milestones in the evolution of cloud computing that aren't relevant to your business. The real purpose of understanding the history of cloud computing is to understand the answer to, "Why now?"

In the early 1990s, the idea of grid or utility computing started to become reality. This was essentially the idea that we could make computing power as easy to access as the electric power grid. The main practical result for most of us was monthly Internet access as opposed to privately run bulletin boards like AOL and CompuServe.

In the late '90s, the terminology shifted to application service providers or ASPs. To oversimplify it, ASPs would bulk license applications and host the software for end users. Nobody calls them ASPs anymore, instead the language has shifted to software as a service or SAAS (darn it, I said I wouldn't use that term . . . I'll stop now).

In the last 15 years, improvements in browser technology and bandwidth have allowed an explosion of subtly different means of delivering applications, computing power, and data storage to end users. Let's look at some broad categories.

Types of Clouds

Let's use four broad categories of cloud computing. Abacus has used all five over the course of this case study, so it will be helpful to put some of these solutions into buckets. Also, I'm sorry for continually apologizing for oversimplifying, but I'll be using some technical terms in ways that real IT professionals wouldn't agree with. So, if you are one, or if one of them corrects you, I beg forgiveness.

Private Clouds

My son says, "A private cloud is a cloud you build yourself." That's clear. More importantly, a private cloud is one you keep to yourself. Most real IT professionals would argue correctly that private clouds don't belong in a discussion of cloud computing. That doesn't bother me, I'm not a real IT professional. As a small RIA, a private cloud is an indispensable step on the path to freedom from the tyranny of servers.

In grown-up talk, for our purposes here, a private cloud is essentially the same as having servers in your kitchen, but they can be accessed from the Internet without being in the same location as the servers. There are two types of private clouds, "do it yourself" and "done for you" (those aren't those technical terms I was talking about . . .).

Done for You

There are a host of vendors out there that own data centers and servers, and they'd love to give you access to them. Depending on the vendor, you'll either rent your own actual servers or you'll get a virtual server (or three). For your purposes, there's no difference. Virtualized servers are not lesser than actual servers; in fact, I prefer them for flexibility. Regardless, you're renting, so just like when you're at a hotel, if the servers stop working, you move to a different one with very little work required by you. The key aspect of this kind of server is that you have a reserved amount of computing power and data storage. You'll understand why that's important when we discuss shared servers.

The company that rents you the server also acts as your IT department, performing server maintenance, security, application installation, data backups, and even IT help desk and training for your staff. We'll talk more about choosing a vendor later in the chapter.

The applications are accessed using some sort of remote access technology where you either use a virtual desktop or virtual applications. A virtual desktop looks like a windows desktop in a special window on your screen. It's basically remotely controlling another computer. A virtual application appears to be the application running on your computer, but it's really just a window where you're remotely controlling the application from far away.

Most RIAs could easily move to a private cloud, save gobs of money, and never need to explore the other types of cloud implementations (the ones that real IT professionals would call the real cloud).

The cost of this type of solution starts around $1,000 per month for a couple of users and rises significantly as you add users and additional servers. Twenty to thirty users with a SQL server could cost around $5,000 per month.

Do It Yourself

If you own a big company with 100,000 workers around the world, it makes a lot of economic sense to build a data center, staff it with the required techies, buy a pile of servers, and create your own private cloud. I've even spoken to RIAs that have rented space in a shared data center themselves and maintain their servers themselves. If you have a decent sized tech staff, this may be a viable option, but it won't be appropriate for many of us.

The cost of this type of solution runs from an initial purchase cost of $20,000 to $100,000 with ongoing maintenance costs.

Shared Servers

Shared servers are probably the most familiar of the types of cloud implementations. Your website is almost certainly hosted on a shared server by your web hosting company. On a shared server, you have a secure and reserved amount of data storage, but the bandwidth and computing power is shared. This means that if another tenant on your shared server has a website that starts getting a lot of traffic, then your website may crash. Shared servers are only appropriate for applications that are not mission critical like websites. If you can't live without it for a few days, don't put it on a shared server.

Space on a shared server can be had for as little as $6 per month.

Software as a Service (aka SaaS, Multitenancy, the Real Cloud)

I keep using SaaS. I give up. You'll hear about SaaS all over the place, so you may as well get used to it. Most of the cloud applications that you see out there are SaaS. These include communication applications like Gmail, Skype, and iContact; CRM applications such as Salesforce.com, Zoho, and Redtail; RIA-specific applications Black Diamond, Orion, Tamarac, and Morningstar Advisor Workstation; or business applications like Google Docs, Quickbooks Online, Expensify, MindMeister, and Evernote. This list of applications is not meant to be comprehensive, but rather to illustrate, by example, what an SaaS app is.

Through technical wizardry beyond the scope of this chapter, SaaS allows you to avoid the setup and overhead of a private cloud solution and enjoy the costs similar to a shared server without the disadvantages.

SaaS applications generally are billed at a per-user per-month fee. As your firm grows, so does the cost. As an example, Gmail costs $5 per month per user and Salesforce.com Enterprise Edition costs $125 per user per month. It can add up, so plan carefully.

Platform Providers

I avoided the use of platform as a service (PaaS) because it reminds me of easter eggs. Platform providers are very similar to SaaS providers, but they generally offer a specialized solution instead of a whole package. Hmmm, that definitely doesn't pass the eight-year-old test. Said another way, you can *do* something with an SaaS product, you can *build* something on a platform. The most common platform providers offer file storage, database storage, or a special easy-to-build application development language. Amazon pioneered its file storage platform, Simple Storage Service or S3 in 2006, and now many SaaS providers use it to store your data. Salesforce.com, in addition to its SaaS CRM offering, markets a popular database platform as well as an application platform. Document management providers like NetDocuments and Docupace fall in between platform and software providers.

Nine out of ten RIAs will never need to consider using a platform provider. The one that will use one is likely sophisticated enough to not need my summary description.

The cost of a platform provider almost always depends on usage, although some use per-user per-month pricing.

BIG BUSINESS VS. SMALL BUSINESS

While the concepts are the same, the types of implementations and tools that small business uses are vastly different from big business. I can only speak from the small business user perspective, not the big business issues that require a professional IT staff. If, as you are Googling around looking for cool cloud apps, you see the terms middleware, virtualization, business intelligence, data warehousing, or ETL, click away swiftly; it's not for you.

The Abacus Case Study

In 2003, Abacus Wealth Partners was created through a merger of Sherman Financial in Philadelphia and San Francisco and Abacus Wealth Management in Los Angeles. By 2006, the firm had doubled in size and was experiencing serious growing pains. Each of the three offices had its own distinct CRM database, its own file server, and its own business processes. The two firms had been beautifully integrated culturally, but the difficulties of implementing consistent processes and technological systems for three offices with thousands of miles between them proved beyond the capabilities of a company with no professional management and no full-time IT staff.

The founders of Abacus had the foresight and humility to seek advice from some of the best thinkers in the industry and started the process of hiring a management team and building technology systems. They were advised that the CRM was the most important part of the puzzle, so they started by reviewing their CRM.

Right after the merger in 2003, rather than setting up in-house e-mail servers, our founders instead chose a hosted Microsoft Exchange server. At the time, this technology was still pretty new, and most IT professionals still mistrusted the idea. It worked out very well, however, and our e-mail was the only one of our systems that worked consistently (if slowly).

Based on their experience with cloud-based e-mail (although the term "cloud" was not yet in wide use in 2006), they looked for a cloud-based CRM to meet their needs. We were then using Sage ACT! in each of our offices, and every night, the co-founder and president of the company logged into the server and made the attempt to sync the data between the three offices. The sync even worked some of the time. It certainly was not the best and most productive use of our president's time.

Abacus hired an IT strategist (that's like a consultant who gets paid extra) to help select and implement a system. We eventually chose Salesforce.com with a customized Salesforce app to tailor the CRM to the wealth management industry. The Salesforce platform would allow for easy access to all of our data, and the custom app would integrate our Portfolio Center data and link all of our documents to a structured database. It was the solution to all our problems.

Like every technology implementation that I've been involved with, the promises never match the ultimate reality. Salesforce was indeed easy to access, but the custom app was never fully implemented by the consultants, and we never experienced the integration with Portfolio Center or the structured documents.

I joined the firm in 2007, shortly after the implementation team stopped work. I quickly noted the lack of certain features that were supposed to exist, and I called the IT strategist to find out what happened. When I asked for a copy of the project plan, there was a long silence.

Now that you know how our path to the cloud started, let's pause and discuss some of the benefits and drawbacks that we noted as we walked the path. I'll continue to refer back to the case study as we continue.

Benefits and Drawbacks of Cloud Computing

Here's a handy chart listing all the benefits and drawbacks I'll be discussing. I'll detail the benefit and the associated drawback together to highlight the trade-offs.

Benefits	Drawbacks
Scalability	Data portability
Variable costs	Potential higher expense
Automation	Control
Mobility	Reliability
Integration	Integration
Implementation speed	Training
Collaboration	Privacy and security

As we detail each of these benefits and drawbacks, I'll dive into our case study to illustrate how Abacus has enjoyed the benefits and suffered the drawbacks.

Scalability vs. Data Portability

The number one reason for true cloud applications to exist is to have limitless scalability. The ability to add users to an application in an instant without thinking about the performance hit has long been the dream of business managers. It's absolutely true that the cloud providers have achieved this dream. For any small to medium-size business, there's no limit to processing speed, file storage, database size, or number of users. In reality, someone is still considering how to add capacity and is concerned about server loads, but with the cloud, that person isn't you, which is all that matters.

However, that limitless storage for files and databases does cause issues. Because you are only renting space, and because each provider codes its data slightly (or significantly) differently, you may not be able to access your data easily. You may end up locked-in to a provider that you don't like just because the cost and time to extract your data and convert it to a usable format is prohibitive. This is a big issue that we will more fully address when we discuss compliance and security.

CASE STUDY NOTE

A great example of the power of scalability is in e-mail. In 2006, Abacus used Hosted Exchange e-mail with Outlook as a client. Even though it was on a hosted server, when each user's local e-mail database grew larger than 1 gigabyte of data, Outlook slowed to a crawl. I spent countless hours searching for large attachments to delete to shrink the size of my.pst file. After switching to Gmail, I'm now happily growing my e-mail box past 9 gigabytes out of my 25 gigabyte storage capacity. If I need more, I just call Google and increase it.

The drawback of data portability hit us hard when we were switching our e-mail retention service. Both providers had stated that the data they retained was fully portable. What we didn't know is that the old provider would charge us a lot of money to export the data from its system, and the new provider would charge us significant money to import the data to the new system. It ended up being cheaper to just have the old provider keep the data for the remainder of the five-year retention requirement instead of importing. Not an ideal situation, and I wish I had known about those costs prior to being forced into it.

Variable Costs vs. Potential Higher Expense

I'd like to make a confession. I love variable costs. I love being able to predict my profit margin, even if the margin has to be slightly lower. Luckily, cloud computing feeds my variable cost fetish. Nearly all cloud providers charge based on usage as opposed to fixed fees. Most charge per user, but some charge based on storage or processing cycles. A few providers even charge using a basis point fee schedule. This kind of fee structure makes financial projections simple and means that your expenses are 100 percent predictable. You don't have to worry about a server breaking and having an unexpected repair expense. Everything is included.

The drawback is, just like an all-inclusive vacation, you may end up paying more than you originally thought. There are two traps to be aware of.

First, when comparing your variable costs to your fixed costs, you need to build in your expectations for growth. As an example, let's suppose you're looking to buy an e-mail server that can handle 100 users and you have 80 users. You need to compare the cost of the server not only to the cost for your 80 users on a cloud-based e-mail system but also to the cost of any expected new users that you expect to hire over the life of the server.

	Local Solution	Hosted Solution
Current users	80	80
Maximum users	100	∞
Expected growth in users over useful life of local server	15	15
Up-front cost	$20,000	0
Useful life	5 years	N/A
Cost per user per year	$0	$50
Total cost over 5 years for current users	$20,000	$20,000 (80 × $50 × 5 years)
Additional cost for growth in users	$0	$1,875 (15 × $50 × 2.5 years average)
Total cost	$21,000	$21,875

The hosted solution ended up costing more, even though it appeared to be the same cost at first blush. Of course, with the local solution, if you go over 100 users, costs go up tremendously.

Second, beware of third-party services that enhance your cloud application. These aren't always provided by the cloud provider, but are built to work specifically with them. These include browser extensions, integration tools, and gadgets. These can vastly increase the cost of your cloud product. I use several Gmail enhancements that cost two to three times the cost of Gmail itself. These can make your cloud application work like a charm for your specific needs, but make sure you budget the costs of all these extras.

CASE STUDY NOTE

Nearly all of Abacus's IT spending is based on a per-user charge. When I budget for a new hire, I know exactly what the IT burden will be. It's certainly caused me to rethink some of my hiring decisions now that the full costs are staring me in the face. Our cost for IT spending per employee is close to $2,500 per year. That's just the variable costs for our cloud apps and doesn't include some of the fixed costs or the specialty applications that only a few users access (like financial planning software).

Automation vs. Control

A lot of IT professionals hate the cloud for one reason. They no longer get to control when they upgrade their systems. With cloud systems, upgrades are not optional, and sometimes the users don't even know when they are going to happen. This is a blessing and a curse. Does anyone (besides me) enjoy upgrading his or her software? It's great to have someone do it for you. You log in and suddenly find a new feature you've been hoping for or a bug that that's been bugging you has been fixed. It's awesome! But what if the upgrade breaks or removes a favorite feature? What if the new cool feature isn't something you like? Facebook Timeline?

When you decide to go cloud, you are deciding to put your faith in the developers of the cloud systems. Their vision for their software is critical to your success. You should do three things before you sign on to any new cloud system that is critical to your operations.

First, if you can, get a developer or product manager on the phone (or e-mail) and find out whatever you can about their road map. Be careful, because you'll hear a lot of pie-in-the-sky dreams about where they are taking their system. Do not base any buying decision on features that might come in the future. I've been burned countless times by hope for future features. So, never say yes to a system because of future promises. But, understanding the future road map may cause you to say no. If you use Salesforce, and the developers of a potential system are actively developing an integration with Microsoft CRM, you might want to instead find a system that is working on a Salesforce integration (or better yet, already has one). If the system you are looking at is focusing all development on enterprise features and you're a four-person firm, then find someone whose vision matches your company's growth plan.

Second, read all of the release notes for the past several years' worth of releases. You can see where a system is going by seeing where it has been. If there hasn't been a release in several years, run away. If some of your critical features are brand-new, you may want to wait for another few release cycles for the new features to get perfected before you start relying on them. If the direction of the releases isn't pointing toward where you want the system to go, find another one.

Third, test-drive the software and see if you enjoy using it. Remember, only make a decision on what is available on the day you implement, not future releases. Any new system should make a positive productivity impact immediately.

CASE STUDY NOTE

We recently implemented Box.com as our cloud file manager/light document management tool. When reviewing the system, one of my primary concerns was that Box didn't have any ability to enforce metadata fields or folder structure. The company promised that it was about to release the ability to do this in the next few months. We implemented the system and are still waiting for the feature with no idea if or when we might see it.

Mobility vs. Reliability

You can use cloud systems anywhere. I once approved client trades from my car outside a Starbucks while on a road trip from Los Angeles to San Francisco. In that moment, my mobility dreams were realized.

Another time, I was looking at a potential new office lease, and I tried to pull up the trade system on my iPad. No service. So, I walked a mile away, restarted the iPad, logged in, and got kicked off a couple times, and then finally approved trades 40 minutes later.

When it works it works brilliantly. Our expectations for uptime are high and when those expectations aren't realized, we feel betrayed. The reality is that most cloud systems are more reliable than any server you have in your office, but it doesn't always feel that way, especially when the downtime takes longer than an hour to come back up. There are more moving parts in cloud systems (your Internet connection, their Internet connection, all the routers in between, their multiple servers, your browser, etc.) and the whole thing feels very out of your control.

Integration vs. Integration

Back in the old days, we never worried about integration. The systems I used at the beginning of my career were generally built to work together and we didn't have an expectation of totally different systems working together in any meaningful way.

Now, the collective dream is to take a pile of unrelated systems and weave them into a unified whole. I, for one, get incredibly irate when I find out that two systems I like don't play nicely together. I want my clients' portfolio data inside my CRM and their estate documents linked to their records in the CRM and an automatic upload of every e-mail they send me or I send them stored in the CRM with an instant speed search that only returns relevant results. I guess what I really want is the *Star Trek* computer that can make the blurry picture clear when I say "Computer, improve color and texture."

The reality is that integration is extremely difficult to make work well, and even the best and easiest integration needs careful planning. I'm not here to discuss integration strategies, but cloud solutions have two unique integration issues that on-premise software does not have.

First, the good part. Most cloud software applications have an application programming interface or API. Basically, an API is a published means of pulling data out of and putting data into the software. Software vendors build these hooks into their software to allow other software vendors to create applications that work closely with each other. The apps on an iPhone use the iPhone's API to do things like use the camera or the volume buttons. Some cloud software has very robust app stores like the Salesforce AppExchange and Google's App Marketplace. Cloud apps use something called a "web service" to talk to each other securely over the public Internet. The availability of these web services combined with an API means that you can build a integration with Salesforce without calling Salesforce to coordinate the development. This allows for unprecedented flexibility to build integrations, which is why Salesforce.com has over a thousand apps listed on its AppExchange.

Second is the bad part. You don't control the cloud app, so if there's data in the system that isn't available using the API, you're out of luck. Sometimes the software developers don't want to allow integration partners to access everything. Apple's iPhone has a public API for everyone to use, and a private API that only Apple is allowed to use. The company keeps anything private that it feels gives it a competitive advantage. As an example, for years, Apple denied others the ability to use the volume button as a camera shutter.

Implementation Speed vs. Training

Back in my days of implementing big accounting systems, we would put about two weeks' to a month's worth of training in the project plan. The vendors would come with big binders and hold in-depth training with all the users. We'd get big manuals with detailed instructions on how to do anything we could imagine needing to do.

These implementations generally lasted for months, and took months of planning before we even started.

On the other hand, I recently implemented a new expense reporting system in eight minutes. I didn't have to install anything, and I just had to type 30 e-mail addresses into a window to add all my users. Of course, nobody knew how to use it, and I didn't have any binders or detailed instructions to give them.

Cloud apps reduce implementation time by several orders of magnitude. It's just easier to e-mail 30 people a link than it is to set up servers and then install and keep software updated on 30 terminals.

With that time savings on the implementation, you get a patchwork of training strategies by the various vendors. Unless you are using an all-in-one solution, you have to figure out how to weave all the pieces together and teach your employees how to use this new stuff productively. Training is a major part of any new system, and it's made harder because there's nobody you can hire to do it for you. Only you know how to communicate your vision of how the new online expense reporting system works with QuickBooks Online.

Collaboration vs. Privacy and Security

Because there's no software to install, it's easy to grant access to your files, your portfolio data, and your financial data to your clients, your CPA, and your other trusted partners. It's also easy to grant that data to the wrong clients and people other than your trusted partners. I'm not speaking of the ease of hacking into cloud apps. I believe that your average cloud app is more secure than your average on-premise system. However, the typical collaboration features that are prevalent in cloud apps can easily create a privacy disaster.

Imagine a system like Box.com, where you can create client folders and give clients access to a system where you can deliver documents, let the clients' CPA upload their tax returns, and offer a secure encrypted vault for the clients to store their financial data. It's a great value add for the clients, and saves us tremendous time gathering data and retrieving it later. Now imagine that all you need to do to grant access to that folder is to type in someone's e-mail address and hit enter. Now imagine the most technologically innocent employee in your firm having that power. Now imagine that there is a parent folder that holds all your clients' files, and that folder also allows your technologically innocent employee to type in an e-mail address and share everyone's files with someone.

That's exactly how Box.com works if you don't take precautions to limit some of the collaboration permissions. The collaborative aspects of cloud apps that are selling points for a software development firm sound great at first and can, indeed, create great efficiencies. They also need to be very carefully considered when implementing to avoid a severe privacy issue.

Implementing and Maintaining a Cloud Infrastructure

Before I jump back into the Abacus case study, let's talk through the first two steps of implementing new technology.

Project Manager

The first thing you need to do is determine if you have the implementation expertise and capacity in-house or if you need to hire a short-term consultant. In order to do an implementation justice, you need someone who understands the business process, understands technology, and has project manager skills. The individual also needs to be able to dedicate the majority of his or her time to this project. If this doesn't describe one of your employees, hire a consultant. Do not assume that you can learn this on the job. Also, don't be afraid of the dollar cost of hiring a consultant. If the owner of the firm takes on this job, the opportunity cost of not looking for new clients and not servicing existing clients can be huge.

Needs Assessment

Step two is to understand exactly what you need to implement to make your business better. A good consultant will do this first, and your in-house project manager should, as well. If you don't clearly understand the vision for what you are creating, you'll end up with a mess of applications that don't serve you and are a drain on profitability and productivity.

Every project manager will approach a needs assessment differently, and some will call it something different. Once everyone completely understands what the business needs to ultimately have implemented before anyone starts implementing, then this step can be marked complete.

BACK TO THE CASE STUDY

Back to 2007, when Abacus had recently implemented Salesforce. Salesforce was still being used as a glorified shared contact manager and note storage database, definitely not living up to its potential. We still could not easily share our files across the firm (we did have a virtual private network to allow access to our files, but it only worked about half the time) and had no real organization or document management capability. Our portfolio management system, Portfolio Center, was hosted on a single server in someone's figurative garage, and our clients' data was in three separate databases. Rebalancing was done using several Excel spreadsheets (not necessarily the same versions).

The first step for Abacus to improve our situation was to figure out our primary needs.

Abacus's 2007 top five oversimplified needs:

1. A CRM that could track all client requests and all prospecting activity.
2. A single repository for all files, with remote access capability.
3. A portfolio accounting system that combined all client data into one database, and allowed client electronic access.
4. Automated trading and rebalancing.
5. 24/7 IT help desk for employees.

This wasn't the end of our needs assessment, but it allowed us to begin prioritizing our vision into discrete steps.

Core vs. Ancillary Applications

I believe in categorizing your technology applications into categories.

Core Applications

Core applications are those that your business relies on to meet client needs. These are the most important applications, and you should build your technology infrastructure around the specifications of your core applications.

Ancillary Applications

Ancillary applications are those applications you need, but aren't critical to your business success. You choose ancillary applications based on your infrastructure and ignore applications that don't fit with the applications you already have.

Gray Area

Some apps are not quite core to your business, but are still very important to all or certain members of your staff. These categories are a sliding scale, not a binary choice.

MORE CASE STUDY

We looked at Abacus's applications and put them into the following categories. We then picked which application we were using in 2007.

Core
- CRM: Salesforce.com
- Portfolio accounting: Portfolio Center
- Rebalancing/trade automation: none

Ancillary
- Web hosting
- Word processing: Microsoft Word
- Financial planning: NaviPlan 9 desktop
- Calendar/scheduling: Salesforce.com and Outlook
- Investment research: Morningstar Principia
- Document management: none

Gray Area
- E-mail: Outlook/Exchange
- Spreadsheet: Microsoft Excel

Many advisors would be surprised at our choice to include financial planning as an ancillary application. It's not that our financial planning software isn't critical to our firm, it just didn't rise to the level of structuring our entire infrastructure around it.

Then we matched our stated needs to our application categories to tried to figure out what out what our real needs were. Let's break down our needs.

- A CRM that could track all client requests and all prospecting activity.

The CRM is a core application, and we had just implemented a new one that theoretically could do everything we needed if it were implemented correctly and adopted by all staff. Further, since we felt committed to Salesforce.com and Salesforce .com was a core application, we needed to build our infrastructure around Salesforce.com. The critical next step was to implement the case and opportunity tracking features in Salesforce.com and train users.

- A single repository for all files, with remote access capability.

Document management was an ancillary application, and as we weren't using anything, we had nothing to replace. We needed to find a document management system that met our specific needs and that would work well with our other core applications, particularly Salesforce.com. The critical next step was to define our exact business needs (beyond the single sentence above).

- A portfolio accounting system that combined all client data into one database and allowed client electronic access.

We already had Portfolio Center, but it didn't allow for electronic access. We had to either purchase or develop an add-on feature that allowed for electronic access or replace the system. This was a core application, so if we weren't going to replace the system, we needed to make sure our technology infrastructure was also built around it. The critical next step was to identify whether we were sticking with Portfolio Center or switching to a new system.

- Automated trading and rebalancing.

We had no rebalancing system, so we needed to find one that worked with both Portfolio Center and Salesforce. However, this was a core application, so whichever system we chose, we needed to change the infrastructure to allow for its use.

- 24/7 IT help desk for employees.

Based on this requirement, our infrastructure needed some level of outsourced help desk assistance.

Based on the above, we reached the following conclusions:

(*Continued*)

> We needed a technology infrastructure that was a mix of locally installed and cloud applications. We needed to find a rebalancing system and document management system that worked with Salesforce and Portfolio Center (or its replacement). We needed outside help to allow for our expanded help desk needs.
>
> We tabled the review of our ancillary applications until we had a better sense of our ultimate infrastructure solution.
>
> Our hunt was on.

How to Put a Plan Together

By this point in your own personal story, you'll need to have found a competent project manager (either consultant or in-house) and have done a preliminary, high-level needs assessment. At this point, I'm going to gloss over the project management advice and really focus the discussion on how this relates to cloud applications.

Fundamentally, you have one of three possible cloud infrastructures.

1. You have on-premise applications with local servers (non-cloud).
2. You have installed applications on remote servers (private cloud).
3. You are 100 percent in the public cloud (public cloud).
4. It's wet everywhere (rain cloud).

On either number one or number two, you can sprinkle some cloud applications in with your installed applications. You can't sprinkle in some installed applications in number three. In number four, it's just sprinkling.

EVEN MORE CASE STUDY

We ended up choosing option two, the private cloud. It gave us all the benefits of the cloud, namely the ability for anyone in any office (or at home) to access all applications and all files. Our vendor was able to provide 24/7 help desk, and the nature of the system meant that we didn't need to replace any of our ancillary applications. Everything just worked within the walls of the platform. All our problems were solved (at least it felt that way at the time).

In my opinion, if you have any servers in your office, it is critical that you at least explore the option of moving the servers to a private cloud. Abacus saved $60,000 in the first year simply by reducing our on-site IT help desk bill. It's not right for everyone, but do yourself a favor and explore the idea. Abacus's vendor at the time was External IT, which we continue to use as of the date of this writing.

As time went on, we realized that some problems lingered.

1. External IT was able to manage all of our installed software, but not our cloud apps like Salesforce.com. We were on our own for managing that.

2. Accessing files on a private cloud is better than trying to access them on a server in your office across the country, but it's less convenient than accessing them on a public cloud service like Box.com or NetDocuments.
3. E-mail was still slow.
4. We still didn't have a real document management system, electronic reporting for our client, or a rebalancing system.

We had only solved two of our problems: infrastructure and help desk.

Over the course of the next five years, we slowly began solving the rest of the problems.

- We replaced Outlook/Exchange with Google Apps (a public cloud app).
- iRebal (an on-premise app) was chosen as our rebalancing solution.
- We implemented Box.com (public cloud) to store our files.
- We replaced Portfolio Center with Orion (public cloud).
- We replaced NaviPlan 9 with NaviPlan Select and Money Guide Pro (both public cloud).
- We replaced Morningstar Principia with Morningstar Advisor Workstation (public cloud).

At this point, the only listed apps that aren't public cloud are iRebal and Microsoft Word and Excel. Half of our staff has experimented with Google apps to replace Microsoft Word and Excel, but we haven't made that switch yet. I can't imagine replacing iRebal, but once they figure out a cloud version, then we'll be able to move our infrastructure to 100 percent public cloud and close our private cloud.

We learned many lessons about implementing cloud applications as we went through our journey to the cloud, and before I begin discussing the issues with maintaining a cloud infrastructure, I'll share those lessons in the hope that you can avoid some of our missteps.

Lessons Learned

In no particular order, here are some of the most critical areas that we would address differently if we had a time machine.

Cloud Is Not a Feature

When selecting applications, pay attention to your core vs. ancillary categories, pay attention to how the application fits into your infrastructure, but don't let the fact that an application is a cloud application sway you in any way.

Here's a partial list of why you might select a cloud application:

- It works within your technology infrastructure.
- It works with other core applications.

- It solves a business need.
- The costs are within your budget.
- It has variable costs instead of fixed costs.
- Your brother-in-law is the salesman.

Nowhere in that list is the fact that the application lives in the cloud. Cloud apps tend to have variable and lower costs, integrate well with other applications, and employ brothers-in-law, so they are frequently chosen over on-premise applications, but the fact that they are cloud shouldn't be a factor.

Make a Written Project Plan

I don't care how easy the implementation is. I don't care if it's a simple expense report system that you could implement in a day. Create a written project plan that breaks down every step of the project from the initial review to the final day of training. It seems like more work, but someday it will save your hide, and if we ever meet in person, you will offer to buy me a drink just for this piece of advice alone.

Use Small Pilot Groups

As part of your project plan, include a lengthy trial period where two to four people test the system first. Half of the systems I test this way end up not being chosen. Sometimes the idea of a system is better than the actual system itself. Most of those times we don't even end up picking a different system. We realize in the testing that we never really needed an application with those types of features for that process. At Abacus, this happened when testing time sheets, online project management tools, 360-degree employee reviews, a client document vault, flowchart software, travel tracking, proposal automation, client data gathering forms, a social intranet, tax planning software, and compliance automation. We test a lot of applications.

Some applications don't work well with small pilot groups. Document management and CRM are pretty tough to implement across a small portion of your firm. A switch to a private cloud is impossible to pilot. However, we were very successful with piloting iRebal, where we added one distinct population of clients before rolling it out to everyone. It also worked with the performance reporting switch to Orion and our switch to Gmail. Among the smaller applications that we have piloted or are piloting are Cloud Factor (an application that links Salesforce and Gmail), Attachments.me (an application that saves Gmail attachments to Box.com), and Expensify (an expense reporting system that downloads to Quickbooks).

Process is more important than platform.

You can't rely on an application to create a disciplined business process. If you replace an on-premise disorganized file server with a slick new document management system, but you neglect to document the process around storing the right kinds of documents, then you'll find yourself with a very slick, very pretty, and very disorganized document management system.

You need to define your process first, and only then start the process of finding applications that can automate your processes to create efficiencies.

I'm still working on consistently doing this. I'm a technophile who constantly gets enamored with the new and fancy application. I've at least learned to just play with the shiny new apps on my own instead of pushing them across a 30-person firm.

The Three Ts: Training, Training, Training

One of the great masters of science fiction, Robert Heinlein, consistently used the phrase, "tell me three times" throughout his novels. I've learned through my experiments with training my staff that three times is an absolute minimum before something becomes cemented.

Cloud apps tend to be easier to use, and so there is a temptation to skip the basics and let people start using a system with minimum training. This is the biggest mistake I make (and I do it a lot). You should hold an initial training session before launch, then do another session right at launch, and then another one somewhat after launch.

Focus on how people learn best. I generally try and do live online group sessions, one-on-one in-person sessions, recorded video sessions, sessions where I demonstrate, sessions where I make the user control the screen, and written manuals. Everyone has a different optimal learning pattern.

Again, be diligent about holding training, be compassionate with people who aren't as technically proficient, and be ruthless with making sure that people use the new system correctly and don't fall back on using an old system because it's more familiar.

That's enough lessons for today, kids. Let's talk about administration and maintenance, the hard part of cloud.

Maintaining Your Infrastructure

There are five pieces to maintaining and administrating your cloud infrastructure.

1. User Administration
2. Integration
3. Backups
4. Help Desk
5. Compliance and Security

Private Clouds

Private clouds are vastly easier to maintain than a collection of unrelated public cloud apps. For the most part, the private cloud vendors offer help desk, user administration, and backups. A good private cloud vendor is very secure by design. They also generally can provide resources to help with integration.

Really the only things left are to provide one on-site person to help when a hardware issue happens, designate a person to coordinate with the vendor when new users come on board or new applications need to be installed, and deal with any compliance issues like five-year data retention.

Moving toward a 100-Percent Cloud Infrastructure

User Administration

One issue with multiple public cloud apps is that whenever you add a user, you have to add that user to each and every application that you want them to have access to. Unlike a server-based infrastructure, where excellent tools for centrally managing users have been developed over decades, there aren't any good standard tools for adding users to every application you use.

Abacus has a long checklist for adding/removing users to/from our system, with a lot of steps that our IT guy has to accomplish. As you'll come to see as we go through this section, a 100-percent cloud infrastructure needs a lot more in-house capability than a private cloud.

Integrations

There are three major categories of integration (according to me . . .)

Single Sign-On

Single sign-on can alleviate some of your user administration work and make things much more convenient for your users. Single sign-on means that you log in to a platform like Salesforce or Google, and then you don't need to log in to other apps. The new apps know that you are already logged in and bypass the log-in screen. For example, I don't need to log in to Box.com, TripIt, or Expensify. They all use my Google password. You've probably also seen the "log in with Facebook" button scattered around the Internet. Lots of applications work inside of Salesforce.

Data Sync

Most of the good functional integrations in the RIA industry fall into this category. On a regular schedule or on-demand, one application pulls data from another application and uses it in some way. This can happen over the Internet using public APIs and web services as I previously described. It can also happen through custom-built integrations written with the cooperation of both of the applications' developers. Some of these integrations are one-way, and others pass data back and forth.

For the most part, these integrations are built by the application developers themselves and don't need sophisticated IT staff to keep going. However, depending on the nature of the sync, there can be conflicts and other serious sync issues that need a savvy staff member to solve.

Some of the data sync integrations that Abacus has used are:

- iRebal and Portfolio Center/Orion (built by iRebal)
- Salesforce.com and Box.com (built by Box.com)
- Google and Salesforce.com (using a third-party tool called Cloud Factor)
- Google and Box.com (using a third-party tool called Attachments.me)
- Orion and Salesforce.com (built by Orion)
- Orion and MoneyGuidePro (built by MoneyGuidePro)

Shared Database

This kind of integration means that instead of sharing data back and forth, the data is all in one place, and multiple applications can access it. Generally, the all-in-one systems that combine portfolio management, CRM, financial planning, and so forth are this type of integration. This can also describe applications that are written using an existing platform, like Salesforce's. The accounting software FinancialForce is an example of an application that was fully written using Salesforce's database and interface.

Backups

Data management on cloud applications are both simple and extraordinarily complex at the same time. Most cloud application providers have extremely sophisticated backup and recovery systems that are invisible to the end user. If your provider is large enough, you just don't have to deal with this issue.

However, if you want to keep separate backups outside of the system, you may have an extremely difficult time getting your data out on a regular basis. Some of the smaller cloud providers make it almost impossible. This is less of an issue for backups, but as you will see, it can be a huge issue for compliance.

Help Desk

Help desk is a difficult issue, and, unfortunately, you'll likely need to deal with this in-house. Once you move away from a managed private cloud, only someone deeply involved in your business can understand the intricacies of how each of your systems work together. Even if you are partially on a private cloud with a few public cloud apps mixed in, you'll have to have someone acting as help desk for the public cloud apps. Your private cloud help desk people don't have expertise in applications outside their playground.

Compliance and Security

Security

Cloud apps run the gamut from the most secure application money can buy to a dodgy server in someone's garage. It's up to you as the user to do your due diligence and make sure that you're dealing with an application provider with adequate security.

One way to gain comfort is to ask for a Statement on Auditing Standards (SAS) 70 letter. An SAS 70 letter generally means that the application provider has gone through an extensive audit of its internal controls, including controls around IT systems, security, and backup. At the very least, it tells you that the company has sufficient resources to pay for an expensive independent audit and doesn't keep its server in the garage.

You should also determine how the data is encrypted, if the company has ever had a security breach and how it was handled, and read everything the company will provide about its security protocols.

Of course, if the system does not contain sensitive client data, then you can worry less about security. I'm not concerned about the security of my flowchart application that I only use to draw business processes. If that data gets shared with the world, the worst that can happen is an epidemic of people falling asleep at their computers.

Honestly, the greatest possibility of a security breach is not on the side of the application provider, it's internal to your firm. I would bet that you have someone on your staff who keeps his or her passwords on a Post-it note stuck to the monitor, a piece of paper under the keyboard, in a drawer, or listed in an unencrypted spreadsheet. It's an epidemic. Do your best to educate your staff to choose strong passwords and keep them in a secure, encrypted location. Personally, I use an application called 1Password to store my passwords in an encrypted file. LastPass is another good option.

Data Retention

The SEC and FINRA have very specific data retention requirements. I won't pretend to be an expert on the various state and federal compliance requirements, so I will simply say that it is critical to involve your compliance staff or consultants in every decision around new applications, and ensure that they have documented how your firm will meet each of your compliance obligations. Enough said.

Conclusion

I'd like to end our time together with some encouragement. As much as I tried to give you the silver linings and the thunderstorms of cloud computing, I will now admit that I am a true believer in the power of the cloud to make our lives easier and more productive. I love approving trades at the beach on my iPad.

As incentive to move more to the cloud, let me tell you a story.

It was eight hours before my flight to the T3 conference in Dallas. I was working on my presentation when my computer crashed and wouldn't start up again. I quickly drove down to the Apple store and grabbed a new laptop. I was home 45 minutes later, started up my new computer, installed two utilities, and logged into my private cloud website. Immediately, the application I had been working on popped up and my cursor was in the same place as it was when I left off. I continued working, losing only an hour of time, made my flight, and had a successful presentation.

Remember, feel free to contact me via twitter (jdbrucecpa) or LinkedIn (jdbruce), or via the Abacus website, www.abacuswealth.com.

CHAPTER 10

Digital Signature Technology

Dan Skiles

Executive Vice President, Shareholders Service Group

The evaluation and understanding of electronic signature (e-signature) technology involves some of the most complex issues that a business owner must face in creating the infrastructure for doing business. The due diligence process before using e-signatures should involve all of these areas: hardware needs, software interfaces, databases in use, network infrastructure, and of course, legal, and compliance oversight.

Generally speaking, e-signature technology has been around in various forms for a number of years. The first industry to broadly adopt e-signature technology was the consumer retail sector (Home Depot, Best Buy, etc.). This started with consumers signing credit card slips using a stylus on an electronic pad that recorded their signatures. Overall, this was a fairly straightforward process, and consumers could ask questions of the retail employee if they didn't understand how to use the new technology. In fact, in the consumers' eyes this wasn't much of a change—their signatures looked the same as when signing with pen and paper.

Another early form of e-signature technology was a process that validated the client's identity and agreement without having to actually obtain a signature. This was accomplished by asking the client a number of random, personalized questions that the client would answer via a computer. Each question would require a specific answer that, by design, only the actual individual could answer. An example would be: "Your credit card balance on your last statement was:" and the system would list four or five different dollar amounts as possible answers. Each question would need to be successfully answered in order for the client to pass the process. Then, upon successfully answering the questions, it was determined that this was the actual individual. At this point, the client could execute agreements and other documents that traditionally would require his or her signature for confirmation. Usually, the client would check boxes and other fields to acknowledge agreement.

Given that the capability of using e-signatures has been with us for a while, it is interesting that the advisor community has been slow to adopt this technology. There are a number of good reasons why the use of e-signatures has not yet become a standard practice, and we shouldn't expect e-signature technology to take over the advisor community yet, as it has, for example, in the consumer retail sector. In other industries that have higher adoption of e-signature technology, the consumer or user is generally using the technology in a self-directed manner. This means that the consumer expects to control most of the experience and is comfortable being more hands-on with the process. For advisors, generally your clients fall under the delegator category, which is part of the reason that they have selected to work with your firm in the first place, and so their intentions are not always as clearly defined nor as limited in scope as when they are in the checkout line at the grocery store. However, there are still many opportunities for advisors to realize benefits and ultimately be more efficient by utilizing e-signature technology, regardless of the type of client you serve. You may be able to process more documents per hour, per employee, and have them more readily available when you need them by using e-signatures. And more importantly, you may see more clients sign up with your firm more quickly and more easily. The key is very similar to achieving success with other technology solutions—it involves evaluation across business practices and technology platforms. Achieving success with e-signature technology will not happen by accident. You need to have a clear strategy and a thoughtful plan in addition to selecting the right e-signature technology provider for your specific firm.

Today, there are several common forms of e-signatures. A client typing his or her name in an acknowledgment field on an electronic form could be an e-signature. An e-signature could also be a distinct pin number that was selected by the client. Furthermore, an e-signature could be the client actually signing his or her name directly on the electronic form using a mouse or other method. Each of these methods offers its own unique benefits. Therefore, it is important to evaluate which one would work best for your clients and your firm.

E-Signature Technology Core Offering

There are a number of core features that should be included in any e-signature technology solution. These features include:

- ESIGN Compliant: The Electronic Signatures in Global and National Commerce Act (ESIGN Act) was enacted on October 1, 2000. This granted online electronic signatures the same legal status as a written signature.
- Templates: This feature allows you to create ready-made documents with automated workflow, signature boxes, and other items that are repeatedly used.
- Multiple Platforms Supported: This e-signature technology works on various platforms including web-based, tablet devices, and smart phones.
- System Integration: Integration with commonly used software (Microsoft Office, Adobe, etc.) in order to create templates and forms.

- Custom Branding and E-mail: Include your branding and customize the message content in the e-mail sent to the document recipients.
- Document Storage: All documents are archived on the system with search and other filter tools.
- Custom Workflow Routing: User-defined workflow of how the documents are routed after each step is completed.
- Alerts: System sends alerts to the parties involved (sender, receiver, etc.) as changes to the document occur and signatures are recorded.
- Progress Status: System shows the user where they are in the process of completing the form and how much work is remaining.
- Security and Audit Trail: 256-bit SSL encryption as well as a detailed audit trail of who, when, and how each user interacted with the document.

The pricing for e-signature technology solutions is generally based on several components. These components will include the number of users (senders), the number of templates, overall level of customization required to install the solution in your working environment, interfaces with other services you use, data transmission needs, and the level of customer support desired. Many e-signature technology solutions will charge their fees monthly and might also offer a discount when you sign up for an annual plan. Furthermore, depending on how your needs change and evolve, it is possible to start small and later upgrade to a more extensive plan with the same provider. It is also certainly possible to change e-signature technology providers, if you discover that your needs have outgrown your current provider. However, it is important to understand that there could be significant switching and conversion costs when you decide to leave one e-signature technology solution for another provider. The level of these costs (both direct and indirect) will be influenced by many factors including the number of documents, templates, and overall customization involved.

Evaluating E-Signature Technology Solutions

There are several fairly well-known e-signature technology solutions available for advisors to evaluate. Examples include DocuSign, EchoSign, and RightSignature. Because e-signatures are not yet in use in many industries, it is also an evolving technology and more providers will become available as the barriers to entry decrease. This is consistent with other technology solutions available to advisors. It generally starts with one or two companies offering a technology solution that addresses a specific need and then other companies enter the market as more opportunity for growth is expected. This is a very important business dynamic to be aware of, because more choices should lead to better solutions and improved value as the technology becomes more widely adopted. With e-signature technology, this is critical to understand given that this technology is not only influenced by the software needs (the design and process for retrieving the signature), but also the hardware needs (the device used to run the software). Both these areas continue to greatly change and evolve. Therefore, with any e-signature technology provider that you select, you need to evaluate how the provider will adapt to continuing changes in the marketplace.

For example, if you had selected an e-signature technology provider back in 2008 whose solution could only work on web-based platforms, then you would have dramatically limited your opportunity to work with tablet-based devices that were broadly introduced a short two years later. It is unlikely that you can forecast these types of market changes and their overall adoption by consumers. However, you can focus on selecting an e-signature technology provider that has demonstrated the capability for introducing consistent upgrades and new features. Ask these questions about vendors you are evaluating: How has its solution evolved in the past with the changes in the marketplace, such as new operating systems, or new interfaces to other vendors you might work with? As new hardware devices have been introduced, such as tablets and smart phones, how has the e-signature provider responded? The answers to these questions should assist you with understanding how the e-signature technology provider will likely respond and evolve with future changes in the marketplace.

Advisors have multiple options in working with e-signature technology providers. You can work with these providers directly or potentially utilize the relationship that they may have with your document processing company, your custodian, or broker-dealer. The cost for the solution is certainly a factor in the decision-making process, but be sure to not give cost an overly high weighting versus other decision criteria, especially at the outset in your due diligence. Selecting the right e-signature technology provider involves many other factors. The core features offered are important as well as integration with your other systems, how intuitive and easy it is to use the solution, flexibility with a variety of different forms and documents, overall scalability, customer support, and the training programs available. This list is just the start and depending on the specific needs of your firm, each item might have a higher or lower weighting.

Another significant component of the evaluation criteria that deserves its own attention is how your clients will use the e-signature technology. You can make all the right decisions with the above list of evaluation criteria, but if you don't consider the process that will work best with a majority of your clients, you will limit your overall success with e-signature technology. There may be a certain client-type that is right for using this technology, and there are certain situations that are suited for utilizing e-signature technology. Specific questions that you should ask include: Are your clients generally tech savvy and comfortable with technology? How much hand-holding do you do today helping a client complete forms and applications? Do your clients already respond well to your current technology offering, for example, electronic reports, statements, confirms, prospectuses, file-sharing, and so on. Do you know the type of devices your clients use—PC or Apple based? How different are the answers to these questions when you consider your current clients versus your prospective clients? E-signature technology is essentially a replacement solution. Meaning, instead of using the traditional method of signing (pen to paper), its goal is to provide a more efficient way of accomplishing the same task using technology.

Therefore, it is critically important to carefully evaluate the process through the eyes of your client. If your clients don't like using e-signatures, or don't feel it is secure, if they don't feel in control or worse, if they just don't understand how to use the e-signature technology, they will just simply switch back to the old way of doing business and your opportunity for increased efficiency will be lost.

Before You Start—Other Considerations

There are several other considerations that need to be evaluated prior to moving forward with utilizing e-signature technology. One area to consider is your firm's current adoption of paperless systems. Do you currently scan and electronically store all of your documents? Do you take in client data from a website or from another digital source? If your office is currently paperless, how quickly do you scan new documents? In order to be prepared to embrace e-signature technology, you need to be relatively proficient with your imaging and data capture technology. Put simply, an electronically signed document will not yield the same efficiency gains if you ultimately have to print it out and store it in a paper form. Therefore, your firm must have a strong paperless office foundation already in place in order to be adequately prepared to leverage e-signature technology. Also use this opportunity to evaluate your current workflow processes and procedures for your paperless system. If everything is in good order, then introducing e-signature technology should be a logical addition to meeting your paperless goals and improving your workflow management.

It is also a good idea to contact your paperless provider (imaging system) to learn if it has any e-signature solutions that already work well with its systems. There are many natural process connections between an imaging system and an e-signature technology solution that you want to ensure you are able to leverage. When designed properly, these connections not only make the implementation process easier, but they should also derive benefits with ongoing support and maintenance. Specifically, the two providers should work more closely together in managing the impacts (if any) with upgrades between the imaging system and the e-signature technology solution.

Another consideration that should be evaluated prior to moving forward with e-signature technology is the capabilities and skills of your employees. These individuals will not only have to understand the technology but will also need to be able to explain it to your clients. Their comfort and confidence with the e-signature technology will be a key component in your firm's success with the solution. Given the importance of their role in the success of any new technology, be sure you consider whether or not your employees are ready for this new responsibility. Is there time available in their schedules to be properly trained on the e-signature technology? During their training, make sure your employees have the opportunity to fully test drive the e-signature technology solution. This includes using the product as if they were the client as well as understanding the possible error messages and trouble spots that might occur. The goal with this training is to minimize any surprises and again build your employees' confidence with the solution. Unfortunately, training is an area that can easily be overlooked and can create lots of frustration if your employees feel like they are not prepared. It is well worth the time to prepare and train your employees, in order to ensure that your investment in the new technology will pay off.

Getting Started

Once you have evaluated the e-signature technology systems available and have addressed the other considerations, it is now time to get started with a solution. The first step is to review all the forms that you currently use and decide which ones are candidates for using the e-signature technology. On the surface, this might appear to be a very simple task. However, you must still use a critical eye to ensure it makes sense for a document to be signed electronically versus a traditional method. This includes not only your proprietary forms but also the forms provided by your custodian, broker-dealer, or other service providers, as well. For example, which of your forms should be eligible to be signed electronically? Does the e-signature technology work well with your fee agreement, investment policy statement, privacy policy, and so forth? It is critical that the experience with using the e-signature technology is consistent, regardless of the type of form that is being completed. And you might consider adjusting where a client actually signs on the document to better facilitate the e-signature technology. Of course, it is a different experience signing a document electronically on a computer or tablet versus having the paper document in front of you. Therefore, be flexible with making formatting changes to improve the experience with using the e-signature technology.

If you plan to utilize e-signature capabilities for a certain process task, then it is important that the client can sign all forms using the e-signature technology. This includes your forms, the custodian's forms, whatever is necessary to complete the task. And it needs to be relatively seamless as the client goes through the process. You want to avoid a broken process where the client signs one form a certain way and another form a very different way. This may not make much sense and can often lead to confusion on behalf of the client. Therefore, where and how they provide their initials, signatures, and select check boxes needs to be consistent and clear. The e-signature technology solution should highlight each area that requires your client's input, which is similar to the traditional "sign here" sticky tape that you see on paper documents. In addition, it needs to be very clear to your clients where they are in the overall process as they review and electronically sign each document. Furthermore, remember that many forms require signatures from multiple individuals. For example, perhaps you are working with a joint account that requires signatures from both individuals on the account. This is relatively easy to accommodate if both individuals are electronically signing at the same time. However, it becomes a little more challenging if they will be electronically signing at different times. This is certainly possible to facilitate with e-signature technology as long as you understand how to adjust the process.

E-Signature Workflows

The types of accounts that you normally open and work with can also impact how you utilize e-signature technology. As previously discussed, the most common types of e-signature technology involve your client selecting a ready-made signature (created by the system) or your client actually signing the document electronically using a mouse on a computer screen or even a finger on a touchpad or on a tablet or mobile device. For certain types of accounts, it may be necessary to obtain the client's actual signature, whether through an electronic means or a traditional pen to paper method. Therefore, simply verifying that it is really signed by the client and generating a ready-made signature will not work appropriately in all situations. For example, it may be important for your custodian or your client's bank to know what your client's signature looks like if the client plans to use check-writing features or bank wires with his or her account. It would be very challenging for your custodian to verify if a check was signed by your client and not forged if there were no signature on file. Most importantly, you don't want to go through the process of adopting e-signature technology, but then inadvertently limit the account solutions available because of the type of e-signature utilized. This can quickly compromise any efficiency benefits previously gained if you have to go back and resubmit forms that now must include the client's actual signature. Given the potential risk with this situation, consider in advance the overall account requirements of your clients, and then use the e-signature technology that best meets these needs.

Frequently, the new account opening process is the first area considered for evaluating e-signature technology solutions. Generally speaking, this process most likely includes the highest number of times that your client must initial and sign in one setting. The new account opening process, of course, involves your firm's own client agreement forms and the new account forms provided by your custodian, and any other forms that are directly required by your firm or other firms you work with. Furthermore, the new account process is generally the first "paperwork" experience as a prospect is converted to a new client. Advisors clearly want to control all aspects of this experience to ensure it goes smoothly. Advisors are also trying to minimize the time it takes to complete the process. Certainly, one of the contributing factors is the amount of time lost when the new account forms are mailed between the advisor and the client. When done well, leveraging e-signature technology in the account-opening process should speed up the process and improve the overall experience for the client. However, it is also the process that potentially has the highest risk of an unsatisfactory experience given the number of forms involved and the fact that clients might be doing a majority of the work on their own. This is another reason to select an e-signature provider that has a presentation and capture process that will meld smoothly with your practices and other firms whose forms you use regularly.

It is also important to remember that the new account opening process occurs in a very fluid environment. Specifically, it is not uncommon for forms to be added or deleted, existing documents modified, and other changes to occur throughout the entire process. These changes can happen on the same day, or on a couple of days, or even over weeks. It is critical that your e-signature technology solution can accommodate all of these potential changes. For example, it is quite possible that you will have already sent electronically the new account packet of information requesting your client's e-signature, and then you realize that you missed a form or document. Or your client calls you after receiving the new account packet for his or her individual taxable account and now wants to also open a Roth IRA. Of course you want to minimize any work that needs to be redone. Ideally you would want to simply append the original new account packet with the goal of highlighting what has changed and therefore present to the client only what still needs to be electronically signed. Because there are many variables that can occur during the new account opening process, and because it takes time to set up all the special asset management features and put into place all the terms of your engagement with the client, your e-signature technology should ultimately make it easier to address these needs and help make such changes more intuitive and efficient.

The new account opening process is a good example of a complex workflow for using an e-signature technology solution. There are also a significant number of much simpler workflow tasks where e-signature technology can offer many benefits. An example would include processing a cash wire request for your client. In most cases it is fairly simple: You complete the necessary fields on a form and then send the document to your client requesting an e-signature. Once the client signs electronically, the document is ready for you to retrieve and submit for processing. Overall, this is a fairly straightforward and simple task to process, and the e-signature technology improves the speed and efficiency. Other simpler workflow tasks where e-signature technology can provide benefits include your client acknowledging an update to an investment policy statement, processing distributions from retirement accounts, and facilitating a variety of letter of authorization requests.

Another workflow task where you should consider utilizing e-signature technology is exchanging documents with other professional intermediaries. For example, you can use e-signature technology for completing agreements that you draft with technology providers, compliance firms, and other professional companies. The e-signature technology can also assist when each party needs to sign a document in a predefined order. Take, for example, a situation where three parties need to sign a document in a distinct order. Once the first party electronically signs the document, it can then be routed to the second signing party and then ultimately to the final signer. Each of these action steps will be clearly tracked and accounted for, making it very easy to identify where you are in the process. This is especially helpful when you are on a tight timeline and can't afford any delay in the process.

Introducing E-Signature Technology to Your Clients

The first introduction of e-signature technology to your clients must be a thoroughly planned exercise. In fact, it can be argued that it is much less work to select and install a new e-signature technology solution for your firm than it is to successfully introduce the technology to your clients. When it comes to presenting the new technology to your clients, it is all about execution. Therefore, as previously discussed, try to identify the right type of client who will most easily embrace the technology. Consider selecting a handful of clients who you know will be comfortable with the technology and who will also provide you with valuable feedback on the experience. These early adopter clients are a great resource to help you understand how intuitive it is for them to use the e-signature technology. They can provide clear feedback on the process and help you make the right changes to improve the overall experience. It is also a best practice to start with one of your less complex workflow processes to make it a little easier to get going. There is a lot to be gained when you strategically introduce a new technology with the assistance from the right group of clients. Most importantly, avoid the fire hose approach in which you aggressively introduce the e-signature technology for a number of tasks when you have limited real-life experience with the technology. Frequently, this will lead to disappointment and even embarrassment for your firm when problems arise that you didn't plan for or expect. Therefore, starting out slow is a good idea as you and your clients learn the particulars of the technology.

E-Signature Technology Adoption

After all the effort of evaluating e-signature technology solutions, selecting your provider, defining your workflow process, introducing the technology to your clients, you now move into the next phase, which is tracking your adoption of the technology. First, it is important to recognize that successfully utilizing e-signature technology is not easy to do. It certainly is attractive technology, and it promises great benefits. But that doesn't mean that you should expect significant adoption early in your use of the technology. Therefore, be careful in setting the right expectations with both your staff and your clients. You can accomplish this by how you approach setting your goals and objectives with the e-signature technology solution.

The first step in achieving your e-signature technology adoption goals is to be sure to assign an owner who is responsible for monitoring the success of the initiative. Without a clear owner, it will become very easy for your employees to fall back on conducting business the old way. That is, they may choose not to use the e-signature technology because of the change involved and also because they believe that it is not very important. A clear owner will make sure that the initiative remains in the forefront of importance and doesn't get lost with other goals and objectives.

When tracking your e-signature technology adoption, be very specific about how you plan to measure success. For each of your defined workflows, identify an e-delivery percentage goal that you would like to achieve. Make sure that the adoption goal is realistic and recognizes potential growth as you have more experience with the technology. For example, set a goal of reaching 10 percent adoption of utilizing e-signature technology for processing letters of instruction within the first three months of introducing the technology. Then, set a goal of reaching 25 percent adoption during the next three months. Each workflow adoption goal should take into account the overall complexity in using the e-signature technology with that specific process.

Next, it is important to consistently measure your adoption throughout the time period. Perhaps tracking your e-signature technology adoption results once a week is appropriate. This should be a very visible effort for your employees. When the adoption numbers are progressing as you expect, celebrate this early progress and use the momentum created to further the effort. If some of the numbers are not as positive as you had hoped, this is a great opportunity to understand why and then make the necessary adjustments. Sometimes, the technology is working great, but it is the process being followed that potentially needs some adjustment. As you review and discuss the e-signature technology adoption results, this will provide a perfect forum to dive into these details.

One of the interesting challenges for advisors in utilizing e-signature technology is understanding when it is best to use it and when it is better to rely on traditional methods. You should not expect to achieve 100 percent adoption. Advisors work with a variety of variables in managing their client relationships—which I know is definitely an understatement! Some client engagements are well-suited for leveraging an e-signature technology solution, and others might add complexity that compromises the expected benefits and efficiency gains. Therefore, be very strategic about how and when you adopt e-signature technology. E-signature technology definitely offers tremendous benefits and time savings when implemented and utilized effectively. And achieving success will deliver ongoing dividends to your firm for years to come.

CHAPTER 11

Innovative Software and Technologies Implemented at One of the United States' Leading Advisory Firms

Louis P. Stanasolovich, CFP

CCO, CEO, Founder, and President, Legend Financial Advisors, Inc. and EmergingWealth Investment Management, Inc.

Christopher J. Kail,

Director of Marketing

Sherri M. Slafka,

Communications Coordinator

Daniel D. Kleck,

Marketing Coordinator

Since its founding in 1994, Legend Financial Advisors, Inc. (Legend), based in Pittsburgh, Pennsylvania, has been widely recognized by its peers, and the financial advisory media, as one of the more innovative firms in the country. Legend's technology solutions, some costing as little as $25, have helped create a more efficient and productive workplace. Obviously, creative thinking and technology over the years has propelled the firm forward. Proof of the results lie in the fact that not only have its advisors been selected for over 35 awards as "Best Advisors in the Nation" by national financial publications such as *Worth Magazine*, *Medical Economics*, and others, Legend itself has won numerous business awards and has appeared on the "Inc. 5000" in both 2011 and 2012. Throughout this chapter, many of Legend's innovative uses of technology programs and processes will be profiled.

Background

In January 1994, Legend opened its doors for business. Legend today provides personal financial planning, business financial planning and investment management services to high net worth (generally with investment assets over $1,000,000) clients.

In 2010, the shareholders of Legend launched a second registered investment advisory firm, EmergingWealth Investment Management, Inc. (EmergingWealth). EmergingWealth provides investment management services only to clients whose wealth is emerging (generally investment assets of $300,000 or more).

In November 2004, serving as editor, Louis Stanasolovich, in conjunction with Wealth Advisor Publishing, Inc., a firm with outside private ownership but operated by Legend, launched Risk-Controlled Investing, a subscription service and newsletter for financial advisors. The service and newsletter, which is delivered in a PDF format, focuses on creating portfolios with low volatility.

In March 2012, again serving as editor, Stanasolovich, in conjunction with Wealth Advisor Publishing, Inc., launched *Global Economic & Investment Analytics*, a weekly research-oriented newsletter that is e-mailed to approximately 330,000 financial advisors and related professionals. The website is www.globaleconomic andinvestmentanalytics.com.

As a result of operating three companies and their many tasks and services that are mentioned below, Legend and its affiliates extend their reach by utilizing extensive amounts of technology.

Another key to Legend and its affiliates' development and usage of technology over the years is its incorporation of interns into its daily operations. Legend believes in utilizing interns to supplement its regular staff of 22. Since 1994, Legend has hired approximately 300 (that number is not a typo!) interns (mostly college students but that number includes approximately 20 high school students, who provide mostly administrative support to Legend's staff). Generally, Legend employs between 10 and 20 interns at any one time.

All internships are paid and are year round. Interns work approximately 1,200 hours per year. As a result, they perform many tasks that use technology extensively but also require large amounts of training. College interns are recruited in their freshman and sophomore years and the better performers are invited to stay until they graduate. Graduates may be offered full-time positions after graduation.

Interns usually plan to major in finance, marketing and communications, information technology, business management, and/or human resources, but in most cases, being so young, they have not yet taken any courses in their major, and Legend expects to train interns extensively through a combination of technology and one-on-one training. The goal is for the interns to build their skill sets and resumes while benefiting the company and its affiliates. Interns receive approximately 150-plus hours of training annually in their respective specialties including investment management and financial planning, marketing and communications, information technology, business management, human resources, and accounting. Out of 22 regular staff members at Legend, there are currently 11 former interns employed full-time at Legend.

Legend takes pride in advancing employee knowledge and improving efficiency across the entire firm. Through technology, Legend continuously enhances its client service capabilities and creates engaging marketing initiatives to attract prospective clients. In fact, Legend has a technology committee that meets on a weekly basis to discuss the company's technology challenges, opportunities, and new ideas to enhance productivity. Members of Legend's tech committee are voracious readers, consuming dozens of technology-related periodicals on a monthly basis including, of course, *Technology Tools for Today*. Firm members believe that being on the cutting edge of technology is a prominent reason why Legend is considered one of the leading financial advisory firms in the country.

Video Training

Legend has created training videos, which are produced by employees themselves, as a tool to educate all of its staff, including interns. Legend utilizes video film clips to record all of its internal processes. This includes everything from nontechnology procedures such as how to greet a client at the door and set up a conference room for a client meeting to using a complicated piece of software such as BNA Income Tax Planner or an information service such as Bloomberg Investment Research Service.

Camtasia

For creating videos that capture software and service uses, Legend uses the software program Camtasia, which is a video screen capture program, published by TechSmith (www.techsmith.com/camtasia.html). The program allows the user to define the area of the screen or the window that is to be captured before voice recording begins. A user can also talk and use a webcam to record activities of firm members. This software allows the firm to create its own training videos by combining voice and screen interface recordings. These videos have proven to be incredibly effective by providing an interactive and hands-on approach to employee training. The videos allow the staff to become more time efficient by preventing them from spending huge amounts of time conducting repetitive one-on-one training. In effect, employees can place a laptop playing the videos next to their desktop computers so that they can simultaneously practice what they learn. They can stop the video when needed as they move through each step, and practice or work on their regular desktop computers. Legend now has an extensive library of over 2,000 training videos available for employees and interns. Generally, these videos have a duration of five minutes or less. Segmenting the videos into very short clips allows them to be updated whenever a software change or internal process is changed without having to change the entire training film on a software package. This innovative training process has fostered an environment of continuous learning and development. Current pricing is $299 per single-user license for up to four licenses.

Office Suite Software

Legend utilizes the Microsoft 2010 Office Suite, including Word, Excel, PowerPoint, Publisher, Access, and Outlook. Microsoft Access is used mostly for billing and reporting, while Outlook is used to a more limited degree. Publisher is used for the monthly client letter and various other newsletters, charts, and graphs.

Audio Media Solutions

AudioGenerator

AudioGenerator is an audio recording and hosting service. Audio messages are automatically converted into a single line of code that can be uploaded to any website. AudioGenerator files can also be published as podcasts online. AudioGenerator hosts the audio messages on its servers and allows for 24-hour access. Legend's advisory team uses this service to record audio messages, typically to create Legend's Securities Market Overview recordings, which the company's marketing department sends via e-mail to clients. These audio messages can provide clients with updates to portfolio changes or the latest information on the current economic and investment environment. The AudioGenerator website is www.audiogenerator.com. The cost is approximately $19.95 per month.

TextAloud

Legend uses the TextAloud GhostReader program from NextUp.com to convert electronic documents such as articles on the Internet into audio files to create internal training programs and courses. TextAloud GhostReader is text-to-speech software for the Windows PC that converts text from Microsoft Word documents, e-mails, web pages, and PDF files into natural-sounding speech. Files can be played on a personal computer or on MP3 players, iPods, iPhones, and other portable audio devices. TextAloud can even automatically sync to iTunes. Legend has used this tool to create educational materials for investing, business management, and technology. You can learn more by going to www.nextup.com/textaloud/. Pricing for TextAloud's GhostReader is $39.95. TextAloud 3 (a more limited product only compatible with Microsoft software) costs $25.95.

FreeConferenceCall.com

Conference call services are obviously a necessity, whether to facilitate a meeting for staff separated geographically or to partner with vendors or clients. This type of service can also be utilized to address a large audience on a webcast, as well. Legend uses FreeConferenceCall.com (www.freeconferencecall.com), which it has found to be a reliable and cost-efficient service. Legend utilizes the free Unlimited Audio Conferencing service. Callers dial into a non-800 number to use the service, which does not require a reservation and is therefore especially useful for last-minute audio conference calls. The number and ID number are preassigned. Up to 96 callers may participate on a call and free call recording is optional.

The toll-free conferencing option also does not require reservations and allows up to 1,000 participants and offers optional call recording. This service costs 3.9 cents per minute per caller. FreeConferenceCall.com also has screen sharing for online meetings for up to 50 participants with instant online meetings, which cost $19.95 per month.

Dictation Service

Copytalk

Legend utilizes a dictation service (this is not a software program) called Copytalk, which allows messages to be recorded by phone. This allows the company to dictate large amounts of information quickly and inexpensively. While there are other services that financial advisors can utilize, Copytalk in our view, offers the best combination of flexibility, price, speed, and accuracy.

Copytalk is a cost-effective mobile documentation, digital dictation, and transcription service. The service allows the dictator to use any phone for dictation without installing any new equipment.

Legend immediately implemented Copytalk for two primary purposes: to dictate client notes to help track all client communications and action items and to dictate employee reviews for human resource purposes. Periodically, the firm has used the service to dictate letters and articles, as well. This service sends dictations to Legend via e-mail usually within one hour and, at the latest, the very next day. The e-mail messages are then converted to Microsoft Word documents. To learn more about Copytalk, visit www.copytalk.com/mobilescribe.po. The cost for the service starts at $49.95 per month although Legend has a number of monthly subscriptions that will vary at times in number. There are no long-term contracts. The service is contracted for on a monthly basis.

Webcasts

GoToWebinar.com

In late 2008, due to the stock market crashing, Legend launched a series of webcasts for clients, prospects, and other professionals. The firm adopted webcast technology to communicate to its clients amidst one of the more challenging economic and market downturns in financial market history. Legend continues to conduct monthly educational webcasts.

The GoToWebinar.com service (www.gotomeeting.com/fec/webinar) includes the ability to create an unlimited number of webcasts. The monthly service plan allows up to 1,000 participants to attend each webcast presentation. Costs start at $99.00 per month. With this service, a video and audio recording of the presentation can be made without any additional charge. The recording can then be archived on a firm's website or be put on a CD/DVD for clients and/or prospects. While the service is relatively easy to use, we would advise numerous practice runs prior to its first live usage. Also, contingency plans (what you plan to say to the audience) in the event of problems and possible reschedule dates in the event of power, hard drive, Internet, and phone disruption/failures need to be developed. The service has many additional features too numerous to mention here.

GoToMeeting.com

Legend also uses GoToMeeting.com for one-on-one web conference meetings with clients. This interactive platform gives clients the option of having Legend advisors demonstrate investment and financial planning concepts online as opposed to traveling to our office for a meeting. This is a convenient alternative for clients who want to discuss their investment management reports, investment recommendations, as well as various financial planning issues from the comfort of their own computer. Obviously, this is perceived as a valuable service for those clients who do not live in close proximity to Legend. The website is www.gotomeeting.com/fec/webinar. The starting cost is $49.00. This is a necessary tool for Legend since approximately 25 percent of its clients live 50 miles or more from Pittsburgh.

Organizing Online Data

Evernote

Evernote is a service designed for note-taking and archival. A note can be a piece of formattable text, a full webpage or webpage excerpt, a photograph, a voice memo, or a handwritten note. Notes can also have file attachments. Notes can be sorted into folders, tagged, annotated, edited, commented on, and searched. Evernote is a service that Legend is just starting to utilize. Evernote allows employees to capture thoughts, ideas, and inspiration in one place. Employees can access everything stored in the service, at any time, from their personal computers. Evernote's website is www .evernote.com. The service is free for small amounts of data or you can upgrade to premium service for $5.00 per month or $45.00 per year. Legend uses the premium service. Unfortunately, there is no enterprise service offering.

Hardware

Mac Pro Computers

This year, Legend and its affiliated companies purchased two Apple Mac Pro computers to assist in efficiently and creatively designing and producing various publications. The current starting price is $2,499.

The firm uses the Mac Pro computers running Adobe Dreamweaver to produce its newsletters. Some of the features within Dreamweaver could not be fully utilized on a typical PC. The Mac Pros offer a much faster user experience than a traditional PC. You can learn more at www.apple.com/macpro/.

Security Technologies

IronPort E-mail Encryption

In order to keep documents secure, Legend employees send e-mail to clients via an encryption product called IronPort C160, from IronPort Systems, Inc. (a division of Cisco Systems). This program enables secure two-way communication with e-mail recipients. In addition to e-mail encryption, the software offers numerous other services that protect company and client data. E-mail encryption protects against hackers who may attempt to intercept messages to and from clients that may contain sensitive personal information. While the firm doesn't expect its e-mail server to be hacked, it believes it is best to take a proactive approach to ensure that client information is kept safe and secure. Legend also provides clients with a step-by-step procedure for accessing an encrypted e-mail. Some additional features include antispam, Sophos Anti-Virus, and Platinum Support. To learn more about IronPort, visit www.cisco.com/web/about/ac49/ac0/ac1/ac259/ironport.html. The pricing is approximately $9,000 for a three-year single appliance enterprise bundle.

SpectorSoft Keylogger Software

The firm also utilizes SpectorSoft Keylogger keystroke screen capture software to monitor and deter inappropriate Internet browsing and computer usage by its employees. In addition, e-mail correspondence is strictly monitored and reviewed to prevent unethical, improper, and/or mistaken advice. Spectorsoft also provides detailed reporting of Internet usage including specific websites visited by employees.

Legend utilizes the screen capture software portion of the software, as well. It, in effect, takes a picture periodically (in Legend's case—every 30 seconds) of each user's screen. This allows monitoring of a user's computer usage.

Pricing is approximately $3,000, which allows for up to 55 users.

FortiGate Firewall Protection

Legend utilizes FortiGate for the firm's firewall to protect its computer network. FortiGate is a worldwide provider of network security appliances and a market leader in unified threat management. The FortiGate service provides the latest findings on global Internet threats and attacks in real time. Legend also uses FortiGate to block targeted websites from being visited by employees. Pricing is approximately $900 for a one-year subscription.

Security Cameras and Door Locks

Sonitrol technology protects Legend's employees and buildings. The firm uses key fobs and electronic door locks at every entrance to the office. This technology solution protects employees and clients, as well as their privacy, and the firm's equipment and furniture.

Legend also uses state-of-the-art security cameras, which are installed throughout its offices to keep a watchful eye on every entryway and corridor on a 24-hour basis. Outside of normal business hours, all of the doors and common areas are locked and monitored by video cameras and the firm's security system. Sonitrol of Pittsburgh's website is www.sonitrolpgh.com. Please contact Sonitrol directly for pricing.

Phone Messaging Technology

VoiceShot

Approximately 50 of Legend's clients do not have e-mail. Those that do may not always read their e-mail in a timely manner. Therefore, Legend uses an automated phone messaging technology service called VoiceShot to send urgent messages via customized, prerecorded messages. The service can send text messages to groups, as well. VoiceShot allows users to record a message via phone or computer and send it to an uploaded list of contacts with phone numbers, eliminating the need to call each client individually. The technology is useful for making mass announcements, allowing all clients to receive a message in a timely manner. While e-mail might be able to accomplish this, a client still has to open an e-mail to obtain a message. Voice messaging technology ensures the intended recipient will receive the message in a timely manner. Typically messages are sent to a client's home and/or cell phone numbers. Messages communicated via VoiceShot typically include information about an upcoming company event; a general financial planning and/or investment portfolio issue affecting all clients; a newsworthy item of interest, such as market decline and what our thoughts are; or even an advisor's TV or radio show appearance. If end users do not answer the call, the message will automatically be sent to their voicemail.

VoiceShot's service also includes text messaging, appointment reminders, virtual office phone system, a virtual receptionist, enhanced toll-free and local numbers, as well as XML voice alert and notification services. VoiceShot also has a group text messaging service that allows you to send and receive text message alerts to and from one or more members of your personal or professional group. You can send and receive text messages while managing the entire process straight from the web.

VoiceShot is a popular service often used during election campaigns to promote various candidates. However, for Legend, it is a useful tool to promote urgent or time-sensitive information to its key audiences. Legend has received many positive comments on the service. Visit www.voiceshot.com to learn more.

Legend utilizes VoiceShot for outbound calls within the United States at a rate of $0.12 per successful call. This includes a personalized message that is 60 seconds or less in length. VoiceShot is a prepaid service, and charges only apply to all successfully delivered calls. Pricing for international rates and additional services are available at www.voiceshot.com/public/outboundcalls.asp.

Recording Pen Technology

Echo Smartpens

In an effort to ensure accuracy at all levels, and to address all details brought up in client and internal meetings, Legend uses Echo smartpens by Livescribe. The smartpens are used in all client and internal meetings and on all conference calls, which occur over speakerphone where the notes taken are handwritten within special notebooks (pricing is listed below). Legend staff members begin a conference call by making introductions (stating each participant's name), stating the date, and notifying all parties on the line that the call will be recorded (this is a legal requirement). These pens are able to transfer written and audio files to computers and can be stored in programs such as Evernote. The pens can be recharged using a standard USB cable connection. A built-in speaker produces sound to play back recorded audio. The smartpens ensure that Legend captures all participants' talking points and requests. The Echo smartpens allow for specific playback points by touching the note written during a meeting or conference call. The pen then plays back the entire conversation on a Livescribe Paper Tablet. The tablet in conjunction with the smartpen allows you to control when to record, pause, or stop the recording. It also controls the playback speed and volume. Legend has found that data and points of disagreement (especially internal meetings) are solved significantly more easily when using this technology and accuracy improves tremendously. Furthermore, the more detailed the note taking the easier it is to locate specific comments. Instead of the special notebook, which generally cost approximately $10 in stores, various forms of notebooks, including extra large and Post-it notes are also available to write on. Current pricing levels start at $119.95. Visit www.livescribe.com/en-us/smartpen/echo/ to learn more.

Video Conferencing

Skype

Legend Skypes . . . do you? Legend has implemented Skype videoconferencing to conduct long-distance meetings with clients. This allows Legend to talk to its clients and other parties face-to-face without having to spend money on travel expenses. Videoconferencing allows two or more locations to simultaneously interact via two-way video and audio transmissions. Currently, as many as 10 locations can participate in a Skype conversation. Skype also includes instant messaging, texting, and calling. Most Skype services are free, while calls to both traditional landline telephones and mobile phones can be made for a fee using a debit-based user account system.

Legend uses Skype to conduct video conversations with remote clients and prospects. Another great use is to conduct face-to-face hiring interviews with employment candidates. This is especially useful for initial interviews before bringing a candidate in for an interview that lasts an entire day can cost $1,000 or more.

As with all Legend communications, Skype videoconferencing was selected because it is a secure service. Because Skype uses the Internet to transport voice calls and text messages and sometimes these calls are routed through other peers, all information is encrypted so that no one can eavesdrop.

All that is needed to use this service is a computer, a webcam, and a Skype account. Current pricing service plans may be free and depending on additional features desired, paid plans include pay-as-you-go (from 2.3 cents per minute), subscription plans from 1.2 cents per minute, and the Skype Premium plan is $4.99 per month (pricing may vary). You can learn more about Skype and its available services by visiting its website at www.skype.com.

Scanning

DocuXplorer

DocuXplorer is an industry-leading state-of-the-art document management software application designed for organizations of all sizes. It is designed to secure and manage the lifecycle of documents, records, images, e-mail, faxes, or any other paper or electronic files a company may have. Its website is www.docuxplorer.com.

Legend uses DocuXplorer to achieve the goal of becoming a more paperless office. DocuXplorer's scanning system stores all pertinent client and prospect financial planning and investment documents. Legend maintains organized electronic file cabinets of documents stored within docuXplorer, which has helped to eliminate the need for physical storage space. All scanned documents are backed up both on- and off-site on a daily basis. Protection of client documents and information is one of the most important tasks of the firm. Current pricing plans include $500 per single-user license and $250 for the required import engine. Additional support fees may be required.

Customer Relationship Management

Salesforce

This year, Legend transitioned from its customer relationship management (CRM) system to Salesforce.com, one of the up-and-coming platforms in the financial advisory profession and certainly one much more established outside our industry. It is used to help sell products or services more effectively by facilitating better sales tracking and real-time visibility. Salesforce provides Legend with the ability to track new business opportunities from phone calls and e-mails. The data is also tracked in one place and in real-time, so employees can stay on top of opportunities and build stronger relationships with clients or prospects. Salesforce is also integrated with TD Ameritrade's custodial platform and conveniently linked to Veo. Legend's goal in using Salesforce is to make smarter business decisions and produce higher close rates via the sales tracking features.

Legend used ProTracker as its CRM tool for 14 years and although it served the firm well, the staff wanted to have a CRM located on a web-based platform. We understand that ProTracker is currently building its own web-based version.

Website Hosting

Advisor Products Inc.

Advisor Products is a leading financial services client communications and marketing company, serving more than 1,800 independent financial advisors. Among many other marketing services, it creates cutting-edge websites. Advisor Products hosts Legend's website, www.legend-financial.com. Legend's website was originally designed in 2000 and has had minor tweaks and updates since, but Legend has put off a major redesign for a number of years due to other priorities in the firm. Legend plans a total revamp of its website in 2014. In 2013, its sister company, Emerging-Wealth Investment Management will have its first website constructed.

Advisor Products offers customers three options when developing a website: a custom website, a designer website, and a template website. Each of these options allows a company to develop a website that best reflects company aesthetics. Advisor Products and its website services are a relatively easy way to manage and produce a professional website without spending a large sum of money. The company also offers a large menu of content to select from. Advisor Products also offers a variety of products from branding development to newsletter production. For pricing options available, please contact Advisor Products or visit www.advisorproducts.com.

Make It A Great Day, Inc.

Make It A Great Day, Inc. (MIAGD) is a website design and hosting company catering to financial advisory and other firms to help streamline and grow their businesses. MIAGD provided Legend's affiliated company, Wealth Advisor Publishing, Inc., with an effective website design for one of the company's leading online publications, *Global Economic & Investment Analytics*.

Global Economic & Investment Analytics is a cutting-edge publication that provides economic and investment-oriented research and analysis, and is delivered on a weekly basis to a nationwide audience of financial advisory professionals. You can view the publication's website by going to www.globaleconomincandinvestmentanalytics.com. AdvisorFlex 2.0 is the back-office component of MIAGD that maintains and updates the website content and design as necessary. AdvisorFlex 2.0 is used to maintain a polished, professional-looking, well-functioning website. For pricing information, please contact Make It A Great Day, Inc. You can visit their website at www.MIAGD.com.

E-mail Marketing

CoolerEmail

Legend has used CoolerEmail 3.0 with a goal of providing the best and broadest e-mail delivery campaigns at the most economic price possible. While there are many competitors for this type of service, Legend's marketing department has grown comfortable with CoolerEmail's enhancements over the years and believes that it's more inexpensive than many of its competitors yet just as effective. Legend uses CoolerEmail to deliver various personalized promotional announcements and newsletters to clients, prospects, and other professionals.

CoolerEmail's web-based e-mail marketing software, established in 2000, enables Legend's marketing department to easily create and deliver professional, graphic-rich e-mails. Pricing is based on quantity of e-mail usage. Through Legend's research and competitive analyses, CoolerEmail has proved to be one of the more inexpensive e-mail service providers on the market.

Additionally, CoolerEmail allows Legend to send updates and reminders for upcoming events. CoolerEmail provides templates to help create professional HTML e-mails, or companies can upload their own. CoolerEmail's main function is to help manage contacts through its multi-e-mail list feature (ability to manage and send E-mail to multiple lists), making it easy to target specific demographics.

Some of CoolerEmail's other features include the ability to track recipients' responses in real time. The software allows Legend to preview real-time charts and statistics in order to confirm the success of the campaign. CoolerEmail can also process this data in summary format, which allows Legend to see who is reading and who has unsubscribed from the mailing list. CoolerEmail also provides confirmation once each e-mail campaign has been successfully delivered to the desired list audience.

Additional benefits of CoolerEmail include:

- It allows other communication software such as Microsoft Outlook, Sage ACT!, Goldmine, and more to be incorporated.

- Automatic subscribe/unsubscribe capabilities.
- Schedule or event-driven automatic delivery.

CoolerEmail has provided Legend with an easy way to build, send, and track e-mail sent to clients. To learn more, visit www.cooleremail.com. For pricing, please contact CoolerEmail.

YouSendIt

YouSendIt is secure, online file sharing software that allows companies to easily send large files and e-mail attachments. YouSendIt helps Legend and its affiliated companies easily send files from anywhere. Wealth Advisor Publishing uses YouSendIt to distribute its monthly advisor newsletter, *Risk-Controlled Investing*, a 40- to 50-page plus publication that includes graphics-rich charts, graphs, and text. You can visit YouSendIt's website at www.yousendit.com.

Mozilla Thunderbird

Mozilla Thunderbird is Legend's primary e-mail system. It is a free program and loaded with unique features. Thunderbird provides fast review, tagging, and delivery of e-mail messages. Its user friendly settings help boost productivity across the firm. Among the features it offers are personalized e-mail addresses, one-click address book, attachment reminder, quick filter toolbar, message archiving, smart folders, and activity manager, just to name a few. You can visit Mozilla Thunderbird's website at www.mozilla.org/en-US/thunderbird/.

Design Software

Adobe InDesign

Adobe InDesign is a desktop publishing software program used to design professional layouts for print and digital publishing purposes. To learn more, visit www.adobe .com/indesign. Current pricing is $699 for the full package.

Adobe Dreamweaver

Adobe Dreamweaver web design software is a visual interface used for editing HTML websites and mobile applications. Dreamweaver is compatible with both Mac and Windows operating systems. Legend's affiliated company, Wealth Advisor Publishing uses Dreamweaver to produce its weekly newsletter, *Global Economic & Investment Analytics*. Dreamweaver is relatively easy to use and cuts down on outsourcing costs. To learn more about Adobe Dreamweaver, visit www.adobe.com/Dreamweaver. Dreamweaver costs $399. A free trial of the product is available at www.adobe.com/cfusion/tdrc/index.cfm?Product=dreamweaver&loc=en_us.

FileZilla Server

FileZilla is a two-part server system that has a server side and client side. FileZilla supports FTP and SSL/TLS in order to provide secure, encrypted connections to the server. The benefit of using software that supports SSL, is that SSL is the same level of encryption supported by your web browser. Wealth Advisor Publishing uses this software to modify its website and its newsletter by uploading files. When making alterations to either the website or the newsletter, the data is encrypted so that others are unable to see the confidential information. FileZilla permits the company to update the weekly newsletter while prohibiting outside viewers from seeing these updates until the publication is officially released.

TV and Web Video Production

Legend is in the process of building its own video production studio with state-of-the-art equipment to enhance its capabilities in the digital age of marketing. Videos will be created to enhance the reputation of Legend and its affiliated companies, EmergingWealth Investment Management and Wealth Advisor Publishing. Videos ranging from conversational interviews, in which an advisor will be interviewed by a professional journalist, to profiles of advisors speaking by themselves, can accomplish various objectives including introducing the newest features of a publication, explaining an interesting chart or graph, or just providing basic tips and strategies for advisors and investors, alike. Previously, Legend's staff would have to travel locally to a professional studio for live remote interviews or to create custom recorded videos. Now, they can conveniently achieve this at their own office with a soundproof video studio utilizing state-of-the-art camera and teleprompter equipment.

Probably in 2014, as a spin-off into one of its other companies, Legend envisions selling its TV studio recording and programming services to other businesses, including advisory firms, which they can use for their own marketing purposes.

Additionally, there will be two recording rooms with Camtasia production, a control room, and a SMART board. Future purchases for the firm include having dual cameras for different shot angles (frontal view, side view), a short throw projector, as well as the top-of-the-line Apple computer built for video editing and Apple's Final Cut Pro video editing software.

Accounting Software

QuickBooks

QuickBooks is a leading small business financial software package that for many years has helped Legend maintain its bookkeeping and accounting records. QuickBooks software allows a company to put its sales, expenses, and customer and vendor profiles at its fingertips. As a result, Legend's accounting staff can quickly find what they need when they need it. Legend and its affiliated companies use QuickBooks to prepare all of its financial statements. In addition to tracking revenue and expenses, QuickBooks assists the firm with record keeping for tax time. QuickBooks Pro 2012 costs approximately $200 for the complete software package. You can learn more at http://quickbooks.intuit.com.

Investment Research

Bloomberg Investment Research Service

Legend has been using the Bloomberg Investment Research Service for approximately 10 years. As a result, Legend significantly improved its investment research capabilities in numerous areas. The Bloomberg Investment Research Service is a data stream service that delivers real-time statistics and provides access to all news, economic and investment analytics, communications, chart and graphic creation capabilities, and liquidity and securities trade execution services. In today's challenging and volatile investment environment, all clients indirectly continue to benefit from the Bloomberg service, which enables our advisors to view and/or obtain up-to-the-minute information on financial markets and economic developments. This includes in-depth company news, insider trades, corporate legal actions, interest rate fluctuations, financial market movements, and economic information. Bloomberg's service is highly regarded and widely recognized as one of the most comprehensive research services in the investment industry. It provides information regarding individual stocks and bonds. It can also provide research on options, derivatives, commodities, certificates of deposits, and mutual funds. Such a research service can be cost prohibitive for many advisory firms. The cost for one terminal can range from $6,000 to $22,000 depending upon discounts received. It is best to contact Bloomberg for pricing. Some firms that accept soft dollars can use these monies for this service.

Morningstar Principia Pro

Morningstar Principia Pro is a flexible investment research and portfolio management software program that Legend uses for its powerful research database, which includes mutual funds, stocks, variable annuities, exchange-traded products, closed-end funds, and separate accounts. Using Principia Pro, Legend conducts advanced research and analysis, monitors portfolios, manages client accounts, and proposes investment strategies for clients and prospective clients. The advisory staff performs intensive searches and screens across multiple investment types to determine the most suitable securities for client portfolios. Annual pricing is approximately $1,400 when including monthly updates for the entire Principia Suite.

Thomson InvestmentView

Legend uses Thomson InvestmentView primarily to build cost basis information on mutual funds when new clients bring in mutual funds where the cost basis is missing.

It can also be used for due diligence purposes, conducting mutual fund research to analyze existing and potential mutual funds for client investment portfolios.

InvestmentView provides information on open-end, closed-end, and exchange-traded funds, indexes, variable annuity, and variable life contracts. The annual cost is approximately $600.

Investment Portfolio Reporting

PortfolioCenter

Schwab's PortfolioCenter is a well-known user-friendly solution for independent advisors managing client investment portfolios. Legend uses PortfolioCenter as its primary investment portfolio reporting software for clients. PortfolioCenter is a software application that provides the functionality needed to manage financial data, run the back office, and serve clients. PortfolioCenter gives advisors a single, consolidated view of all financial assets, regardless of where they are held. Its capabilities include:

- Portfolio data management
- Performance measurement
- Decision support tools
- Accounting
- Reporting
- Billing

PortfolioCenter is both networked and built on Microsoft's Windows-based SQL Server database platform. It provides the following:

- Tools to enhance security. With tools such as secure logins, needs-based access levels, and other customized settings, you can control which kinds of data are accessible to which authorized users.
- Technology that adapts to a financial advisory practice. Adding new client accounts and authorized users is easy and has no impact on overall performance; PortfolioCenter has been engineered to adapt quickly to the changing needs of your firm.

The software can be customized to fit firm needs. Some option levels of customization include:

- Display, sort, and filter data from multiple account views, based on analytic objectives.
- Create customized firmwide management reports and client presentations to reflect the information desired to be included.
- Generate billing statements with flexible features that reflect a firm's unique pricing structure and policies.

Investment Portfolio Rebalancing

iRebal

Legend utilizes iRebal rebalancing technology from TD Ameritrade. During the mid-2000s, one of the company's goals as a growing financial advisory firm was to provide the best client service solutions possible. Legend was one of the first nine firms in the country to utilize iRebal, a software technology program that rebalances investment portfolios across various accounts. In addition, iRebal is designed to help manage cash flows into and out of a portfolio.

iRebal has been dubbed the "intelligent rebalancer" and is a rules-based application that automates the generation of trade tickets for multiple account (family-level) portfolio rebalancing, cash management, and tax loss harvesting.

Additional benefits of iRebal include:

- Automated back-office operations.
- Ability to retain electronic audit trails to assist with regulatory audits.
- Provides companywide consistency and operational efficiency.
- Potential to increase client returns by leveraging iRebal research—including tolerance bands and "look frequently" rebalancing.
- Leverage industry best practices incorporated into the product.

For more information go to www.irebal.com. Exact pricing can be obtained from iRebal.

iRebal was built and founded by Gobind Daryanani, president of Digiqual Inc. Daryanani, CFP, PhD, is a consultant who specializes in high-end financial planning tools, and technologies. In 2007, iRebal was acquired by TD Ameritrade.

Financial Planning Software

Money Tree

Legend uses Money Tree Software's TOTAL Planning Suite to provide goal-based personal financial planning for its clients. Money Tree Total Planning Suite can also provide in-depth, complete accumulation phase reporting. Legend relies on Money Tree's other software programs, including Golden Years, to provide clients with detailed retirement projections. Legend uses Money Tree's Easy Money to provide clients with net worth statements, cash flow projections, and education planning and survivor projections. The Money Tree website (www.moneytree.com) outlines its list of top features as follows:

- Determine retirement needs.
- Show multiple solutions to retirement shortfall.
- 10,000 Monte Carlo simulations.

- Analyze life insurance, disability, and long-term care needs.
- Project education funding requirements.
- Calculate net worth and cash flows.
- Display audit trail for validating report numbers.

The Money Tree software package is approximately $1,890.

BNA Income Tax Planner

BNA Income Tax Planner, now owned by Bloomberg, is used by Legend's advisors and assistant advisors primarily to create income tax projections for its financial planning clients. A tax planning software solution, BNA Income Tax Planner is used by tax, financial planning, and legal professionals in firms of all sizes including the Big Four accounting firms. Legend views the BNA Income Tax Planner as a leader in software support as they provide free, unlimited telephone technical support.

BNA Income Tax Planner analyzes the full, potential tax implications of life and financial changes such as marriage, Roth conversions, retirement, and stock sales including multistate ramifications. With BNA Income Tax Planner, Legend's advisors can accurately and efficiently show clients what their tax situation looks like with in-depth analysis and comparison of multiple, side-by-side scenarios. Calculations, analytics, and regulatory compliance are all handled automatically, with greater dependability than traditional spreadsheets, tax preparation software, and/or financial planning packages. The advisory team believes this software has helped to increase productivity and retain clients, while helping to build and preserve wealth for the most complex of clients.

BNA Income Tax Planner provides extensive features that are designed to handle simple to very complex tax scenarios and provides professionals with a wide array of tax planning and tax projection tools including:

- Multiple tax scenarios help you compare side-by-side what-ifs to determine best tax savings.
- 20 planning years of potential projection capability.
- Drill-down analysis capabilities allow you to precisely manage the tax ramifications of marriage and divorce, real estate transactions, stock options, and more.
- Up-to-date calculations assure you are working with the latest tax law.
- Prior-year tax calculations going back to 1987 help you effectively manage audits, adjustments, and back-tax engagements.

For more information, visit www.bnasoftware.com. Current pricing is approximately $2,200 for one year.

TValue

Legend uses TValue, which stands for time value, a comprehensive resource for determining mortgage and loan amortization schedules for clients. TValue is a loan amortization software package that is used to structure loans, loan modifications, leases, troubled debt restructurings and to solve any time value of money calculations in seconds. For structuring or amortizing loans with irregular payments, balloons, or rate changes, TValue has proven to be a great, inexpensive tool. The initial cost is $149 for single-user access. There is an additional annual maintenance fee of $35 per user. A major benefit for Legend's advisors is that this software can automatically generate an amortization schedule with just a click of the mouse.

TValue is recognized as the best and most accurate amortization software available. Today, all of the Top 100 accounting firms and more than 500,000 financial professionals worldwide rely on its accuracy and flexibility to generate detailed amortization schedules.

Advisor Products' AdvisorVault

Advisor Products' AdvisorVault is an extremely helpful technology tool for Legend and its clients. It is used to post client financial reports and documents online. AdvisorVault is simple to use and provides excellent security. Files are encrypted while being uploaded or downloaded and they are also stored using high encryption—a feature not available from most other online storage vendors. In addition, the system sits behind multiple firewalls. AdvisorVault is available with an Advisor Products website or as a stand-alone product.

To build better client relationships, Legend wanted to provide its clients access to personal folders where they could store important financial documents online, including financial plans, net-worth statements, insurance policies, wills, tax returns, and trust documents. AdvisorVault transforms an advisory firm's website into a practical tool that can be used by clients. In making a clients' personal documents accessible 24/7 on the web, AdvisorVault offers clients an extra level of service and convenience. Some features include:

- 256-bit encrypted secure document management
- .NET platform using Microsoft SharePoint technology
- Secure access for additional staff and outside professionals
- Automatic document expiration
- Globally shared folders
- Drag and drop documents from desktop to vault
- Fully redundant infrastructure

You can learn more by visiting www.advisorproducts.com/advisorvaultct.aspx. Pricing for a one year subscription is approximately $1,400.

ByAllAccounts

Legend will soon implement the ByAllAccounts service. This account aggregation software eliminates manual data entry on retirement accounts, 401(k), and other held-away assets. In fact, ByAllAccounts aggregates account data from virtually any online financial source, and then, using its patented process, enhances and normalizes the data into a reconciliation-ready format that feeds into the most popular back-office systems. These systems include portfolio management systems, CRMs, accounting systems, reporting systems, personal trading applications, and rebalancing tools.

ByAllAccounts provides transaction-level detail, data quality, and custodian coverage specifically required for professional wealth managers and financial advisors. ByAllAccounts lets advisors scale their businesses and increase revenues by billing on held-away assets. Each night, collectively hundreds of billions of dollars and millions of financial records flow through the patented data aggregation engine. With ByAllaccounts, advisors can have one feed to capture all client accounts including 401k's, retirement, 529s, annuities, and other hard to reach assets. ByAllAccounts' portfolio management system is currently priced at $750 per quarter for up to 25 accounts, with a set-up fee of $1,000 plus in the first year. Additionally, its CRM software allows for unlimited positions for $900 per quarter with a $250 onetime set-up fee.

CHAPTER 12

Virtual Staff Sparks Growth, Profitability, and Scalability

Jennifer Goldman, CFP

President, My Virtual COO

As more CEOs and owners of financial advisory practices seek to grow their practices, scalability has become a vital component differentiating practices that successfully make this transition from those that don't. Many top-performing CEOs/owners who are scaling their practices, adding assets under management (AUM), and increasing the number of high net worth families served find that outsourcing tasks, functions, and jobs to virtual staff in addition to upgraded and enhanced technology helps manage that change. By adding the key technology and outsourced staff that scale a financial advisory practice, advisors achieve increased profitability and productivity.

Benefits of Virtual Staffing

In discussions with those advisors, I've found that virtual staffing—along with the right technology—aids productivity and profitability in multiple ways. For advisors who have the ability and interest to delegate specific tasks or entire job functions to experts who aren't physically located in their offices, virtual staff members offer a number of advantages over full-time or even part-time staff members who work on site. Virtual staff members offer advantages to financial advisory practices, including:

- Eliminates overhead costs such as computer terminals, desk, chairs, square footage, and utilities.
- Frees up CEO/owner's time from training and managing staff directly on a day-to-day basis.

- Provides mastery of a specific skill set and brings best practices and insider knowledge from the industry to your practice.
- Allows you and your staff to focus on the tasks that you do best and that add the most value to your practice—client acquisition and client engagement—rather than continually being distracted by noncore tasks.
- Adds staff who can immediately jump in and perform complex tasks without training and a learning curve.
- Gives flexibility in that many virtual staff members can scale their workload up or down depending on how busy you are and how much work you need from them.
- Permits you to try out an outsourcer with some small, noncritical tasks to see how that type of expert performs and fits in with your team in a specific role.
- Manages costs effectively as you are only paying for the time of virtual staff members, not benefits such as vacation, health insurance, retirement plans, and the employer's cost for Social Security and Medicare.

In terms of what virtual staff will provide the most bang for your buck, it's clear that subject-matter specialists with experience tailored to just what your firm needs are best. Fortunately, many such consultants who have gone out on their own are available and can provide mastery of a specific skill set and bring best practices and insider knowledge from the industry to your practice. Experienced virtual staff members usually can immediately jump in and perform complex tasks without training and a learning curve. If you're unsure about whether working with a virtual staff member is right for your practice, you can try out an outsourcer—many advisors start with a virtual assistant—with small, noncritical tasks to see how that staff member performs and fits in with your team in a specific role. As your practice grows, virtual staff members provide a lot of flexibility because many can scale their workload up or down depending on how busy you are and how much work you need from them.

Partnering with one or more virtual staff members offers the opportunity to grow your practice in a strategic way. Growth for the sake of growth often doesn't accrete to the bottom line. By implementing processes around tasks, partnering with the best virtual staff members in the business and scaling growth in a cost-effective way, growth can translate into increased profitability, satisfied employees and clients, and a happier CEO.

Otherwise, growth can create as many problems as it solves. That's because advisory firms that aren't prepared and find themselves scrambling to service the additional clients and principals work more hours without gaining an increase in income. A 2008 Moss Adams survey revealed that advisors' income actually tends to flatten along with profit margins as their firms grow. This flattening of profitability also occurs because advisors tend to increase operating costs with bigger offices, more travel, enhanced services, and more staff members.

A solution that many advisors rely on—combining operations with other advisors into an ensemble firm—can actually serve to depress profitability and increase the workload. This happens when advisors and their staff members aren't well positioned to cope with additional work and costs and there hasn't been much thought put into how to blend two sets of processes, two sets of technologies, and overlapping staff skill sets. Instead of bringing costs down, owners and staff find themselves working more hours, while the owner's take-home pay and profitability suffer.

By controlling—or cutting—costs via outsourcing, advisors can handle their new clients and the increased workload without sacrificing their profit margins. Implementing a strategic plan around growth and expenses that includes virtual staffing is one of the best ways to ensure that growth adds to the bottom line rather than subtracts from it. This requires investing in the right technology, the right outsourcing partners and the right mix of services to attract and retain clients.

Finally, outsourcing can yield significant work/life balance benefits. Many CEOs/owners go independent because they want more control over their business and personal lives. But as a practice grows, the increased demands of servicing clients, interacting with and supervising staff, and the ever-present need to acquire new clients translates into more hours at the office and fewer hours at home. These CEOs/owners can find themselves increasingly unhappy as their families see less of them and they feel pressured at home and at work. Hiring virtual staff can free up time spent on operational, compliance, administrative, marketing, technology, and supervision tasks to focus on core competencies at work and time spent at home with families.

While there are numerous virtual roles that you can outsource, I've focused on the ones that I find are the most valuable to financial advisors today. These include virtual financial planner, virtual chief operations officer, virtual assistant, virtual portfolio back office, virtual portfolio manager, virtual marketing, and virtual compliance. By making use of even one of these staff members, you can increase operational efficiency in your office and free yourself and your staff members from some of the onerous time-sucking operational activities that interrupt your schedule daily.

If you're looking for specific companies or experts to fill any of these or other virtual staffing roles, I recommend that you check out Virtual Solutions for Advisors (www.VirtualSolutionsForAdvisors.com), a group of outsourcers who are experts in working with financial advisors and financial advisory firms. This website is a free directory that provides a continuously updated list of outsourcers in every aspect of virtual staffing and can steer you in the best direction to meet your outsourced staffing needs.

Virtual Financial Planner

An outsourced virtual financial planner will work with your staff to prepare a complete financial plan with recommendations based on documentations and notes from client meetings. Outsourced planners are very familiar with a variety of financial planning software so there is no time wasted getting the virtual planner up to speed. A virtual planner can handle overflow on an as-needed basis if a staff member is on vacation and you need temporary help. Accountants and investment advisors who are adding financial planning services to their practices can also outsource financial planning to a virtual planner until they have enough critical mass within the practice to hire a full-time planner to assume these responsibilities.

To retain a virtual financial planner, you can expect to pay an hourly rate of $100 to $150. Many virtual planners charge by the project. One virtual planner quoted a rate of $2,000 to $2,500 a month to fill in for a staff planner who was on leave. That same planner handles updates, reports, and plan reviews for advisory firms and charges a flat fee of $3,100 per client per year.

To get an idea of the time you're spending on financial planning tasks that you might be able to spend elsewhere, such as on client acquisition or client engagement, the Financial Planning Association's (FPA) survey in October 2010[1] found that FPA members spend 19 percent of their time developing a financial plan for clients (see Figure 12.1). For a CEO/owner of a multiperson firm earning $200,000—according to the FPA's 2010–11 Compensation Survey—compensation for time spent on financial plans is $38,000 a year for financial planning services delivered by CEOs/owners. If financial planning services are delivered by staff members who are not the CEO/owner of the firm, a senior planner's time would be worth $20,000, while a junior planner's time would be worth $11,000 a year. The FPA survey also revealed that the creation of an individual financial plan consumes between 2 and 10 hours of the FPA members' surveyed time.

In contrast to what it would cost to outsource financial planning tasks to a virtual planner, consider what it would cost to hire a planner in-house. Typical salary for an in-house planner on staff who can handle a full range of financial planning tasks is between $60,000 and $113,000.

As far as services offered, an outsourced planner can handle a number of specific tasks including preparation of a plan with recommendations, delivery of a financial plan to the client, and interaction with the client to request documents and information needed to prepare the plan. To ensure confidentiality and compliance, the outsourced planner should sign a contract and a nondisclosure agreement.

FIGURE 12.1   Cost of Financial Planning Personnel

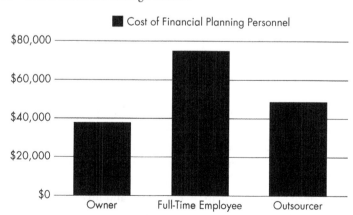

The technology most commonly used to communicate includes CRM, document management, and planning tools. These systems provide the ability to receive assigned tasks and documents, upload notifications via e-mail, and allow the planner to access the documents without needing anyone to e-mail them to him or her. Most financial planning software licenses allow an outsourced planner access as an assistant for free.

Ultimately, by outsourcing financial planning tasks on an as-needed basis, an advisor can take advantage of an expert planner's education, software experience and expertise, and knowledge gained in the industry for less than half the cost of bringing on a staff member.

Virtual Chief Operations Officer or Operations Manager

A virtual chief operations officer (COO), interim COO, or operations manager handles a firm's operational backbone. An expert in processes and operations by nature, a COO acts as the manager of workflow and workflow accountability for an advisory firm and the in-house and virtual staff. Handing over operational tasks to a professional manager, whether part time or full time, virtual or in-house, allows the owner(s) of the firm to step aside from operational matters and focus on client-facing and acquisition activities. It also allows a firm to build scale in a way that isn't possible when the firm's founder directly controls operational and administrative matters.

CEOs/owners consistently underestimate how much time they spend on operational tasks. That's because the nature of operational problems is that they crop up when least expected and stealthily rob an advisor of the time and energy needed to grow a practice via client-facing activities. A typical CEO/owner can spend 50 percent of his or her time attending to operational tasks; however, that time could be better spent building the practice. Experienced COOs find that there is a huge opportunity cost for financial advisors who manage all of their own operations.

An *interim* onsite COO costs approximately $10,000 per month and assists for three to six months to realign the operations. A *virtual* COO typically charges a retainer starting at $1,000 a month and is based on the expected number of hours, level of staff management needed, and the complexity of the realignment of operations. The salary and benefits for a chief operations officer is, according to the *InvestmentNews*/Moss Adams Survey, $130,000 a year.

An in-house or outsourced COO can handle a number of tasks including management of staff and consultants, creation of processes in all aspects of practice management including client acquisition, client service and marketing to scale your business, leveraging technology to automate work, developing a culture of accountability, and ensuring projects have deadlines and team members are working effectively.

A big part of the COO's job is to evaluate current processes, employ automation to reduce the workload of the staff, and manage expenses wisely so the firm can add more clients and services without necessarily adding more costs or staff. A COO will also suggest technological improvements, staff, and virtual staff to meet the needs of a practice as it grows and scales.

Ultimately, the COO is in charge of creating and maintaining the workflow processes that will scale the practice over time.

As far as return on investment goes, an investment in virtual or interim operations management staff will pay off significantly. Without implementation of processes, it is impossible to gain the scalability to grow a practice significantly. Not only is the owner's time freed up when there is an outsourcing to operational staff, but the whole practice also gains clarity around what, how, and when to delegate tasks.

Virtual Assistant

A virtual assistant (VA) is currently the most common staff position outsourced by financial advisors. Although the hourly cost may seem high compared to hiring in-house, the VA firms that specialize in financial services are extremely efficient in managing onboarding clients, providing ongoing servicing of clients, and navigating the custodian(s)' service departments for the right answers when a client has a problem. They also share best practices they gain from working with other financial advisory firms.

The hourly rate for an experienced VA runs $55 to $75 per hour. That's in contrast to the average salary for an administrative assistant, which is about $45,000. This figure doesn't include benefits and overhead such as a desk, computer, benefits, vacation, or the time the CEO spends on staff management. A typical virtual assistant engagement can range from $750 to $2,500 per month or $9,000 to $30,000 a year. (see Figure 12.2). Personnel that staff VA firms come from the industry or have been thoroughly trained. VAs are experts in handling the paperwork in onboarding new clients and they do it in less time than it would take to complete a new in-house hire in your office with no financial services experience. Most experienced VAs have

FIGURE 12.2   Cost of an Administrative Assistant

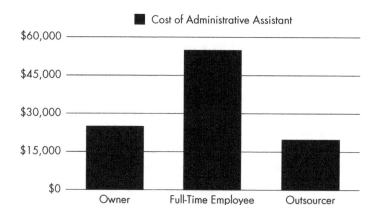

established a direct line of communication with the best customer service members at each custodian and they know the quickest way to get tasks accomplished.

The range of services offered includes account applications, transfers, forms; client communications and customer relationship management; quarterly reporting; receptionist and executive assistance services and custodian interaction. For compliance purposes, execute a contract and nondisclosure agreement with your virtual assistant. It also pays to get a background check. The technology needed to interface with a VA includes a CRM, a document management system, and an e-mail address.

In terms of workflows, communications flow through tasking in the CRM. Because you may not work with the same VA firm throughout the life of your practice, establish a generic support e-mail address that clients can use to communicate with your VA. This way, if your VA changes, you clients will never know there is a change and won't have any idea that the VA isn't a full-time staff member.

Most advisors find the return on investment in hiring a VA compelling. Rather than managing a staff member on site and paying a salary and benefits, a VA firm can be hired for as little time as you want per month and can provide more hours as your practice grows. You can also start working with a VA firm and outsource small tasks, then send more work their way as your confidence grows in their ability to interact with your clients and handle administrative tasks.

Virtual Compliance

As compliance gets more complex in an ever-changing regulatory environment, managing compliance in a financial advisory firm is becoming more difficult for CEO/owners. That's why it can make a big difference to outsource compliance tasks from something as seemingly simple as the annual completion and filing of Form ADV to your entire compliance to-do list.

Compliance outsourcers, whether individual vendors or larger firms, are intimately familiar with deadlines, issues, and requirements of state regulators, the Financial Industry Regulatory Authority (FINRA), and the U.S. Securities and Exchange Commission (SEC). Outsourcing compliance tasks relieves you of the responsibility to manage the day-to-day details, though you or another senior advisor needs to retain overall responsibility as the firm's chief compliance officer.

There are various levels of services provided by outsourced compliance firms. The highest and most expensive level is paying an outsourced firm a retainer to manage most, if not all, of your compliance functions. Such a firm will be proactive in managing your compliance, creating checklists, and managing projects. If you are required to have staff compliance meetings, compliance outsourcers will schedule them for you and run the meetings and annotate them, ensuring all the required points are covered.

A step down from complete outsourcing is contracting with a firm or individual compliance consultant to manage specific projects, such as an internal compliance audit, creating a compliance calendar for you to follow, or filling out and filing specific forms with regulators. In this type of situation, you can do as much or as little as you want with the consultant, depending on your needs.

For the highest level of service, ongoing compliance management, the cost runs about $20,000 to $30,000 a year. That can make sense for a firm with a minimum of $75 million in assets under management. On the lower end, to hire an individual consultant to manage an internal audit and some other smaller tasks, the cost would be in the range of $3,500 to $5,000 a year.

Contrast this to the salary and benefits you'd need to pay to a full-time chief compliance officer. The 2011 *InvestmentNews*/Moss Adams quotes an average full-time salary and benefits package at $85,000 per year. If the CEO/owner is handling compliance—which consumes a minimum of 5 percent of his or her time—that $200,000 executive is spending $10,000 worth of time on compliance alone. Not only is the CEO/owner's time valuable, but compliance time is typically expended during normal business hours, which limits the amount of time spent on client acquisition and engagement activities. (See Figure 12.3.)

To work efficiently with an outsourced compliance provider, you or your operations staff member will need to craft an annual compliance workflow that notes the compliance-related tasks that need to be accomplished each month, where to get the necessary documents and any needed passwords. This workflow should be embedded in your day-to-day task scheduling management system, typically a CRM.

The opportunity cost in trying to manage compliance on your own is pretty high. Think about the SEC, FINRA, or a state regulator coming in and doing an audit and all the time you'll spend finding documents and, after the audit is over, following up to bring your office up to their compliance standard. It makes sense to outsource the aggravation or potential aggravation to someone who is an expert in the field and can

FIGURE 12.3   Cost of Compliance Personnel

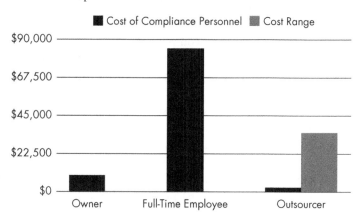

keep up with changing regulatory requirements and represent your firm, if necessary, in a case or issue involving the SEC, FINRA, or state regulators.

Virtual Portfolio Back Office

Managing a portfolio back office comes at a major cost to financial advisory firms, and one that too many advisors underestimate. Reconciling portfolios is a specialized skill set that requires about a half an hour of time a day, two weeks at the end of each quarter, and three to four weeks at year end, and this time does not include the CEO but, rather, just the support staff's time.

Many advisors hire this function in-house. However, this is not the best use of in-house resources because typically there isn't enough portfolio back-office work to keep that staff member busy all day. Also, his or her skill set to perform this job accurately is not necessarily transferrable to working with clients or to other tasks within the office. A staff member with this skill set, which is mostly accounting-oriented, has to be extremely detail-oriented and wouldn't be well suited to handle another job such as marketing or even routine administrative assistant tasks.

In terms of hard numbers, it makes sense for any firm with assets under management of $50 million or more to outsource this function. By outsourcing the function to a large firm that specializes in portfolio back-office management, you receive web-based performance reporting, expert reconciliation, billing, and other services. Overall, outsourced portfolio back-office firms can cost $7,500 to $45,000 a year and upward based on the number of accounts. (See Figure 12.4.) This outsourced cost pales in comparison to hiring and retaining in-house staff to perform the same function. FPA quotes a salary (no benefits) of $80,000, and the 2011 *InvestmentNews*/Moss Adams quotes this position with a salary of $75,000. This type

FIGURE 12.4　Cost of Portfolio Back-Office Personnel

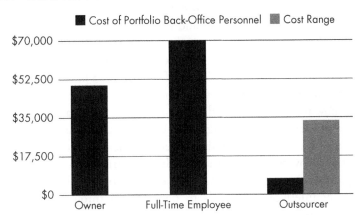

of outsourcing frees up an enormous amount of time, which can be directed toward activities such as client engagement or acquisition or enhanced work/life balance.

A white paper produced by Black Diamond Performance Reporting (now Advent) in conjunction with Nexus Strategy, LLC, reported that a firm with $150 million in assets under management can save $53,000 a year by using an outsourced portfolio back-office solution instead of a web-based software solution. Orion Advisor Solutions, another outsourced portfolio back-office solution, suggests that an advisory firm can save $12,882, a 21.4 percent savings, by switching to a service bureau over a software solution.

A major advantage of outsourcing these functions—besides the obvious cost savings—is that firms that are experts in this area can catch all the nuances coming in through the reporting from the custodians in terms of capital gains and dividends and spot any problems and resolve them quickly. From the compliance perspective, if you get the numbers wrong when a staff member performs reconciliation, you could end up going out of business due to faulty performance reporting. With an outsourced solution, you leave the technical details to the experts while retaining the ability to go into the system and look at any numbers that you want at any time. A number of firms that handle these tasks at a variety of price points and service offerings are available at Virtual Solutions for Advisors.

On the positive side in terms of making a good impression for client engagement and client acquisition, professional-looking statements that reflect all aspects of a client's portfolio—including their holdings and performance—can only benefit your firm. If you are currently passing on the client's statement directly from your custodian, it probably isn't making a great impression. Instead, by working with a portfolio back-office solution you will able to place your own brand on your statement, which will leave a positive impression in your clients' minds.

Virtual Portfolio Manager

As markets get more complex and investment alternatives proliferate, more advisors are considering outsourcing at least part of the investment management function. Outsourcing all or part of your portfolio management is a two-part process: finding the right outsourced portfolio manager and then ensuring the manager has access to your clients' portfolio holdings via a custodian's data feed or aggregation tool.

Typically, advisors build the costs of outsourcing into the fee they charge clients. Outsourced portfolio managers typically cost from 50 to 75 basis points with outliers of 20 and 125 basis points for this service. The typical outsourced portfolio manager includes the following services in its offering: investment research, modeling, selection of investment products, and trading. The communication between advisor and portfolio manager is best achieved with quarterly phone calls and a workflow of steps that both parties follow throughout the year. It is important to understand that some outsourced portfolio managers will not manage the portfolio back office, so that's another point of interface that needs to be managed through workflows, verbal communications, and technology.

The act of rebalancing and the tools used to perform this important part of outsourcing investment management should not be overlooked. Managing rebalancing in-house involves the cost of an investment research tool, which can cost $2,500 per year per user, and a software rebalancing tool, which can cost between $5,000 and $50,000 per year. Furthermore, the cost of the technology and staff doesn't include the time it takes for the staff and the CEO to manage the rebalancing process and execute the trades.

In terms of cost savings, the FPA 2010–2011 Compensation survey noted that the average salary, bonus, and incentive for an in-house investment specialist/portfolio construction specialist was $90,000 in 2011. The 2011 *InvestmentNews*/Moss Adams survey pegs the salary and benefits for a chief investment officer at $140,000; the same for a senior investment/portfolio manager at $115,000; and the same for an investment/portfolio manager at $75,000.

An FPA Fall 2010 survey found CEO/owners spend, on average, 8 percent of their time on trading and asset management and 7 percent of their time on investment research, for a total of 15 percent. At the average founder's compensation of $200,000, that translates into $30,000 of the CEO's time spent on investment management tasks. When the cost of time spent on reconciliation, reporting, billing, the cost of liability for placing trades, and the cost of rebalancing software to manage a growing AUM business is added in, costs can exceed $100,000 a year.

An outsourced portfolio manager takes much of the compliance concern related to investment management off of your shoulders. From the perspective of managing that relationship in a compliant fashion, the best way is to set up workflows in your portfolio management system to regularly check holdings balances and performance as well as manage investment reporting to clients.

Outsourced Chief Marketing Officer

Marketing is one of the most critical client acquisition activities, but one that is often given short shrift by CEO/owners of financial advisory practices. Too often, advisors fail to create a marketing plan or fail to execute the marketing plan that they put together. By outsourcing project marketing on a part-time or full-time basis to a virtual staff member experienced in the industry, the CEO/owner can focus on core competencies such as client acquisition, increased client interactions, and nurturing relationships with referral sources.

Virtual marketing services come in many forms. At the top end is a virtual chief marketing officer (CMO) who will handle all planning and execution of marketing-related tasks. Such a staffer can be hired full-time, part-time, or on a project or temporary basis. Other marketing jobs that can be handled by outsourced staff include social media marketing; writing and creation of marketing collateral such as website copy, brochures, white papers and case studies; public relations outreach to the media; and coordination and project management of marketing strategies.

The *InvestmentNews*/Moss Adams 2011 Staffing and Compensation Survey pegs the salary of a chief marketing officer for a financial advisory practice at $88,026. The costs to hire a CMO can run from $125 to $200 an hour, depending on locale and the expertise of the consultant. The typical range of fees for marketing assistance in writing, media, graphic design, and client events can range from $1,500 to $4,000 a month. Marketing consultants frequently charge by the project, with the fee dependent on the type and scope of the project, the number of staff members involved in approving the work, and the number of revisions requested. There are also many writers, graphic artists, marketing consultants, and social media experts who work by the project or by the hour.

When seeking an outsourced CMO or marketing consultant, look for someone with industry experience who is experienced with compliance. You don't want to get in trouble with FINRA, the SEC, or a state regulator by hiring someone who isn't familiar with financial services compliance issues and publishes copy that recommends investments or violates compliance guidelines in some other way.

In terms of compliance, a contract and nondisclosure agreement is a good idea. You don't want a marketing contractor to share your proprietary information with other advisors in the industry. In the contract, specify details regarding which party owns the writing or other work product (your company should). As for technology, we recommend you set up workflows in the CRM that notify the marketing staff member. Most marketing contractors work in Microsoft Word.

In summary, outsourcing marketing to a virtual staff member can benefit your practice in many ways. When you formulate a marketing plan in concert with a client acquisition plan and execute that plan well internally and externally, your practice is more likely to experience growth in assets under management and in numbers of high net worth families served. Many CEO/owners aren't comfortable or experienced in marketing and tend to approach it haphazardly or put it off. With the financial advisory industry becoming more competitive than ever and clients demanding more services for less, it's never a good idea to leave a critical client acquisition and practice growth activity to chance or to staff members who aren't experts.

In Closing

There's no end to the roles that virtual staff members can play in your practice. From performing specific tasks on an occasional basis to taking over an entire job description and running with it, virtual experts such as those at Virtual Solutions for Advisors offer unparalleled expertise and experience for a fraction of the cost and ongoing management hassles of onsite staff.

As the financial advisory industry continues to evolve, flexibility is the key to staying ahead of the curve. Advisors who can leverage the skills of highly productive, experienced, and well-connected virtual staff members can add expertise and increased revenue-generating potential to their staff without significantly increasing overhead.

Depending on how your practice grows, you may cycle through different out-sourced staff members who fulfill various needs at different times. As long as you are flexible and willing to take a big-picture view and consider all the options, a long-term mix of full-time, part-time, on-site and off-site staff members will give your practice the best opportunity to achieve the operational scalability that will produce maximum profits and employee, client, and owner satisfaction.

The key here is the increased return on investment that results when you can successfully find, retain, delegate to, and grow your practice with those best-in-the-business contractors. These virtual staff members are experienced in the industry, eager to grow their own businesses, willing to share industry best practices with you, and eager to partner with you to grow together. In this type of situation, it is a win-win for you, the advisor with a growing practice, and the virtual staff members who will help you achieve that growth.

Note

1. Reprinted with permission by the Financial Planning Association, 2010–2011 Financial Planning Salary Survey. For more information on the Financial Planning Association, please visit www.fpanet.org or call 1–800–322–4237.

CHAPTER 13

ROI—The Holy Grail of the Technology Purchase Decision

Timothy D. Welsh, CFP

President and Founder, Nexus Strategy, LLC

For many advisors, the foundational principal for evaluating any technology is what return on investment (ROI) they will receive by purchasing a new system, adopting an outsourced platform, streamlining a workflow, or incorporating any new business enhancing device or tool.

However, the ability to actually quantify, specifically, what those returns are in terms of real-time savings, lower hard dollar costs, increased capacity, improved service levels, and scalability has been somewhat of a squishy process.

In fact, many advisors express frustration at what was promised to them by smooth talking vendors versus what actually was delivered. Oftentimes, the missing ROI is not the fault of the vendor, but rather the underestimates by the advisor in terms of the amount of time, effort, and training necessary to successfully adopt the new approach.

Therefore, in order to provide a multilevel framework for determining the ROI of any technology, system, or reengineered process, consider using a total business impact analysis (TBIA) approach. A TBIA takes into account not only the savings in terms of current dollars today but also in the future business value generated for tomorrow. It also incorporates the up-front investment in terms of time, effort, and training required to fully embrace and adopt the new tools and processes.

Ultimately, for advisors, the question isn't necessarily how to spend money on software, hardware, and systems; rather it is how to use that technology to get an immediate return on investment (ROI) in terms of simplifying operational tasks, achieving efficiencies in service delivery, and lowering overhead costs.

The good news for advisors is that with new, purpose-built technology applications from leading advisor technology firms, never before has there been such a broad array of solutions to choose from that are customized and affordable to meet the specifications of their independent advisor business models. Ten years ago, that wasn't necessarily the case. Now, with the growing recognition of the importance of the independent wealth management industry, innovation in advisor technology is flourishing, and there is literally a new gold rush for technology firms to bring new solutions to market.

But where do you start? How can you leverage and increase your technology investments in these interesting times? Industry experts all agree that the best approach to building an IT blueprint is to begin with a plan.

The Technology Plan

Just like financial advisors develop long-term financial plans to help their clients make intelligent financial decisions, so, too, should advisors develop IT plans so that they can make the right technology purchase decisions that make the most of limited resources.

Recent research reports from industry consultants and custodians have identified the most effective technology investments that provide the most improvements in efficiency and where the highest return on investment (ROI) lies. Top of the list are automating client information, systematizing workflows, streamlining client reporting, managing paper and digital documents, as well as automating aspects of client service.

Accordingly, the top technology systems that can directly apply to these activities include CRM software, portfolio management and performance reporting platforms, client service portals, and document management systems. Additional technology solutions that also provide a substantial ROI include financial planning systems, portfolio rebalancing tools, account aggregation applications, investment planning and asset allocation tools, along with mobile devices.

Other key areas identified as a success factor were the ability for the various systems to integrate and work together as one system—not as multiple, disassociated applications. These integrated systems, known as "composite applications," reduce manual data entry and automate many of the manual workflows required to process business or provide service.

The rise of the composite application that integrates multiple pieces of technology into one process is the next advisor technology paradigm to grab hold of the industry. Evidence of this can already be seen in the massive technology integration projects initiated by all of the major custodians to combine brokerage platforms, CRM technology, portfolio management systems, and other applications to automate workflows.

The reason that the above technology features and integrations score the highest on ROI and efficiency gains is that for the typical advisory firm, these systems streamline the activities that make up the most manual efforts and are what histori-cally has been "the way we do business."

To combat that status quo thinking, your technology plan should be considered as an investment in your firm's growth and ultimate business value. When advisors think of it in this strategic way they quickly realize that not only should they be smart in how they allocate their technology dollars, but also they should actually *increase* their spending on technology, because there is a direct correlation between lowering overhead expenses and creating business value.

In fact, when looked at from a business valuation point of view, leading firms are realizing that the more scale, capacity, and efficiency they build into their firms, the higher the value they can monetize when they exit the business and sell their equity either internally to a junior partner or externally to a third party.

According to leading industry and valuation experts, advisory firms today are being valued at approximately 5 to 15 times cash flow (also known as EBITDA), depending on how large a firm is and other factors. In the case of a technology decision, if the new system lowers overhead and increases cash flow, then the return on that investment in terms of business value can be quite dramatic, beyond just the annual cost savings.

For example, consider the case of a medium-size firm of $1,000,000 in revenue. If a technology implementation will lower overhead costs by a net 10 percent ($100,000) per year, these savings drop directly to the bottom line, increasing profits and cash flow by a corresponding amount. When a business value multiple (conser-vative estimate of 10 times in the case of a $1 million firm) is applied to this increased profitability, then the net business value increase achieved is $1,000,000! Not bad for a $20,000, $50,000, or even $100,000 software purchase.

When viewed in the light of the business value multiple, then just about any investment in technology that will save staff time and increase capacity becomes a very simple decision.

Other things to consider when looking for ROI are to constantly rethink the way you are processing business. When asked, leading advisors say that the key to their success in building efficient businesses is to continually challenge their assumptions as to why and how certain things are done. This process of self-examination can have a dramatic impact.

As an example, consider the recent experience of a successful independent advisory firm in Southern California that was growing rapidly. As part of its history, the firm prided itself on its reporting and communication with clients to service their entire financial picture.

Inherent in that, however, was a vast, manual reporting system they had cobbled together through the years that was quickly becoming an operational burden and nightmare to manage. Because they had continued to do business as usual, they were beginning to fall behind in service, while communications and reports provided as their standard service model were taking them over a month every quarter to complete.

Just before they reached a breaking point, however, employees started to chal-lenge their way of providing reports in a paper fashion and invested in building a composite application to automate that process by integrating document management technology with their portfolio management system and CRM software.

This integration allowed the firm to publish its reports electronically to private, secure client websites (known as a client service portal), triggering e-mail to clients informing them that their reports were ready to be viewed.

What they had thought would be a service decrease by going to electronic delivery actually wasn't a decrease at all. In reality it was a service increase as the information was much more timely. The firm communicated this difference in service approach in a "going green" message (no more paper, no carbon generated in delivering paper reports) that was well received by clients. Because they could track the e-mail opening and report downloading, what the firm discovered was that fewer than 1 in 10 of their clients actually viewed the reports. Additionally, the firm realized that it had completely misunderstood its real value proposition to its clients. It was clearly not in providing quarterly reports!

By challenging its assumptions and existing ways of doing business, the new technology saved the firm roughly three weeks per quarter of staff time and tens of thousands of dollars in annual printing, collating, and mailing costs. It also provided the team with added scalability to grow the firm without adding additional back-office staff.

Looking back, the firm realized that had it viewed the cost of the technology as an added expense, it might never have invested in the first place. This realization was critical to its continued success and it is now looking for ways to automate virtually every process in the firm.

Other key ways to stretch technology can be seen in thinking differently about the types of solutions used and to understand the true costs of a process. Operational costs include not only the actual dollars expended for the software, hardware, and systems, but also the staff time it takes to run that software, including operational time, training, management, maintenance, and so on.

An example of this can be seen with some of the daily processes related to account maintenance and data reconciliation. Typically, many firms are using in-house systems that require manual work to accomplish these tasks in-house, despite the availability of advancements in technology and new, outsourced service models that can efficiently handle these manual steps with a higher accuracy rate and much less staff time.

According to the 2011 Asset Management Operations and Compensation Survey by the Advent User's Group and the Investment Adviser Association, advisory firms using in-house systems spend 25 hours per month for small firms, 60 hours per month for medium-size firms, and 160 hours per month for larger firms on account reconciliation.

Contrast this in-house process with an outsourced portfolio management and performance reporting system that automatically performs account reconciliation on a daily basis via electronic feeds from custodians and other data providers as part of its service model and virtually all of these tasks and staff costs are eliminated, with a much higher confidence rate and fewer errors.

Thinking differently in this case creates capacity by outsourcing what was once a core internal process to those who can do it better, faster, and cheaper due to advancements in advisor, purpose-built technology.

To further illustrate these points and to provide specific dollar and time savings of various technologies under a TBIA approach, consider the following four common software solutions and related composite applications that make up a majority of functionality advisors use on a daily basis:

1. Customer Relationship Management
2. Client Service Portals
3. Portfolio Accounting and Performance Reporting
4. Document Management

Nexus Strategy, LLC has been a pioneer in quantifying the ROI of advisor technology and has developed multiple white papers and research projects on these topics. Pulling from these TBIA analyses provides multiple examples of ROI and the incredible opportunity firms have at their disposal to build profitable businesses that can scale with growth.

Customer Relationship Management

It's no surprise that CRM systems provide a substantial ROI to advisory firms based on a number of factors, including streamlining client service, automating workflows, and of course providing new revenue opportunities by systematizing business development, marketing, and sales.

According to the "CRM as Total Firm Technology" industry white paper developed by Junxure and Nexus Strategy, LLC, there are also a number of other benefits offered by CRM that enhance ROI. These include business intelligence, back- and front-office efficiencies, as well as in streamlining quarterly reporting.

By extending CRM with additional features and functionality to also keep track and manage operational tasks, advisory firms now have a view of not only clients but also the workflow and back office.

By querying the database, a "dashboard" for the firm is available to provide a strategic view of firm operations. This ability to see how client service is being delivered by each type of person in the firm (back office, professional, and principal) provides the key business intelligence to be able to optimally allocate resources and make the most out of staff.

To show the impact of this business intelligence on optimally allocating resources, consider that for firms that do not optimize CRM technology (according to Schwab Advisor Services research), the average principal spends 35 percent of his or her time on client service, 12 percent on operations, and 12 percent on business development. However, those firms that have adopted CRM technology are able to reduce their amount of time spent on operations to 7 percent and increase the amount of time they spend on client service to 38 percent and time spent on business development to 16 percent.

This reduction in operational focus for principals translates into significant opportunities to ensure that the right people are working on the right tasks, increasing the capacity of the firm for not only handling higher volumes with fewer staff members, but also freeing up the valuable business development resources of principals to continue to grow the firm.

The many back-office and workflow features that CRM provides also can translate into extremely valuable efficiencies in the segmentation and delivery of service to clients. Many advisors use some sort of segmentation scheme to label those clients who are of most value and importance, such as assets under management (AUM), revenues, profitability, ability to refer, and so on, putting them into A, B, and C categories or Platinum, Gold, and Silver, and the like.

In order to attract and retain the most valued types of clients, the ability to segment and deliver a higher service level is critical. CRM technology enables firms to efficiently define, track, and provide different levels of client service, which can be very important to ensure the right clients receive investments in differentiated services. Conversely, the ability to understand client value also saves costs and resources by preventing over-servicing or provision of benefits to C clients who don't qualify for them.

Another key aspect that is becoming increasingly important as clients move toward the "de-accumulation" stage of retirement is in the ability for firms to leverage CRM to monitor, automate, and execute upon client-specific needs for maintaining enough cash for retirement distributions. Through a reporting capability, alerts can be generated on a daily basis for those clients who will need to execute trades in their portfolio to cover cash withdrawals mandated by minimum distribution requirements or other needs.

As firms grow and the proportion of clients who need retirement income distribution planning increases, it will become even more critical for advisors to have an automated approach to managing this to continue to profitably grow without adding additional infrastructure.

One of the more powerful applications of CRM is its ability to integrate with other systems such as e-mail, word processing, and forms packages, along with document management systems to create composite applications, eliminating the redundant tasks of manually entering the same data over and over. An example of how compelling CRM can be is in the process of streamlining the constant need to create targeted client communications, such as updating holders of certain securities about issues or opportunities, and other communications. By querying the CRM database, lists of clients are easily identified and pulled, with their contact information dropped into e-mail or word processing templates. Through integrations with document management systems, these documents are automatically placed in the firm's repository and filed into the appropriate client folder.

To see how efficient this process can be, consider one firm's approach to year-end gifts for clients. Consistent with their segmentation approach, they provide three different types of gifts for their A, B, and C clients. Because of their CRM, they are able to quickly identify and pull the three lists, dropping their information into a preset letter template at the same time sending a file with contact information to an outside vendor for fulfillment. What once took a week or more to accomplish is now completed in a couple of hours.

Client Portals

According to the "Live Client Portals: Extend Your Advisory Services Through the Web" industry white paper developed by Junxure and Nexus Strategy, LLC, improvements in technology have enabled advisors to take advantage of new capabilities to create secure "document vaults" or "client service portals" for the storage of electronic documents, copies of financial statements, tax returns, wills, and other financial and personal information. These vaults also allow advisors to post statements, financial planning documents, and investment performance reports as well as provide a way to interact with clients' other professionals such as their accountants and attorneys.

These client portals enable clients to log on to their private web address, using secure, password-protected online access to see their relevant information, post electronic documents, and download their financial and investment planning statements and reports. Additionally, clients are able to use these client portals as online "safety deposit boxes" to back up any important paper documents, such as insurance policies, passports, birth certificates, title deeds, and the like.

By integrating their websites to their CRM and office management systems to create a composite application, advisors are able to broaden their client portal to include client collaboration tools to create tasks for their advisor or service team to follow up on as well as publish real-time information of client holdings.

The CRM integration allows advisors to host client data on their servers and directly link through their CRM to the client portal. The integration allows clients to then initiate tasks directly to a service contact or if the client is a priority client, directly to his or her advisor. This service-tiering model provides the firm with flexibility in offering its best clients a higher service level and ensures the task will be completed and will not fall through the cracks, as it will be automatically tracked in the same place where all of the firm's workflow is stored.

Additionally, through integrations with CRM and portfolio management systems (PMS) to create composite applications, daily positions and values can be automatically published to the client portal, allowing clients to have the latest information whenever they like and often saving firms from incoming client phone calls and incremental service requests.

Another benefit of having client portals originate from the CRM is that quarterly performance reports and statements can be automatically produced and assembled electronically and then directly published to each client's portal. By using a document assembly tool, the many manual steps required for posting information to client portals hosted by third-party vendors are eliminated. For clients who require printed statements, they can be segmented out in the batch processing and only those are printed for subsequent mailing.

This streamlining of the quarterly reporting process can save advisory firms thousands of dollars every quarter and add tremendous efficiencies, freeing up staff to focus on higher value, client-facing activities.

To quantify the annual cost savings for the quarterly reporting process, consider the data in Table 13.1 from the 2011 Asset Management Operations and Compensation Survey by the Advent Users Group and the Investment Adviser Association. This table highlights the manual costs required to mail quarterly statements to clients, based on the size of a firm's assets under management. As you can see, even small firms can generate tens of thousands of dollars in savings every year, and for larger firms, the impacts are even larger.

Portfolio Management and Performance Reporting

According to "A Diamond in the Rough: Technology Savings and ROI in Volatile Markets" developed by Black Diamond Performance Reporting and Nexus Strategy, LLC, the majority of advisory firms have a portfolio management system in place in some form or another, however, the emerging opportunity for ROI in PMS is to outsource the manual and error-prone processes of reconciliation, reporting, and billing.

Currently, many independent advisory firms are using in-house processes combined with software applications to provide these key functions. The lack of flexibility inherent in this approach is creating inefficiencies in their back offices and is limiting their ability to respond to the dynamic, volatile markets of today. While clients are demanding timely information on the status of their portfolios, many advisory firms are stuck with the ability to, at best, report on a monthly basis, meanwhile they are inundated with additional work for ad-hoc reports based on client concerns, pushing their back offices to the limit.

TABLE 13.1 Quarterly Reporting Costs

Size of Firm (AUM)	<$500M	$500M–$1B	$1B–$2B
Hours spent per quarter × 4 = annual hours	120	160	292
Cost @ $40 per hour*	$4,800	$6,400	$11,680
Printing/Mailing Costs	$5,000	$10,000	$20,000
Total	$9,800	$16,400	$31,680

*Estimate for the hourly cost of back-office personnel.
Source: Nexus Strategy, LLC.

By outsourcing the many manual steps involved to a third-party with best-in-breed technology and a service model that is dedicated to efficiently providing these services, advisors can quickly realize a much more streamlined back office, smaller IT infrastructure, and the ability to provide performance information on a *daily* basis in a customized, user-friendly, graphic interface that ultimately becomes a valuable competitive advantage.

The bottom-line result is that not only do advisors realize substantial cost savings, they are also empowered with a very robust performance reporting, reconciliation, and billing capability that frees them up to pursue growth.

The costs associated with acquiring a robust and comprehensive in-house system include the core software annual licenses for providing portfolio reporting and accounting, which begin at approximately $30,000 for smaller firms, running upward of $70,000 and higher for larger firms. Combined with additional modules for billing and ongoing consulting services to customize the application for each firm along with the added IT infrastructure, hardware, and disaster recovery/compliance, and even small firms are facing roughly $35,000 in additional annual costs, upward of $75,000 and more for larger firms.

In contrast to these in-house processes, advisors can realize dramatic savings by adopting innovative web-based applications, known as software as a service (SaaS). No longer do advisors need to acquire, maintain, staff, and service expensive IT infrastructure and systems. The resulting savings range from over $25,000 annually for small firms to nearly $70,000 for larger firms as shown in Table 13.2.

Beyond the costs associated with acquiring technology, with in-house processes, advisors must also allocate highly valuable and typically scarce resources to operate their system and perform the manual tasks related to servicing these key function alareas.

These tasks include the many steps involved in account reconciliation such as the time it takes to download data and verify the accuracy of that data through checking the logs and ensuring that all scripts ran. Back-office staff must also set up and map new accounts and related new securities as well as define all aspects of those securities. In addition, staff must also post data and perform exception management processing and research, along with manually making any corrections or adjustments.

Also included in this process is the manual input for noncustodial data feeds, reconciling pricing for nonstandard or unpriced securities, and related performance

TABLE 13.2 Technology Acquisition Costs

Size of Firm (AUM)	$150M	$500M	$1B+
In-house Processes	$63,800	$104,500	$191,300
Software as a Service	$37,500	$75,000	$125,000
Annual Savings	**$26,300 (41.2%)**	**$29,500 (28.2%)**	**$66,300 (34.6%)**

benchmarks. Once all of this is done, staff must then repost the data and run a reconciliation audit to ensure the accuracy of those manual processes.

Performing these tasks via an in-house process is clearly a time-consuming and complex approach that creates many opportunities for errors to be created and is a frequent headache for advisors to manage. According to the Advent User Group study, advisory firms using in-house processes spend 20 hours per month for small firms and 60 hours per month for larger firms on account reconciliation. That is roughly half a week of a staffer's time for small firms and roughly one-and-a-half weeks per month of a staffer's time for larger firms spent on these manual, error-prone tasks.

Contrast these in-house processes with an online performance reporting system that automatically performs account reconciliation on a daily basis via electronic feeds from custodians and other data providers as part of its service model and virtually all of these tasks and staff costs are eliminated, with a much higher accuracy rate.

At a conservative rate of $40 per hour, the cost savings for firms is substantial, ranging from $8,600 to almost $24,000 and more per year as shown in Table 13.3.

For firms using in-house processes for billing activity, there are many manual steps involved in addition to paying extra for an additional module. These include the quarterly process of running billing reports, which include the detailed accounting for cash movements in and out of accounts from contributions and withdrawals. For firms with a large amount of accounts, this accounting in order to accurately calculate billing balances can be a time-consuming, tedious, and sometimes error-prone task. Additionally, once those reports are completed, staff must then export them to their custodians, which can be a cumbersome process for larger firms using multiple custodians.

According to the Advent User Group study, advisory firms using software and manual processes spend roughly 10 hours per quarter on billing for smaller firms and approximately 31 hours per quarter for larger firms.

Contrast these in-house processes with an online performance reporting system that automatically performs many aspects of the billing process, including calculating average daily balances to account for contributions and withdrawals, and this time is reduced by 75 percent with a much higher accuracy rate (see Table 13.4).

TABLE 13.3 Account Reconciliation Costs

Size of Firm (AUM)	$150M	$500M	$1B+
In-house Process	$9,600	$12,000	$28,800
Online System	$1,000	$3,000	$5,000
Annual Savings	**$8,600 (90%)**	**$9,000 (75%)**	**$23,800 (83%)**

TABLE 13.4 Billing Costs

Size of Firm (AUM)	$150M	$500M	$1B
Software/Manual	$1,600	$2,000	$4,960
Online System	$400	$500	$1,240
Annual Savings	**$1,200** (75%)	**$1,500** (75%)	**$3,720** (75%)

Document Management

According to the "ROI for RIAs" industry white paper developed by Laserfiche and Nexus Strategy, LLC, the highly regulated nature of the financial services industry creates a significant amount of paper during the normal course of business; yet, firms often overlook the infrastructure cost necessary to organize, store, and retrieve paper documents.

Leading firms embrace document management (DM) as a critical business tool that provides major advantages:

- Reduced paper storage costs
- Automation of back-office processes
- Integration with CRM software for increased productivity
- Simplified compliance

One of the most visible benefits of document management technology is a reduced need for physical storage space for paper files. Once a firm fully deploys a DM system, it decreases its storage requirements by eliminating the need for filing cabinets. Firms can then move into smaller offices or eliminate the need for additional space as they add more revenue-generating advisors.

Using data from the 2011 *InvestmentNews* RIA Technology Study, on average, firms spend 5 percent to 6 percent of revenue on rent costs. Laserfiche analysis shows the economies of scale produced by space reduction based on firm size. Annual savings in rent costs equate to: $8,000 for emerging firms ($500,000 and lower in revenue) or 25 percent of total average rent costs; $18,000 for established firms ($1 million in revenues) or 30 percent of total average rent costs; and $27,000 for enterprise firms ($4 million or more in revenues) or 35 percent of total average rent costs (see Table 13.5).

Among the most dramatic results of a DM system are the substantial and measurable time savings and efficiency improvements, allowing firms to provide better client service. Digital search and retrieval enables staff to locate critical information in seconds and eliminates lost files, decreasing the labor and time costs associated with getting new client signatures and recreating files. However, the benefits of DM go far beyond search and retrieval. Forward-thinking advisors use DM to automate document retention and destruction, quickly prove adherence to regulatory requirements, automatically route information for review and approval, and automate business processes through workflow engines.

Other firms use DM to automate HR onboarding, contract management, accounts payable processing, new account processing, suitability approval exception handling, and check log creation/review.

Based on working with over 2,000 financial advisors, Laserfiche conservatively estimates that the savings from back-office efficiencies equate to a 20 percent savings in staff time (see Table 13.6). For advisory firms, salaries and associated expenses for back-office staff represents 24 percent of revenue for emerging firms, 27 percent of revenue for established firms, and 23 percent of revenue for enterprise firms. Ultimately, emerging firms realize a 4.8 percent reduction in total overhead costs, established firms realize a 5.4 percent reduction in overhead costs, and enterprise firms realize a 4.6 percent reduction in overhead costs.

Many advisors dread SEC audits, and especially fear surprise audits. With DM, the ability to quickly search and retrieve documents by client, date, type, advisor, product, or any other necessary piece of information streamlines data gathering.

A firm's staff no longer spends days pulling files to get them ready for auditors. Staff can burn documents to a DVD or Blu-ray disc and deliver it to the auditors in less than one business day. Advisors themselves can also quickly pull up the requested documents. Auditors can access a workstation in an advisor's office and search directly for the documents they need during an examination instead of sequestering a firm's conference room. Specific limited-access login IDs for auditors restrict access only to requested files, protecting sensitive documents, such as those with attorney-client privilege.

TABLE 13.5 Rent Savings as a Percentage of Revenues

Size of Firm (AUM)	Emerging (<$500K)	Established ($1M)	Enterprise ($4M+)
Rent Costs	6% ($30,000)	6% ($60,000)	5% ($85,000)
Savings	1.5% ($8,000)	1.8% ($18,000)	1.0% ($27,000)

TABLE 13.6 Back-Office Savings as a Percent of Revenue

Size of Firm (AUM)	Emerging (<$500K)	Established ($1M)	Enterprise ($4M+)
Back-office staff costs as a % of annual revenue	24% ($120,000)	27% ($270,000)	23% ($920,000)
Efficiency savings (annual)	4.8% ($24,000)	5.4% ($54,000)	4.6% ($184,000)

TABLE 13.7 Compliance Time Savings as a Percent of Revenue

Size of Firm	Emerging (<$500K)	Established ($1M)	Enterprise ($4M+)
Compliance Costs	8.6% ($43,000)	7.2% ($72,000)	8.0% ($320,000)
Efficiency Savings	4.8% ($24,000)	4.0% ($40,000)	4.4% ($178,000)

The impact of compliance efficiencies in reducing total overhead costs is substantial and can be quantified in terms of time savings. Emerging firms realize $37,000 in annual savings, while an enterprise firm realizes $178,000 in annual savings as shown in Table 13.7.

Conclusion

These are just a few of the many ways advisors can magnify the return on their investment in technology as they race to build the necessary infrastructure and capacity to efficiently scale and grow their firms to take advantage of the coming opportunity for independent advice.

By implementing purpose-built technology solutions, advisors can automate, streamline, and improve client service dramatically. These simple solutions provide immediate ROI in terms of hundreds of thousands of dollars in cost savings every year combined with millions of dollars in business value created.

Thus, the message is clear: Start with a plan, challenge assumptions, think differently, take advantage of the latest advisor technology solutions, and begin investing now to get the most for your technology dollar today.

CHAPTER 14

Building an Efficient Workflow Management System

David L. Lawrence, RFC, AIF

Founder and President, EfficientPractice.com

If there is one aspect of a financial advisor's daily operations that has drawn questions in light of relatively new computer software offerings, it is workflow. Workflow management is a key way to ensure the smooth and efficient operation of a financial practice while permitting staff to accomplish common sets of tasks associated with a workflow. Workflow management systems vary, but one aspect they share in common is the establishment of a series of tasks that generally can be configured to be automatically assigned based on the completion of a prior task or workflow task set.

The advantage of these systems is the avoidance of missing steps in a workflow process and/or allowing things to slip through the cracks. Consistency and timeliness in accomplishing sets of tasks, particularly where it involves communications with the client, are important aspects of increasing the profitability and decreasing the costs associated with the practice. The reduction and/or elimination of errors and duplication of tasks are other potential advantages.

So, if it is clear that workflow is such a great benefit to financial advisory practices, why is it not more universally used? One reason may be the complexity involved in developing workflow procedures. Another may be the misperception that establishing standardized procedures in a firm detracts from the customized nature of the relationship with the client.

What Is Workflow?

To better understand and apply the concept of workflow to your financial firm, it may be necessary to first understand what workflow is, how it works, and what steps are needed to build workflow systems in your office.

One simple definition of workflow is that a workflow consists of a sequence of connected steps. It is a depiction of a sequence of operations, declared as work of a person, a group of persons, an organization or staff, or one or more simple or complex mechanisms. Workflow is a term used to describe the tasks, procedural steps, organizations or people involved, required input and output information, and tools needed for each step in a business process. A workflow approach to analyzing and managing a business process can be combined with an object-oriented programming approach, which tends to focus on documents and data. In general, workflow management focuses on processes and activities rather than documents. A number of software companies make workflow automation products that allow a company to create a workflow model and components such as online forms and then to use this product as a way to manage and enforce the consistent handling of work. For example, an insurance company could use a workflow automation application to ensure that a claim was handled consistently from initial call to final settlement. The workflow application would ensure that each person handling the claim used the correct online form and successfully completed their step before allowing the process to proceed to the next person and procedural step. In financial services, this could be translated into a workflow process for investment trading, outlining the steps necessary to perform and document the trading process with automated process steps and assignment of tasks to the appropriate employees charged with the responsibility of completing those tasks.

A workflow management system (WFMS) is the component in a workflow automation program that knows all the procedures, steps in a procedure, and rules for each step. The workflow management system determines whether the process is ready to move to the next step. Some vendors sell workflow automation products for particular industries such as financial services, insurance, and banking or for commonly used processes such as handling computer service calls. Proponents of the workflow approach believe that task analysis and workflow modeling in and of themselves are likely to improve business operations. Having an automated task assignment within the workflow environment means substantial gains in efficiency and less likelihood of steps being missed or critical functions being delayed because someone neglected to follow up or assign the next task.

The development of a workflow should have at least three steps: 1) strategic planning, which might include developing a mind map that can sort through all the random thoughts associated with workflows and organize them in some way; 2) organizational steps, in which a flowchart or other similar tool might be used to depict the flow of activities, tasks, and events associated with a particular workflow task set; 3) written steps in the workflow.

Mind Maps and Flowcharts

A mind map is a diagram used to represent words, ideas, tasks, or other items related to a central key word or idea. Mind maps are used to generate, visualize, structure, and classify ideas and as an aid to studying and organizing information, solving problems, making decisions, and writing. The constituent elements of a mind map are arranged according to the importance of the concepts. Elements are classified into groupings, branches, or areas, with the goal of representing semantic or other connections between portions of information.

By presenting ideas in a radial, graphical, nonlinear manner, mind maps encourage a brainstorming approach to planning and organizing tasks. Though the branches of a mind map represent hierarchical tree structures, their radial arrangement disrupts the prioritizing of concepts typically associated with hierarchies presented with more linear visual cues. This orientation toward brainstorming encourages users to enumerate and connect concepts without a tendency to begin within a particular conceptual framework.

Some financial practitioners already use mind maps as a tool with their clients to help organize the clients' priorities with respect to their financial and life goals. However, mind maps should also be considered as an outstanding tool for financial practitioners looking at the workflow processes within their practices.

For purposes of illustration, a mind map might look similar to the one in Figure 14.1.

If you do not already have mind mapping software, you may wish to check out www.mindjet.com, www.mindgenius.com, or the free http://freemind.sourceforge.net. Using the free version can permit you to learn how such a program can benefit you and your firm before outlaying any substantial software cost. Once you reach a certain level of proficiency, you may find it makes sense to purchase a more full-featured product. Many financial advisors have found success with the aforementioned Mind Genius software.

If you already own a version of SmartDraw (www.smartdraw.com), you may already have mind mapping capabilities. The beauty of mind mapping is the ease with which you can rearrange blocks of ideas, information, and topics to create an organized approach. Once organized, you may wish to transfer this to a flowchart to better understand and depict steps in a structural format for a workflow process.

Flowcharting is done to illustrate steps in a series of tasks associated with a workflow. There are several flowchart programs that can be used for this purpose, including the aforementioned SmartDraw.

Figure 14.2 is an example of such a flowchart. This particular one shows a variety of different kinds of elements within each task set.

Developing flowcharts that visually depict workflow task sets in a financial practice is a great training tool for new employees. Many people learn faster by visual references, rather than just lines of text describing the workflow steps. Having both published in a procedures manual (electronic or printed) gives the firm an outstanding

FIGURE 14.1 Mind Map

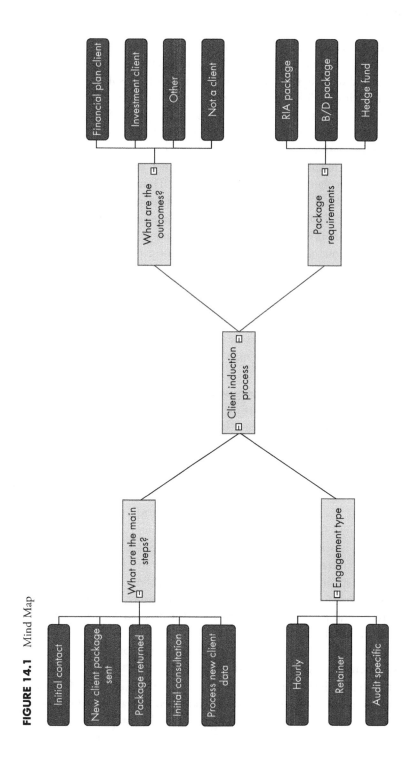

FIGURE 14.2 Sample Client Induction Process

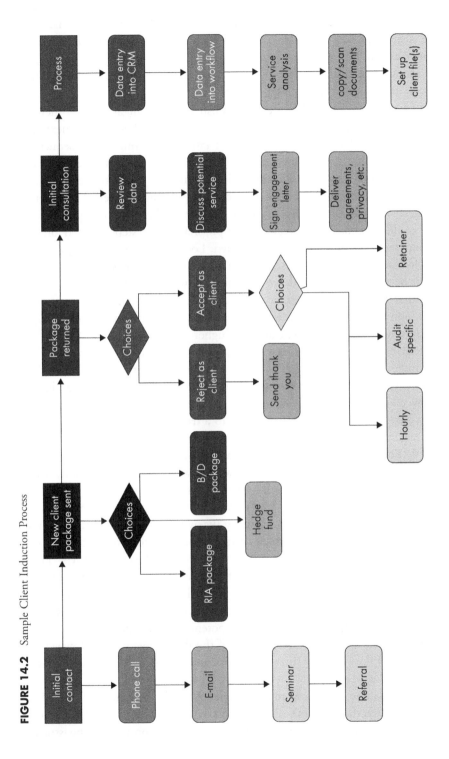

191

training and reference tool. This is not just advantageous for the new employee. It can serve as a reminder to those who perform such workflow tasks on an irregular basis or who are needed to step into a role vacated by a recently departed employee or someone on vacation.

There are at least four possible types of task sets, sequential, nonsequential, decision trees, and loop-backs (see Figure 14.3).

Sequential tasks are tasks that are accomplished one right after the other. In workflow management programs, generally the system fires (begins) the next task based on the successful completion of the last task and so on. In nonsequential (concurrent) tasks, you may have several tasks that need to be accomplished all at the same time. This would be where the completion of one task could trigger the automatic assignment of several tasks at once. In decision trees, what happened in the prior task might determine which of a list of future tasks must then be accomplished and the system could automatically create the appropriate next step(s) based on the how the prior step was completed or determined. Loop-backs are where a process is interrupted for some reason and must be restarted from an earlier point. An example of this might be the insurance underwriting process, where during the process, it is determined that the contract must be a rated policy. In this example, it may be necessary to loop back to the application step to apply to a different carrier in hopes that they might not rate the policy, causing a higher premium.

These four typical choices are easy enough, on their own, to understand. The reality of complex workflows though is that a workflow task set very likely could be composed of several different types of tasks, adding to the confusion in developing the workflow.

There is also the issue of tying workflows to a database. With some client relationship management (CRM) software programs, workflow features are available and can be directly tied to the associated client database. This offers several advantages in that if one needs to check on the status of a workflow for a particular client, it can usually be found in the client's record. Advisors Assistant (www.advisorsassistant .com), Junxure (www.junxure.com), ProTracker Advantage (www.protracker.com), Redtail (www.redtailtechnology.com), Upswing (www.upswingcrm.com), Goldmine (www.goldmine.com), and several others contain workflow features (albeit on differing levels of sophistication). However, workflow is not exclusive to CRMs. There are stand-alone workflow programs and workflow features can be found with such document management software as Laserfiche (www.laserfiche.com). One potential drawback to using workflow that is solely associated with a particular function (such as document management) is that it ignores the potential advantages of a broad-based solution that could be applied to every aspect of the firm's operations. However, in cases where the workflow is solely surrounding document management (for instance), such a solution makes sense.

Another stand-alone workflow management system is a company called Perfectforms (www.perfectforms.com). Perfectforms is a stand-alone workflow management solution that can handle simple to complex workflow processes. The issue for

FIGURE 14.3 Four Types of Task Sets

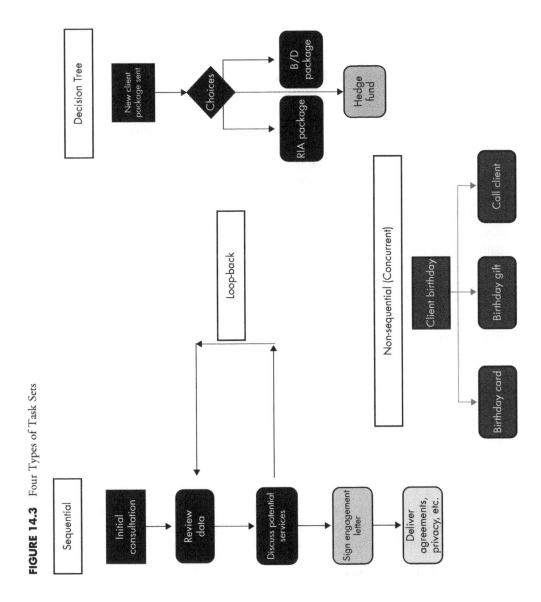

some financial practitioners with respect to nonintegrated solutions (not integrated with their client relationship management software) might be the unwieldy aspect of running a workflow process that must be manually reentered as activities into a CRM database. For this reason, it is recommended, where possible, to use integrated workflow systems (integrated within a client relationship management program if possible).

Managing the Workflow Process

Another key aspect of efficiency in the use of workflows is in the management of the workflow process. Most workflow software products have reporting capabilities that can simplify the process of managing people and resources. Having the ability to view a list of outstanding workflows and/or completed workflows can free a manager from having to constantly ask employees what work is going on in the office. Having the ability to generate FYI-type e-mails can also help; however, in busy offices this can quickly become a burdensome list of e-mails for a manager to have to sift over each day. In those cases, generating a dashboard-type reporting system or building lists for daily viewing is preferred.

In reviewing the lists, it is quick and easy to spot areas where slowdowns are occurring, which can focus a manager's attention on those items for follow-up and review. It may help in spotting training opportunities or system bottlenecks, as well. For the system to work well, managers as well as staff must be trained in how to use it effectively.

According to James Carney, CEO of ByAllAccounts, software "should work like a refrigerator." By this, he meant that software should be easy to use, work the way it is expected, and not require the user to understand how it works as much as that it works. With a refrigerator, we only want to be able to organize it to find things easily and know that it keeps our food and beverages cold. We do not necessarily need to know how the compressor works. In workflow software, the goal is to make the process of accomplishing sets of tasks easier and more efficient, as well as simplifying the management process.

In the end, how efficient workflow can be in a financial advisor's practice is going to depend on the buy-in by all parties involved in the process. With that goal in mind, firms should consider conducting strategic planning sessions with their employees that focus on workflows. In such a session, the agenda might look like the following:

Workflow Planning Session

1. **Introduction**—fleshing out the concept of workflow management, how it works, and how it can benefit the firm and its employees.
2. **Identify the potential workflow task sets**—group discussion on the workflow task sets that could be created inside a workflow management system (this might involve the use of mind mapping software).

3. **Develop the tasks**—list out the various tasks that are inclusive to a task set. In doing this, identifying who does what and when is important. Also, the group needs to define the time required of each step, the method of completion and the identification of the next step(s) in the workflow process.

4. **Results and benefits**—to gain the most buy-in from employees, it is important to not only describe the benefits to clients and the firm, but also to the employees doing the work.

5. **Management oversight**—It is also extremely important to outline management's responsibilities in the workflow process. Employees need to understand how management will oversee the workflow process, how they can spot issues and be able to lend assistance, and so on.

6. **Follow-up**—it is also important in this session to set a predetermined schedule (say quarterly) to revisit the workflows to ensure that what was set up originally continues to be the most efficient way of doing things.

Three questions to be answered in developing workflows should be:

1. Is it simple?
2. Does it work?
3. Are your employees consistently using them?

If the answer to any of those questions is no, then the workflow management system should be reengineered. Gödel's theorem applies: "No matter how perfect or complete a system, rule, or principle, it will generate anomalies at its margin that do not fit in its boundaries. Efforts to enlarge or change the system to allow for anomalies will only make it inconsistent. Thus, all systems are inherently incomplete." Recognizing this, a firm can do its best to create workflow processes with the knowledge that they are always going to be works in progress.

Epilogue

Advisor Technology: Yesterday, Today, and Tomorrow

Joel P. Bruckenstein

This book has been a major departure from the previous two books that Dave Drucker and I have authored. In our previous efforts, all of the ideas and the writing came directly from us. For this book, it dawned upon us that we were uniquely positioned to bring together an all-star group of financial services technology experts, so that's what we did. To the greatest extent possible, we allowed our authors to select their own subject matter. We also edited as lightly as possible because we wanted you to receive their thoughts and perspectives, not ours.

Despite our hands-off approach, we are both thoroughly thrilled with the outcome of our combined efforts. It confirms our long-held belief that if you put together a team of highly skilled individuals, provide them with a clear assignment, and let them do what they do best, the results will exceed expectations.

The responsibility for the last chapter, however, rests with me. In the pages that follow, I'll try to tie together some of the themes in this book and share some of my thoughts on current and future advisor technologies. Before we get to the future, however, a look to the past may be instructive.

One Example from the Archives

In preparation for writing this chapter, I reviewed the first book that Dave Drucker and I collaborated on back in 2001, *Virtual-Office Tools for a High-Margin Practice*. On the very first page of the book, before even the table of contents, is a page entitled, *How to save time, big time*. It contains two flowcharts detailing the traditional way and the virtual way of opening a new account with a custodian or broker-dealer. The old way, which hasn't changed much in the past 12 years, relies totally on paper and manual filing. We estimated that the traditional way took five days and 1.4 advisor hours. The virtual way at that time entailed completing the application, sending it as a PDF to the client, having the client sign it and mail it back to the advisor, who then faxed it to the custodian or broker-dealer, and filed the application digitally. We estimated that process took two days and approximately 0.4 advisor hours.

Now, looking back, there are a few things that come to mind. Perhaps the most distressing is that there is still a small minority of advisors who process their new account applications the traditional way. Those advisors may have survived, but they certainly did not maximize their productivity over the last dozen years.

Today, the account opening workflow is more automated and streamlined. Many custodians and broker-dealers allow their advisors to use form-filling software such as Laser App to prepopulate forms. From there, the forms can be sent electronically to the client for signature and from there routed back to the advisor and the custodian for processing. Form processing technology has improved, but the progress has not been uniform across the industry. That's about to change.

Soon, the process will get even better. With the release of Laser App's new cloud-based product, Laser App Anywhere, straight-through processing, which is only available to a small number of advisors today, will soon become commonplace. Advisors will be able to access electronic forms at any time, from anywhere, from any device, and automatically prepopulate the forms from their CRM or their broker-dealer's account opening system, route the forms securely and electronically to their clients, and then have the signed forms routed back digitally to the broker-dealer for processing with a copy filed to the advisor's document storage system. With straight-through processing, you'll be measuring the time to open an account in hours, and eventually minutes, instead of days, and the amount of time devoted to the whole process will be negligible.

There are a couple of other thoughts I'd like to highlight regarding the this example. The first is that in the near future, almost all of an advisor's paper will originate digitally, drastically reducing the amount of scanning that an advisor's office will be required to do. That's a big change from 12 years ago, when we devoted a substantial portion of *Virtual Office Tools for a High-Margin Practice* to the characteristics and selection of scanners. In this edition, we totally omitted a chapter on scanner selection (although we do cover the topic in the T3 newsletter periodically) in favor of a chapter on digital signatures, a technology we believe will become widely available to advisors over the next few years. When it does, the time required to open an account or process other paperwork will fall dramatically.

Some Lessons Learned

The example I just described also clearly illustrates a few lessons I've learned over the last decade. The first is that the more things change, the more they stay the same. By that I mean that the technologies to run a business can change, sometimes dramatically over time, but the basic business principles that should drive your technology decisions stay the same. You have to be efficient, you have to offer great customer service, and you have to keep your eye on profitability. Technology can help in all of these areas. For example, if you can achieve straight-through processing, you save time, you save money, and you improve client service. That's the role of technology, it is the means to an end, and it should be evaluated as such.

Another example is client communications. Trust is the key to the client relationship, and the best way of maintaining trust is to communicate with clients honestly, clearly, and often. Given that some clients are more receptive to certain forms of communications than others, we think it is a good idea to communicate through multiple channels. It is also essential that you deploy new communications technologies as they become available.

Years ago, Dave and I urged advisors to adopt e-mail as a form of communication. Initially, that message encountered stiff resistance from most advisors. Later, we fought the same battle over advisor websites. In this book, Bill Winterberg discusses relatively new ways of communicating and collaborating with clients. Make no mistake . . . these tools are being used by some of your peers with excellent results. Every advisor should be using some of the communication tools that Bill mentions today.

Another lesson I've learned is that you have to be willing to make mistakes when you purchase technology. I can tell you from experience that not every technology purchase meets expectations, but neither does every employee you hire, car you buy, or restaurant you eat at. I've suffered my share of buyer's remorse even when technology does work as promised. For example, in our first book, I discussed USB flash storage devices, which were new at the time. Back then, a 128-megabyte drive retailed between $150 and $300, depending on the manufacturer. Today, you can find one with 125 times that capacity for less than $10.00. That does not mean that the flash drive I purchased over a decade ago was a bad buy, I got a great deal of use out of it, and having a copy of a presentation on a flash drive saved me numerous times.

Yet another lesson I've learned is that ROI is important, but it is not the only important thing. This book contains an excellent chapter by Tim Welsh on technology ROI, so there is no need for me to make that case. Suffice it to say that the ROI argument for purchasing advisor technology is compelling. As a speaker, writer, and consultant I often emphasize ROI when I discuss technology with advisors because it is such an easy case to make, but it is not the only one. Lifestyle and job satisfaction matter, as well. When Dave and I, independently of each other, attempted to build virtual financial planning firms, we were not exclusively focused on ROI, although we were aware of the financial benefits. For both of us, the virtual office was just as much about lifestyle and job satisfaction. We both wanted to be relieved of mundane tasks that we hated doing, so we either found a technology solution to help us do them, or we outsourced them. Neither one of us liked being tied to a desk at our office, so we adopted technologies that allowed us to work from wherever we wanted to be. Granted, that is much easier today than it was back then, and we had to deal with numerous roadblocks along the way, but the rewards have far outweighed the inconveniences.

We readily acknowledge that many of our peers had, and continue to have, a different set of priorities, but the next generation of planners more closely resembles us than our peers. They want a job that is stimulating and satisfying, they want to work flexible hours, they want to work remotely some of the time, and they expect state of the art technology, because that's what they use in their private lives. If your firm can't offer those things, you will not retain talented employees; they will go work for your competitor who does offer them what they want.

Looking Forward

Hockey great Wayne Gretzky once said, "I skate where the puck is going to be, not where it has been." All too often in our industry, people take too long to make technology decisions and to implement them. The result is that often, by time they have implemented a new technology, they end up where the puck has been instead of where it is going.

Many of the chapters in this book discuss not only today's technologies, but where these technologies are headed. From my unique role as a financial services technology columnist and a coproducer of the Technology Tools for Today conference, I spend a great deal of time thinking about the future of advisor technology. With the disclaimer that predicting the future is impossible, especially for me, I thought it might be useful to discuss some current trends and developments that are likely to shape the future of the advisory business for years to come.

- *The changing financial planning landscape.* As both Dr. Linda Strachan and Bob Curtis discuss in their chapters, professional financial planning and the technology that supports it is evolving. Scalable, goal-based plans can now be better tailored to the needs of the individual client. Smarter software allows you to only enter the data needed for a given situation, and it can generate only the report pages necessary. More importantly, manual data entry is being minimized, and in the case of integrated solutions, eliminated. The ability to produce financial plans more efficiently at a lower cost will open up a whole new market for financial planning professionals. This new group of potential customers desperately needs professional financial planning help, but they previously thought that they could not afford it. By delivering targeted plans through the use of better technologies, the industry has an opportunity to promote financial planning on a scale that was unimaginable a few short years ago.
- *Client reporting will change—for the better.* If I had to select the greatest failing I've seen throughout the profession, it is probably the area of client reporting. Operationally, client reporting is a mess at many firms. They create paper reports through a manual, expensive, time-consuming process. Bill Winterberg's chapter describes how client portals and other technologies allow advisors to deliver digital documents to clients in an automated, cost effective, and secure manner. I firmly believe that within a few years, the vast majority of clients will expect their reports digitally. There's a larger problem associated with reporting that technology can also help solve: The content of the reports themselves. Traditionally, financial advisors have told their clients that financial planning is a long-term, ongoing process. "Don't

worry about short-term market gyrations," we say. "Stay focused on your long-term goals." Unfortunately, the reporting methods of most firms only serve to contradict that message. Typically, firms produce quarterly or semiannual performance reports for clients. These reports track the short-term values of the portfolio against a standard benchmark such as the Standard & Poor's 500 or a custom blended benchmark. In either case, the focus is on short-term performance against a benchmark that tells clients nothing about their progress toward meeting their own long-term goals. There is a better way: Advisors can and should produce periodic reports (delivered digitally, of course) that benchmark a client's portfolio against his or her ability to meet their financial goals. With the integrations now in place between financial planning software, custodians, and performance reporting systems, this type of reporting is now possible. By the time you read this, Orion Advisor Services will be making this type of reporting capability available to its reporting clients through its integration with MoneyGuidePro. I expect this type of report to replace the traditional quarterly report in financial planning firms over the next several years.

- *The mobile revolution will continue.* Historically, financial advisors have not been early adopters; but adoption of the iPad was an exception to the rule. Many advisors purchased iPads before they even knew how they might use them in their businesses, but they have quickly figured it out. Today, we estimate that over 50 percent of advisors use a tablet in their business. Of those, the iPad is the dominant tablet in the advisor space, with about 85 percent of advisors choosing it; that compares with an approximately 65 percent global tablet market share for the iPad, as of this time. Advisors are using iPads in many different, productive ways. They are accessing information from their CRM, portfolio management, financial planning, and custodial platforms via the iPad. In some cases, they are even placing trades with iPads. They are storing internal documents, such as procedure manuals, in digital form so they can be read using an iBook or other similar application. They are using an iPad in conjunction with AirPlay and/or Apple TV to conduct client presentations. Some are handing out iPads to clients at meetings and running presentations on the clients' iPads. iPads may not dominate forever. Windows 8 tablets will be available by the time you read this. Whether they can make a serious dent in Apple's market share remains to be seen, but tablets and other mobile technologies will continue to thrive within the advisor space for years to come, enabling greater mobility for advisors. It is also worth remembering that the clients of advisors use mobile devices, so making your firm mobile friendly, through a mobile-compatible website and an app for your firm are now business essentials.

- *We are all headed for the cloud.* Although many advisors are still apprehensive about the cloud, resistance is starting to fade. That's a good thing, because the software as a service (SaaS) model will dominate in the years to come. Over the last several years, all of the growth in financial planning software and portfolio management software has come from SaaS programs, not traditional desktop/server software. The SaaS model can provide better integration, economies of scale, improved security, and other benefits. Before you buy one more server for your office, ask yourself whether it is really necessary, or whether there is another, more efficient way of running the software and storing the files that you need.

- *Mass market challenges are ahead.* A number of intelligent, wealthy individuals and well-financed firms believe that they can commoditize financial advice and automate it through technology, just as the retail brokerage industry and the retail banking industry have been largely automated and commoditized. Personally, I don't believe that financial advice lends itself to commoditization, but it could happen if the industry is complacent. One thing that the online services do well is technology, and with scale, they can deliver it at a very low cost. The quality of the advice and the ongoing monitoring by a professional is another matter. If this industry continues to focus exclusively on the top 1 percent of the population, it will open the door to the consumer-facing competition. If, on the other hand, we leverage the new technologies at our disposal to reach a larger audience, I feel certain that the value professional advisors deliver will prevail.

- *There may be rough sledding ahead for free and freemium advisor-facing services.* Many companies have been successful in attracting a loyal customer base in the mass market space by adopting a free or a freemium model. With the former, the model is often financed by advertising or some other form of sponsorship. With the latter, the idea is to offer a basic free service, such as e-mail, online storage, account aggregation, and so on, and then try to make money through a premium paid service. It should come as no surprise then that some enterprising individuals are trying to adopt the free or freemium models to financial advisory technology. The pitch is alluring: "Why spend thousands of dollars for financial planning software, portfolio management software, and the like if you can get it for free?" I'll give you a few reasons. First, with respect to some software products like CRM and financial planning software, the annual cost, especially for smaller firms that the free models are most likely to appeal to, is small in the overall scheme of things. So, unless the free product is so far superior to the paid one that advisors would use it anyway, it is just not worth the switch; and if it is clearly better, why offer it for free? In most of the other models I've seen to date, there are inherent conflicts built into the models. Is it possible to overcome these hurdles? I suppose it is, but until I see at least one successful implementation of this model in the financial advisory space, I'll continue to view such endeavors with some skepticism.

- *The pace of technological innovation in our industry will continue to accelerate.* Due to my position, I'm privy to a lot of information about products in development, and I feel very confident that advisor technology will continue to improve, strictly based on what I've seen in the developmental pipeline. It is also worth noting that many of the firms that served independent advisors a decade ago were mom and pop shops with limited financial resources. As this industry has grown, so have our technology vendors. Many are large, publicly traded firms with significant R&D budgets. Others are private, but they, too, have substantial financial strength. Furthermore, as the industry has grown, it has attracted new talent that in the past regarded this market as too small to bother with. For all of these reasons, I feel confident that advisor technology will continue to evolve rapidly to the benefit of all advisors and their clients.

In Closing

For Dave, for myself, and for all the authors who so generously devoted their time and effort to share their insights with you, this book has been a labor of love. We truly believe in this profession, and we sincerely believe that advisors armed with the proper technology and outsourced partners can achieve greater growth, efficiency, profitability, and job satisfaction. If you've taken the time to read this book, you have already taken the first step to improve your business. Don't stop there. Implement one or more of the technologies we've recommended, and begin to reap the benefits today.

About the Authors

David J. Drucker

Under the banner of "Drucker Knowledge Systems," David J. Drucker, MBA, CFP, provides the benefit of his more than 30 years of experience and research to other members of the financial services industry.

He is the co-author of *The Tools & Techniques of Practice Management* (The National Underwriter Company, 2004) and *Virtual Office Tools for a High-Margin Practice: How Client-Centered Financial Advisors Can Cut Paperwork, Overhead, and Wasted Hours* (Bloomberg Press, 2002). He is also editor of the monthly newsletter *Technology Tools for Today* (formerly *Virtual Office News*).

Drucker has written about practice management issues for financial advisors as a columnist or contributor to *Financial Advisor, Financial Planning, Wealth Manager*, and *Research* magazines, as a monthly columnist for MorningstarAdvisor.com and as co-founder of *Technology Tools for Today*.

In addition to his writing and consulting, Drucker is an independent financial advisor who started his own advisory firm in the Washington, D.C., area in 1981 after working as a financial analyst in government and private industry for over 10 years. Drucker still manages the financial affairs of a limited number of high net worth clients as president of Sunset Financial Management, Inc., an Albuquerque, New Mexico, state-registered advisory firm.

Drucker is a member of the Financial Planning Association and the National Association of Personal Financial Advisors (NAPFA), and has served in a variety of NAPFA regional board member and conference planning roles during his many years of membership. He was named by the readers of *Financial Planning* magazine to its 2003 list of Movers, Shakers & Decision-Makers, and by *Worth* magazine as one of the Best Financial Advisors in the United States every year from the beginning of the Worth survey in 1994 through its 2001 listings when Drucker cut back his financial planning activities. In May 1996, he was given the NAPFA Distinguished Service Award for his contributions to the fee-only financial planning community.

He is the original author of INTEGRATE financial planning software used by him and other financial advisors nationwide, now developed and distributed by PlanWare, Inc. Drucker is also a past member of the American Society of Journalists and Authors, serving on its finance committee, as well as the Rydex Funds' Skip Viragh Award Advisory Board.

Joel P. Bruckenstein

Joel P. Bruckenstein is publisher of Technology Tools for Today (www.Technology ToolsforToday.com) and a coproducer of the Technology Tools for Today (T3) Conference, the only annual technology/practice management conference for independent advisors.

Bruckenstein is an internationally acclaimed expert on applied technology as it relates to the financial service industry. He has advised financial service firms of all sizes on improving their technologies, processes, and workflows.

He is co-author of two books with David Drucker: *Virtual Office Tools for a High-Margin Practice: How Client-Centered Financial Advisors Can Cut Paperwork, Overhead, and Wasted Hours* and *Tools & Techniques of Practice Management.*

Bruckenstein was named by the readers of *Financial Planning* magazine to its 2006 list of Movers & Shakers. His expert opinions have appeared in many of the industry's leading publications as well as in the national media. Joel also writes a monthly technology column for *Financial Advisor Magazine* and *Financial Planning Magazine.* In addition, he compiles the annual technology survey for *Financial Planning Magazine.*

About the Contributors

J. D. Bruce, MS, CPA, PFS

President, Abacus Wealth Partners

The reason I got into this profession:

My father was a hippie, so naturally I became a CPA. Being a hippie criminal defense attorney, my father fought "the man" and defended the wrongly accused. He was a defender of the Constitution and an enthusiastic revolutionary. He also didn't like following rules, like the tax code.

When I was 18, studying theater at the local community college, my father had an unfortunate misunderstanding with the IRS. We ended up losing our 4,000-square-foot house by the beach and moving to a much smaller home where privacy was hard to find and secrets were difficult to keep. That's when I started to see through the cracks and learned about how your relationship to money can hurt you.

When I was 20, still a theater student, I steeled myself and asked my father if he had filed his taxes that year. "I'll get to it," he said, which I knew meant "I won't get to it anytime soon, if at all." So, being a computer geek, I drove to the local CompUSA and looked for a box that had the word *tax* on it. I sat my father down, armed with my shiny copy of TurboTax, and filed my first tax return.

The next day, my best friend said, "Wait, you can do taxes?" That day, I became a financial advisor in fact, but didn't yet know that's what it was called.

The path from there to Abacus was filled with twists. It pulled out from UCLA and made a switchback from theater to accounting. It passed through Price Waterhouse with a ponytail. It went up the mountains of initial public offerings (IPOs) and down the valleys of liquidation. It made a stop in advertising and did the express train through consulting. It never stayed in one place long. Then it pulled into a station that felt like home.

The first thing I remember learning about Abacus is that a condition of employment was a willingness to explore the shadow places, both inside myself and in my relationships with others. Here was a place that cared as much (or more) about people as about profit. When I told people that I was joining Abacus, I said, "I'm starting the last job I'll ever have."

Now, my mission is to make every Abacus client say out loud at some point in the future, "Abacus saved my life."

Robert D. Curtis

Founder, President, and CEO of PIEtech, Inc. and Designer of MoneyGuidePro

Bob Curtis has over 30 years' experience as an innovator in the software industry. For the past 20 years, he has designed financial planning software for the financial services industry, and is a leader in developing easy-to-use, interactive software for use by advisors and their clients.

In 1997, Curtis founded PIEtech, Inc. As president and CEO of PIE, Curtis oversees product development, business development, and the day-to-day operations of the company. In addition, he serves as lead designer of PIE's MoneyGuidePro (MGP) financial planning software.

At its debut in 2000, MoneyGuidePro was one of the first financial planning programs created for interactive, web-based use. In 2008, PIE released MGP: G2 (Generation 2), the first financial planning SMARTware, which was selected by Joel Bruckenstein, CFP (in *Morningstar Advisor*), as Software Product of the Year. MoneyGuidePro is currently used by over 25,000 financial services professionals.

Prior to forming PIE, Curtis served as President and CEO of two organizations: Compulife, Inc., an investment and insurance marketing firm, and Compulife Investor Services, a registered broker-dealer. Through its work with bank brokerage firms, Compulife became one of the top 10 marketing organizations in the industry, and was a consistent leader in its use of sales technology.

Before joining Compulife, Curtis owned and operated a software development company, providing accounting software for small businesses.

Curtis is the author of "Monte Carlo Mania," published in *Retirement Income Redesigned: Master Plans for Distribution* by Bloomberg Press in April 2006. In January 2009, he was selected as one of six industry "Movers and Shakers" by *Financial Planning* magazine. He has a BS in finance from Lehigh University.

Jennifer Goldman, CFP

President, My Virtual COO

Jennifer Goldman, CFP, President of My Virtual COO, assists advisors in making their practices more profitable and scalable. COO's team creates processes that maximize the use of technology and virtual staff, implements the process and tech, and maintains operations for firms across the country. The COO team shares their expertise in roles as varied as CEO and COO with growth-oriented firms.

Before founding My Virtual COO, Goldman served in numerous executive and operational roles that prepared her to help advisors run their practices at peak operational efficiency. Her past positions include the Division Coordinator for a 150+-person wealth management and insurance firm, Operations Coordinator for a 45+-person tax and wealth management firm, Certified Planner and Family COO for national business owner clientele, creator of a $22 million advisory business in two years, and Quality Control Manager at M&T Bank.

Goldman has been quoted and published in *Inc.* magazine, *Technology Tools for Today*, *NAPFA Journal*, *Inside Information*, *InvestmentNews*, and other industry publications. She speaks frequently at conferences such as FPA National, FPA local chapters, and T3, and provides webinars to national audiences, sharing her expertise regarding processes, technology, and virtual staff content.

Davis D. Janowski

Technology Reporter at *InvestmentNews*

I have been a journalist for 20 years, the past 13 spent covering technology; I am currently with *InvestmentNews*, where I am both a columnist and reporter. In that role for the past five years I have learned a great deal about financial services, most specifically about the technology in use with or desired by financial advisors. Prior to that I spent almost a decade with *PC* magazine as editor, writer, reviewer, and analyst, where I covered both a wide range of consumer and business technology. I started my career as a medical editor and writer covering the field of epidemiology and infectious diseases, having received training at the Centers for Disease Control. My personal love, though, has been the outdoors. I've been a dually certified National Association of Underwater Instructors (NAUI)-YMCA scuba diver for 25 years with over a thousand dives, the majority in the Gulf of Mexico or the rivers and springs of the Florida Panhandle where I grew up. I've served as a volunteer on the Emanuel Point shipwreck excavation and conservation project and as a volunteer supply diver on the Woodville Karst Plain Project. I regularly enjoy paddling my two Folbot sea kayaks along the Hudson River, many of the lakes and rivers in the Adirondacks, the Gulf of Mexico, and off the coast of Southern California. I've solo backpacked extensively in the Adirondack High Peaks region and the southern Adirondacks, as well as many weeklong jaunts along the Appalachian Trail. I'm a bushwhacker, GPS and geocaching enthusiast, snowshoer, and Eagle Scout.

Christopher J. Kail

Director of Marketing, Legend Financial Advisors, Inc. and EmergingWealth Investment Management, Inc.

Christopher Kail joined Legend Financial Advisors, Inc. full-time in May 2001 and is currently Legend's Director of Marketing and a shareholder with the firm. Kail's primary responsibilities entail strategic planning and execution of the firm's marketing campaigns. This includes managing Legend's marketing databases and media relations efforts, developing search engine optimization and Internet marketing initiatives, creating comprehensive marketing plans, and coordinating the publishing and delivery of Legend's various publications.

His role at Legend also includes developing networking meetings with local attorneys and accountants in order to develop possible referral relationships. Kail is also responsible for reviewing and updating Legend's company website content, conducting market research, seeking article publishing opportunities, and preparing all marketing materials for prospective clients, direct mailings, and company events. Kail also manages and coordinates the efforts of Legend's marketing internship program.

Kail also spearheads many marketing strategies for Wealth Advisor Publishing, Inc., a Pittsburgh, Pennsylvania–based publisher of financially oriented publications and producer of educational webcasts for financial advisors, the financial media, as well as the general public. Chris assists with the company's various publications, including the *Global Economic & Investment Analytics* newsletter, a cutting-edge HTML newsletter directed to financial advisors. The publication provides economic and investment-oriented research, analysis, and educational content for financial advisors. Delivered on a weekly basis, the newsletter is sent to a nationwide audience of financial advisory professionals.

Kail is actively involved in various local professional and charitable organizations, including being a board member for the Northern Allegheny County Chamber of Commerce, where he serves as the chairperson of the Education Committee. Kail is a member of Duquesne University's Marketing Advisory Board. He is frequently invited to speak at local universities on various marketing and public relations topics and internship opportunities for students. He has spoken to Carnegie Mellon University's student chapter of the American Marketing Association (AMA), Duquesne University's chapter of the AMA, and the Public Relations Student Society of America (PRSSA).

Kail's extensive charity work includes being a board member of the Greater Pittsburgh Unit of the American Cancer Society, where he has served on the Executive Committee as assistant treasurer. He also serves as a member of the Larry Richert Celebrity Golf Classic Committee, coordinates an annual Daffodil Days fund-raising campaign, and is a team leader for the "Making Strides Against Breast Cancer" walk event. Kail is a former board member for Variety's Young Professionals (VYP), promoting the mission of Variety, the Children's Charity, throughout southwestern Pennsylvania and providing mobility equipment and assistive technology and communication devices for children with disabilities. In 2008, Kail served as chairperson of the Wheelchair Grand Prix, VYP's signature fund-raising event. Kail is also a past "Pittsburgh's 50 Finest" honoree and has previously served on the 50 Finest Steering Committee for the Cystic Fibrosis Foundation.

Kail graduated from Duquesne University in May 2001 with a bachelor of arts degree in communication studies. Furthermore, he has obtained a master's degree from Duquesne in corporate communications with a concentration in integrated marketing communication. Kail previously worked as a public relations intern at Bozell Kamstra Advertising and Public Relations (now Mullen Advertising & Public Relations) and ultimately became a marketing intern at Legend in November 2000. Kail is a native of Bethel Park, Pennsylvania, and currently resides in the South Side of Pittsburgh.

Mike Kelly

President, Back Office Support Service

Michael Kelly is the President and CEO of Back Office Support Service (BOSS), a company founded in 1996 for the specific purpose of operating portfolio management software for advisors on an outsource basis.

Kelly's academic credentials include a bachelor's degree in engineering management from the U.S. Air Force Academy and a master's degree in systems management from the Air Force Institute of Technology. He received his RIA and Registered Principal licenses in 1978 and his CFP designation in 1979. All licenses were terminated in 1996 when BOSS was established.

Daniel D. Kleck

Marketing Coordinator, Legend Financial Advisors, Inc. and EmergingWealth Investment Management, Inc.

Dan Kleck joined Legend Financial Advisors, Inc. full-time in January 2012 as a marketing coordinator. He graduated from the University of Pittsburgh with a bachelor of arts degree in media and professional communication with a concentration in corporate and community relations.

Kleck's primary responsibilities at Legend include producing electronic publications, managing the content and design of various company websites, and planning and promotion of various educational webcasts presented by Legend and its affiliated companies. In addition, he assists in training and development of staff members. He is also a member of Legend's Marketing Committee.

Kleck also leads the website design and development for Wealth Advisor Publishing, Inc., a Pittsburgh, Pennsylvania–based publisher of financially oriented publications and producer of educational webcasts for financial advisors and the financial media, as well as the general public. Kleck designs and maintains newsletters and websites for the company's various publications, including the *Global Economic & Investment Analytics* newsletter, a cutting-edge HTML newsletter directed to financial advisors.

David L. Lawrence, RFC, AIF

Founder and President, EfficientPractice.com

David Lawrence has over 36 years of experience in leadership. He is a veteran of the U.S. Navy during the Vietnam War, having spent over four years on active duty as a noncommissioned officer and later as a commissioned officer in the Naval Reserves. His service in two war zones, first in South Vietnam near the end of the Vietnam War and later in the Middle East, provides a courageous backdrop to his leadership experiences. His compelling story of military leadership during a time of domestic political unrest is truly inspirational.

Lawrence is a graduate of the University of South Florida in Tampa, with a double undergraduate and master's degree (cum laude). He attended the University of Florida in Gainesville for his doctorate in social behaviorism. Lawrence then spent 18 years with a major financial planning firm as a senior financial advisor, training manager, and district manager. He has also worked for two large independent financial planning and asset management companies in senior management positions. His responsibilities have included managing large numbers of employees as well as setting up employee hiring, training, evaluation, and compensation systems.

His background and experience in integrating technological systems with management needs have given him a unique perspective on the use of technology as a leadership tool. Lawrence has spent the past several years writing and speaking. He founded the Efficient Practice, a consulting company devoted to growth efficiency solutions for financial services institutions and their representatives. His speaking engagements have taken him all across the United States, Canada, and the Far East. Conversant in five languages, he is acutely aware of and sensitive to the need for efficient communications in leadership and in life. David is a current member of the International Speakers Network (ISN). He has been frequently quoted by such national publications as *Barron's*, *Financial Planning Interactive*, *USA Today*, and the *Wall Street Journal Online*, among others. He has written articles for *Practice Lifecycle*, the Investment Management Consultants Association (IMCA) *Investments & Wealth Monitor*, the Virtual Office newsletter, and the Turning Point Inc. newsletter. He has also made frequent appearances on NBC and FOX television affiliates. He is a sought-after public speaker on a variety of leadership, financial, and technical topics.

He is a past president of the Financial Planning Association (FPA) of Tampa Bay and is active in that organization on a national level as past chair of the FPA's National Leadership Council. Further, he was the chair of the FPA's 2006 National Leadership Conference. Lawrence currently is a monthly columnist and contributing editor for *Financial Advisor* magazine (www.fa-mag.com). He carries the professional designations of Registered Financial Consultant (RFC) and Accredited Investment Fiduciary (AIF).

Jason Lindstrom

Managing Partner, AdvisorWebsites.com

Jason Lindstrom is the managing partner at AdvisorWebsites.com, where he manages product development and North American operations. He has over 10 years' experience in the web development industry and has launched hundreds of websites for the commercial, nonprofit, and financial sectors.

Lindstrom received an honors degree in communications and publishing from Simon Fraser University. During his academic career he was recognized as one of the top three entrepreneurs in Canada in the CIBC Student Entrepreneur of the Year Awards for founding Tidal Interactive, a web development agency that focused on large-scale web development projects.

He is passionate about web usability and staying on top of the latest technical standards. Lindstrom is a regular public speaker and likes to speak about both entrepreneurship and web usability.

Lindstrom is married to Opi Lindstrom and loves skiing, cycling, and swimming. In 2009 he competed in the 2009 Triathlon World Championships in Australia.

Jon Patullo

Managing Director, Technology Product Management, TD Ameritrade Institutional

Jon Patullo is responsible for all advisor-facing technology, products, and services for TD Ameritrade Institutional. These responsibilities include oversight of the Veo platform, Advisor Client platform, and third-party technology relationships.

Since joining the company in 1996, Patullo has been focused on building and supporting technology products and services available to the institutional client base, and was a critical force in bringing proprietary and third-party tools and information to clients. He has held multiple management positions in customer support, electronic trading, content management, and product management.

Patullo graduated from Rider University with a degree in finance and is based in Fort Worth, Texas. He currently holds Series 7, 9, 10, and 63 securities representative licenses.

Dan Skiles

Executive Vice President, Shareholders Service Group

As Executive Vice President at Shareholders Service Group (SSG), Dan Skiles is involved in all aspects of managing the firm. Specific areas of focus include technology, compliance, business operations, and strategy. Prior to joining SSG in 2009, Skiles was with the Charles Schwab Corporation, where he had responsibilities with the planning and development of technology solutions for Schwab Institutional and leading Schwab Performance Technologies, Inc., a subsidiary of the Charles Schwab Corporation. In addition, during his eight years at Schwab he visited hundreds of investment advisor offices and spoke frequently at industry events. Before joining Schwab in 2001, he spent eight years with TD Waterhouse and was responsible for implementing technology solutions for the firm's investment advisor clients. Skiles is a leading industry expert who is often quoted in advisor trade publications, and he also writes a monthly article for *Investment Advisor* magazine.

He earned a bachelor's degree and a master's in business from San Diego State University.

Sherri M. Slafka

Marketing and Contracts Coordinator, Publication Operations Coordinator, and Associate Editor, Legend Financial Advisors, Inc. and EmergingWealth Investment Management, Inc.

Sherri Slafka initially began her career with Legend Financial Advisors, Inc. of Pittsburgh, Pennsylvania, while completing her undergraduate degree at Westminster College. Her background includes public relations and marketing, which she utilized during her internship in Legend's marketing department, where she focused on media relations activities, creating media interview opportunities for members of Legend's advisory team, implementing various marketing initiatives, and honing her skills in proofreading and editing. Slafka subsequently made a return to the firm, joining full-time as a Marketing and Contracts Coordinator for Legend. She also serves as the Public Operations Coordinator and Associate Editor for an affiliated company, Wealth Advisor Publishing, Inc. At Wealth Advisor Publishing, Slafka coordinates the proofreading and editing process for *Global Economic & Investment Analytics*, a weekly HTML newsletter directed at financial advisors that provides economic and investment-oriented research, analysis, and educational content.

At Legend, Slafka has been instrumental in her role of overseeing client contracts and vendor agreements. She also manages the tracking of the firm's communications with prospective clients, creates media interview opportunities, and trains other staff members and interns on various marketing responsibilities.

Slafka is a resident of Irwin, Pennsylvania, and enjoys supporting her favorite charities, including the Juvenile Diabetes Research Foundation (JDRF), American Cancer Society, and the Susan G. Komen Breast Cancer Foundation. She is an avid ziplining enthusiast and world traveler.

Louis P. Stanasolovich, CFP

CCO, CEO, Founder and President, Legend Financial Advisors, Inc. and EmergingWealth Investment Management, Inc.

Louis P. Stanasolovich, CFP, is founder, CCO, CEO, and President of Legend Financial Advisors, Inc. and EmergingWealth Investment Management, Inc. Stanasolovich is also the Editor of *Risk-Controlled Investing*, a subscription service that guides financial advisors on how to build investment portfolios with lower risk. He is also the Editor of *Global Economic & Investment Analytics*, a cutting-edge HTML newsletter providing economic and investment-oriented research, analysis, and educational content for financial advisors. Stanasolovich is one of only four advisors nationwide to be selected 12 consecutive times by *Worth* magazine as one of "The Top 100 Wealth Advisors" in the country. Stanasolovich has also been selected eight times by *Medical Economics* magazine as one of "The 150 Best Financial Advisors for Doctors in America," twice as one of "The 100 Great Financial Planners in America" by *Mutual Funds* magazine, twice by *Dental Practice Report* as one of "The Best Financial Advisors for Dentists in America," and once by *Barron's* as one of "The Top 100 Independent Financial Advisors."

Stanasolovich was selected by *Financial Planning* magazine as one of six individuals to receive the inaugural Influencer Awards for 2010. The category that Stanasolovich was selected for was the Wealth Creator award recognizing the advisor who has made the most significant contributions to best practices for portfolio management. He has been named three times to *Investment Advisor* magazine's "IA 25" list, ranking the 25 most influential people in and around the financial advisory profession, as well as being named by *Financial Planning* magazine as one of the country's "Movers & Shakers," recognizing the top individuals who have done the most to advance the financial advisory profession. He has also been named by *Fortune Small Business* magazine as one of "America's Best Bosses." Through Stanasolovich's leadership, Legend was named to the *Inc.* 5,000 list (number 4,235) for the three-year period from 2007 through 2009 as one of the fastest-growing private companies in the United States. Stanasolovich was also selected three consecutive years by *Smart Business Pittsburgh* as a Pacesetter, an award that recognizes outstanding and innovative business and community leaders who have made a significant impact on the region and its future. In 2009, Stanasolovich was selected as a nominee for the Ernst & Young "Entrepreneur of the Year" award for the Upstate New York, western Pennsylvania, and West Virginia region.

Linda Strachan, PhD

Vice President, Product Management, Zywave, Inc.

Linda Strachan has been involved in the development of financial planning and needs analysis software solutions for almost 20 years. She is Senior Vice President of Product Management for Zywave, Inc., where she directs product marketing and strategy for the company's financial planning products, including NaviPlan and Profiles. She previously held a variety of product marketing and senior leadership positions at EISI during her 17-year tenure there prior to Zywave's acquisition of the company. A Certified Financial Planner, Strachan helped direct the firm's financial planning and needs analysis tools from inception. The solutions today continue to be a leading technology choice of financial professionals. Strachan has a PhD in computer science specializing in artificial intelligence from the University of Manitoba.

Marie Swift

Principal, Impact Communications

Marie Swift is a nationally recognized consultant who has for more than 20 years worked exclusively with some of the industry's top financial institutions, training organizations, and investment advisory and financial planning firms. A top-rated speaker at dozens of industry events, including the Financial Planning Association (FPA), National Association of Personal Financial Advisors (NAPFA), TD Ameritrade Institutional, Securities America, Schwab Institutional, NFL Players Association, Financial Network, Investacorp, Transamerica, and Pershing and Lockwood conferences, Marie is dedicated to elevating the conversation in the industry.

Swift is also a prolific writer and contributes to many of the industry's leading publications. Previous multiyear columns were published by AdvisorOne.com ("Transitions"), *Wealth Manager* magazine, *Research* magazine, and Morningstar Advisor.com. You can read Swift's newest content on www.financial-planning.com, where she writes the biweekly "Marketing Maven" column, and on www.advisorone.com/transitions, where her "Transitions" column is housed.

A thought leader for thought leaders, she is known for bringing some of the industry's best and brightest voices together for dialogue and debate. Her *Thought Leader Round Table* series is just one example of how Swift generates interesting conversations with movers and shakers in the financial services industry.

Her *Best Practices in the Financial Services Industry* blog provides additional insights and advice, including podcasts, articles, videos, and other helpful content for independent financial advisors and the institutions that serve them. Find it at www.marieswift.com.

Prior to establishing her own firm in 1993, she served as director of corporate communications for Worldwide Investment Network in Irvine, California, where she helped FNIC's then #1 Top Producer attain and maintain that title for five consecutive years. She managed a staff of 20 who supported two dozen successful registered representatives, estate planners, and wealth managers.

As President and CEO of Impact Communications, Inc., Swift leads a dedicated team of marketing communications and PR professionals serving financial institutions and a select group of independent advisors on an exclusive basis. Swift resides in Leawood, Kansas, and can be reached through her website at www.ImpactCommunications.org.

Kory Wells

Product Director of Data Analytics, Zywave, Inc.

Kory Wells became involved with workers' compensation almost 20 years ago as one of the first programmers of ModMaster, a market-leading software product in the experience rating analysis niche. Now a Product Director of Data Analytics for Zywave, Inc., she edits and frequently contributes to the *WorkCompEdge* blog, where she discusses experience rating basics, changes, and many other factors impacting workers' compensation costs. A published author in both professional and creative genres, she has participated in state and national webinars with the Independent Insurance Agents & Brokers of America (IIABA) and is presenting at the National Workers' Compensation and Disability Conference in November 2012. Visit her blog at www.zywave.com/workcompedgeblog and follow her on Twitter, where she's known as WorkCompEdge.

Timothy D. Welsh, CFP

President and Founder, Nexus Strategy, LLC

Timothy D. Welsh, CFP, is president and founder of Nexus Strategy, LLC, a leading consulting firm to the wealth management industry. Nexus Strategy's primary focus is working with investment advisors on growth strategies as well as partnering with leading financial services and technology firms to distribute products and services through the advisor channel.

Prior to founding Nexus Strategy, Welsh was director of business consulting services for Schwab Advisor Services, where he led the development and marketing of practice management resources for independent advisors, including an award-winning suite of business succession, financing, and mergers and acquisition (M&A) services, along with the industry's leading platform for referral marketing. While at Schwab, Welsh also held senior roles in strategy, marketing, advertising, PR, and event content development.

Prior to joining Schwab, Welsh was vice president at Merrill Lynch, where he was responsible for marketing, product development, and financial advisor training for the financial planning group. Welsh is the author of a number of industry white papers and articles and is a frequent speaker at industry conferences and events. He earned a bachelor's degree in economics from the University of California, Berkeley, and an MBA in finance from the University of Colorado.

Welsh holds the Certified Financial Planner (CFP) designation and is an active member of the Financial Planning Association (FPA), serving in a leadership role on a number of task forces, committees, and most recently as an elected member of the National Board of Directors.

Bill Winterberg, CFP

Consultant, FPPad.com

Bill Winterberg, founder of FPPad.com, is the technology columnist for *Morningstar Advisor* and technology contributor to the *Journal of Financial Planning*. He has been quoted in a variety of leading publications, including *USA Today*, Reuters, the *Wall Street Journal*, *SmartMoney*, *Financial Planning* magazine, and more.

Winterberg has past experience as a registered representative, a registered investment advisor, and an operations manager. He consults with financial professionals in the selection and implementation of the right technology solutions for their practices. Prior to entering the financial services industry, He was an embedded software engineer for Hewlett Packard Co. and LeapFrog Toys.

Bart Wisniowski

Co-Founder and Director, AdvisorWebsites.com

Bart Wisniowski is an entrepreneur and web development specialist committed to creating effective websites for professionals in the financial services industry. As a speaker at various conferences, training sessions, and industry events, he conveys the importance of having a professional online presence.

Wisniowski's mission is to help financial advisors to create effective, user-friendly, customized websites, and his company has a stellar track record for website development. He understands what financial advisors are looking for in a website to help them attract clients and build their business. He has been working in the web development industry since 2000 and exclusively with financial advisors since 2002. In his personal life he likes to spend time with his family, is an avid winter activities participant, and enjoys most team sports.

Wisniowski is a member for the Financial Planning Association and is also on the chapter board of his local financial advisor association as the communications chair.

Index

Printed and bound by CPI Group (UK) Ltd, Croydon, CR0 4YY

16/04/2025

14658509-0004